DESPERATE
SONS

◆◆

Samuel Adams, Patrick Henry,
John Hancock, and the Secret Bands of Radicals
Who Led the Colonies to War

◆◆

◆◆

LES STANDIFORD

HARPER

An Imprint of HarperCollins*Publishers*
www.harpercollins.com

HarperCollins books may be purchased for educational, business, or sales promotional use. For information, please e-mail the Special Markets Department at SPsales@harpercollins.com.

FIRST EDITION

Designed by Fritz Metsch

Library of Congress Cataloging-in-Publication Data
Standiford, Les.
Desperate sons : Samuel Adams, Patrick Henry, John Hancock, and the secret bands of radicals who led the colonies to war / Les Standiford.—1st ed.
p. cm.
ISBN 978-0-06-189955-3 (hardback)
1. Revolutionaries—United States—Biography. 2. Revolutionaries—United States—History—18th century. 3. United States—History—Revolution, 1775–1783. I. Title.
E206.S77 2012
973.3—dc23   2012019551

12 13 14 15 16   OV/RRD   10 9 8 7 6 5 4 3 2 1

CONTENTS

This book is dedicated to don of dons Phil Sullivan,
who taught me to be suspicious of knowledge
and to treasure wisdom.

And to the memory of Zander,
who lived his brief life fully.

I write these things as they seem true to me,
for the stories told by the Greeks
are various and in my opinion absurd.

—HECATAEUS THE MILESIAN,
father of history,
fifth century BC

You haven't got a revolution
that doesn't involve bloodshed.

—MALCOLM X

ACKNOWLEDGMENTS

I am greatly indebted to many who helped me find my way through this undertaking, including my stalwart guide through the stacks both near and far, Adis Beesting, reference librarian at Florida International University. Special thanks are also due James R. Kelly, humanities bibliographer at the W. E. B. Du Bois Library at the University of Massachusetts, who was so helpful during the early floundering days.

Many thanks as well to my editor, Bill Strachan, who believed in this material from the beginning and whose patience and encouragement allowed me to persevere. I am also indebted to my agent, Kim Witherspoon, who unfailingly provided me with assurance that it was possible.

As usual, I could count on James W. Hall and Mitchell Kaplan for careful over-the-shoulder reading and invaluable conceptual advice, and I am equally fortunate to have the careful proofing eyes of Bill Beesting and Brian Sullivan. And as always, I am grateful for the support of so many friends and my family, who have reminded me so often and for so long that such work is worthwhile: Madeleine Blais; Mike and Liz Novak; Steve Leveen; my closest and most faithful reader and mother-in-law, Rhoda Kurzweil; my wife, Kimberly; my son, Jeremy; and my daughter, Hannah. I strive to do you all proud.

AUTHOR'S NOTE

Can there truly be anything left to say about the set of events that compose the American Revolution? Possibly it is an odd question at the beginning of a book about that very subject, but it is also the sort that this writer has asked himself before.

Of course, it is the reader who is best positioned to give the final answer as to whether a book should have been created, but on the other hand, and since there is very little of the slightest historical import that has not been written about well and truly, one might argue that we could, except for the production of the most arcane treatises, leave off the writing of history altogether. I speak theoretically, of course.

If someone asks me just what sort of history it is I aspire to, I might cite E. H. Gombrich and his book *A Little History of the World*, in which he covers most everything of importance from the Stone Age through the atomic bomb in 277 lyrical pages. Ostensibly the book was written for children, though if most of my own graduate students came to class having mastered half of what Gombrich has to give, I'd feel a minder of geniuses. "History begins," Gombrich says, "with a *when* and a *where*. It is 3100 BC, when, as we believe, a king named Menes was ruling over Egypt. If you want to know exactly where Egypt is, I suggest you ask a swallow. Every autumn, when it gets cold, swallows fly south. Over the mountains to Italy, and on across a little stretch of sea, and then they're in Africa, in the part that lies nearest to Europe.

Egypt is close by." My kind of history, if you want to know. Gombrich's purpose is not to remake history but to bring readers to a fresh appreciation of it.

In the present case, the story centers not so much on the individuals whose names have become synonymous with the American Revolution: the activists turned glorified statesmen such as John Hancock, George Washington, Thomas Jefferson, James Madison, and John Adams; and the familiar firebrand heroes such as Paul Revere, Patrick Henry, Nathan Hale, and others. Nor did I wish to tread the familiar ground of the revolutionary battlefield—once I reached the moment where the "shot heard round the world" is fired, I reasoned, I would quit the field. This, in fact, is the story of the group of men who brought the colonies to that pass.

Academic historians have discussed the Sons of Liberty in discrete contexts in numerous books and articles. And certainly a number of the struggles and the exploits sometimes associated with the Sons of Liberty, including the Boston Massacre, the Midnight Ride, and the Boston Tea Party, are prominent in the popular consciousness—as are the names of Revere, John Adams, Hancock, Henry, and others. But despite the drama and the importance of their role, I am aware of no overarching work of narrative history focusing on the Sons of Liberty in readying the colonies for battle against Great Britain, a step of such magnitude that modern readers may find it difficult to truly appreciate: consider for a moment that the counterculture movement of the 1960s had actually been successful in toppling the U.S. government at gunpoint, and one might begin to comprehend the accomplishment of the Sons.

My intention here is to tell the story surrounding a group of men who propelled the country to the breaking point. Some of these men have been termed the "Old Revolutionaries" by one prominent historian who has studied a handful of them in depth, but the title is something of a misnomer. Certainly, it is an epithet none would have ever visited upon themselves while in the thick of it.

These were vigorous men, men of action and of conviction. Most of them were considered dangerous by the majority of the citizenry among whom they lived, and some of them actually were. More than one was willing to commit acts of violence in service of the causes that they espoused.

Yet, by the time a new nation was ready to be formed, few would find places of prominence in its governance. For one thing, it was understood that if these men were willing to destroy one system of government, what was to prevent them from becoming impatient with the new one? True revolutionaries—men willing to risk everything to topple a regime—simply cannot be trusted. Or to put it a different way, one man's patriot is another man's terrorist.

The descriptions of events at the heart of this book are drawn largely from letters, newspapers, historical accounts, broadsides, and other contemporary documents. These materials reflect a growing unrest in the American colonies of the 1760s and 1770s, and nearly simultaneous eruptions of acts of violence and civil disobedience in Boston, New York, Providence, Charleston, and elsewhere. There was a long history of friction between the colonies and the mother country prior to 1765, of course, and although much was made of philosophy and concepts such as liberty and the right to self-governance, a great deal of unrest in the decade prior to the outbreak of war also came down to money.

Lest that all sound too venal, it should be understood that the operative attitude of many colonists in late 1765 was that they were being bled dry by an utterly indifferent British Parliament looking to bail out of its own overspending by exploiting Britain's colonies. The ability to run a successful business—or indeed to earn a living—brave spokesmen such as Samuel Adams complained, was being compromised by the ever-more-onerous tax legislation imposed upon the colonies. Worse yet, the colonists had no say because such matters were being debated thousands of miles away. In fact, when stated in this fashion, the reasons for the discontent of the American colonists sound much like the complaints of the contemporary citizens of Main Street when the possibility of any new tax is mentioned in Congress or during presidential debates.

Nearly 250 years ago, a group of American citizens decided that the conditions under which they were governed were intolerable; eventually they realized that no change would be forthcoming as a result of mere complaint and petition. Action would have to be taken. And because such actions were illegal, often directed at individuals and property, and because they could be punished by imprisonment and even death, their undertakings and the identities of those who carried them out would by necessity be covert. In short, there was an almost simultaneous eruption within the American colonies of cells of a secret radical society committed to imposing forcible change upon the established government.

In some ways, this might sound like a description of what the Western world is facing today in its war against terrorism. Who in recent years has not been chilled by the specter of cells of terrorists springing up around the globe, connected not by a flow of information and orders from some dogma-spewing central leadership but rather by some nearly telepathic or genetic fury and a sense of common purpose that transcend logic?

Many Americans shake their heads at such an incomprehensible scenario. Who *are* these people? Why do they hate us so? How on earth could we have come to such a pass? Why can they not be reasoned with? In fact, the British were asking very similar questions about the American colonists as early as 1765.

Perhaps, then, there is something beyond mere amazement in tracing the story of how the American colonies found their way to independence with a covert group of radicals leading the way. The basic contradiction between means and ends that so perplexed and angered those distant colonists and their patrons has, after all, ignited fierce debate among contemporary Americans as we wage our own wars in defense of democracy.

The men who came to call themselves Sons of Liberty were patriots in their own eyes and are likely to seem so in the eyes of most Americans of this day. In the eyes of the British (and not a few fellow colonists) of the 1760s, however, they were terrorists who deserved to pay dearly for the things they had done.

Certainly, when they undertook to plan and carry out such actions as the Albany "Riots," the burning of the HMS *Gaspée*, and the Boston Tea Party, the Sons of Liberty were not playing at symbolic gestures that would become the stuff of cant and schoolboy legend—they were laying their lives on the line in missions at a time when many of their fellow citizens were straddling the fence between obeisance to their lawful leaders and a commitment to an untested form of republican government.

The danger and the level of intrigue involved were hardly less than those associated with secret operatives and resistance fighters who would do anything to stop the spread of fascism across Europe in the twentieth century. And whatever debate might have existed about their methods, these Sons of Liberty finally led their fellow colonists to kick themselves free of the political gravity that had previously held them and to go to war against their protector, the mightiest nation known to that time.

This is the story, then, of how those forces metamorphosed from murmurings of a vague injustice into focused operations of resistance, led by men who dared to do what most were too fearful even to contemplate. The kindling of the fire of common purpose that would one day bring the British to their knees is the center of this book. The men involved were indeed desperate sons.

DESPERATE SONS

O ALBANY!

M aligning Albany is a very old game," begins the highly re-garded novelist William Kennedy's personal history of his hometown. "The early Dutchmen were targets of derision by visitors who found their city dismal, dingy, and dirty. The English didn't do much better with it. In 1876 the famed architect Stanford White had this to say: 'Misery, wretchedness, ennui and the devil—I've got to spend another evening in Albany. Of all the miserable, wretched, second-class, one-horse towns, this is the most miserable.'"

But despite those slurs heaped upon poor Albany (or perhaps because of them), Kennedy has found sufficient inspiration in the warts, short-comings, and cynical machinations of his hometown to set a number of acclaimed novels there, earning for himself a Pulitzer Prize and compari-sons to James Joyce and Joyce's exploitation of Dublin in the process.

As efficiently and effectively as Kennedy has mined the fictive ore of Albany, however, he has left at least one story untold. Possibly he passed it over because his explorations have centered on more modern Albany; or perhaps he left it alone because, in this tale, Albany plays a different kind of role, the one usually attributed to a grander city, with its famous bell, its Independence Hall, and more. In this real-life nar-rative, wretched Albany takes its place as the true cradle of liberty, for the events of early 1766 that took place there, and the desperate men who fashioned them, helped send the colonies careening toward a war of independence as surely as any other actions and actors of the time.

To begin, let us consider the fate of Henry Van Schaack, one of the early Dutchmen who did not find Albany "dismal, dingy, and dirty." In fact,

Van Schaack found great success there as a merchant in the so-called Detroit, or western, fur trade, an enterprise controlled from the beginning of the eighteenth century on the North American continent largely by the French. In the 1750s, however, as hostilities escalated between the British and the French along the western frontier and the French and Indian War became a reality, business became vastly complicated for Van Schaack.

As a result, he began looking for something more secure, and in 1757 he found it, or at least believed he had: he became the postmaster of Albany, and he fulfilled the gray duties of the office without incident for some ten years—until he made the mistake of considering yet another post offered to him by the king of England, and in doing so fanned passions that would eventually feed the flames of war.

On the Saturday night of January 4, 1766, sometime between 10 and 11, with the temperature in the teens and falling, Van Schaack heard a knock at his door. He opened it to find William Benson, a townsman whom he knew vaguely, standing there with a guarded expression on his face. A number of people were gathered in the public rooms at Thomas Williams's inn, Benson told Van Schaack. The group was eager to speak with him, and wondered if he mightn't be willing to "step over."

When Benson refused to elaborate beyond the addition of the word "immediately," Van Schaack became leery. He was well aware that the City Corporation often entertained at Williams's at holiday times, and although most of the city officials—and the most boisterous component of government, the fire department—were fellow Dutchmen, there was something in Benson's demeanor that put Van Schaack on guard. He told Benson that he would come on over, and in fact he did so, but not before rounding up a couple of his neighbors, just in case.

Van Schaack and his companions made their way to the inn, their breath billowing in the frigid air as they speculated about the nature of this summons. Probably it was just the exuberant firemen who wanted their postmaster there for a round of New Year's toasts, one of his friends told Van Schaack. Everyone knew how the firemen in Albany were about their celebrations.

Or perhaps they'd gotten lathered up and wanted Van Schaack's support for some move to further elevate the fortunes of their department in the coming year, his other companion suggested. Though the group was made up primarily of volunteers, it was nonetheless a mark of some distinction to be invited into the ranks. The department roster was studded with the names of the city's most prominent families (most of them Dutch and including the Beckmans, the Cuylers, the Ten Eycks, the Ten Broecks, the Visschers, et al.); there had just been purchased a second, brand-new fire engine of which everyone in Albany could be proud; and one of the two city servants who actually drew a salary was the department's engine mechanic. Additional to the firemen themselves was the cadre of elected officials called "firemasters," elected annually from each of the city's wards and charged with the task of inspecting the districts' buildings for fire hazards.

In all, the firemen and the firemasters constituted a formidable group of citizenry, and, given the avowed purpose of their organization and the requirement to act quickly and decisively when called upon, they did not tend toward reticence in making their feelings known. They were important, and they knew it. Whatever it was that necessitated his appearance at Williams's—and though Van Schaack was a seasoned enough politician to suspect a matter far more serious than what his companions theorized—the firemen probably had something to do with it.

In fact, he did spot the faces of many firemen as he and his companions entered the crowded hall at the inn. Of the thirty to forty men jammed into the stifling room, perhaps two-thirds were associated with the department. And though he knew the names of many of the men, he also took note that those around him were primarily the sons of his contemporaries, young men in their twenties and early thirties. Their fathers might have held boxes in the balcony of the Dutch Reformed Church, but these were not dour, reserved burghers surrounding him. Van Schaack was among the firebrands.

"Upon my coming in, they give three cheers, with a view, as I imagine, to intimidate me," Van Schaack wrote. And in short order they let him know that their summons was not involved with well-wishing, better pay for firemen, or anything to do with department business whatsoever.

"I was soon made acquainted by Some of them that they had been informed I had apply'd for the Office of Distributor of Stamps," Van Schaack related, and the "stamps" in this case had nothing to do with postage. The Stamp Act of 1765 had been recently foisted by the British Parliament on the colonies—and while it was only the latest in a hundred-year-long series of oppressive measures that had begun in 1660, when the Navigation Act had decreed that only British ships could transport imported goods to the Americas, this was the first attempt to impose a direct tax on colonists.

The act stipulated that all legal documents, permits, commercial contracts, newspapers, wills, pamphlets, and even playing cards produced or employed in the colonies would have to be stamped with the authority of the king, with a fee required for each. In the eyes of Parliament this was simply a just and fair means of recouping some of the enormous costs the British had incurred in carrying out the French and Indian War. Since it was the colonists who had benefited most from that expensive campaign, Parliament reasoned, why should they not help pay down the resultant British debt?

Furthermore, the British had used stamp taxes on at least three previous occasions to raise money within their own borders, and there had been no significant opposition from the country's own citizens. They had no reason to suspect that the colonists would object strenuously, and when Benjamin Franklin, that most able American envoy to England, suggested that there was little to fear from the passage of such legislation, the Stamp Act became law.

Franklin, the fabled Pennsylvania inventor, philosopher, and politician, was one of the colonies' most forceful spokespersons and, as a delegate to the Albany Congress of 1754, devised the so-called Albany Plan, espousing a central government to be headed by a president appointed by the Crown, overseeing a Grand Council of representatives appointed by the various assemblies in each of the colonies. It was the first serious proposal for a central government in the colonies and was put forward largely as a way of addressing concerns over mutual defense and the expense associated with the French and Indian War.

Being the first of its kind, and containing features that were designed to appeal to both the colonists and the British, the plan was almost certain to fail. The colonists were distrustful of any mechanism that centralized taxing authority outside local bounds, and the British were fearful that the creation of any unified government in the colonies would only distance their subjects further from control. To Franklin, the evenhanded rejection was a sign that he was onto something. "The different and contrary reasons of dislike to my plan made me suspect that it was the true medium," he would later say.

Meanwhile, in 1757, he was sent to London by the Pennsylvania Assembly to try to resolve a dispute with the Penn family, the London-based proprietors of the colony, who blithely ignored legislation passed by the colony's assemblymen when disregarding it suited them and routinely ignored requests to pay taxes on their vast landholdings. Pennsylvania, Delaware, and Maryland differed in character from the other ten colonies in that their territories had essentially been given to the families that controlled them by the king. (New Hampshire, New York, New Jersey, Virginia, Georgia, North Carolina, and South Carolina were "royal provinces," under the direct control of the king. Massachusetts, Rhode Island, and Connecticut were "charter" colonies, far more liberally controlled. In fact, the latter two operated very nearly as independent countries, and both would use their original charters as their state constitutions for a number of years following the Revolution. The charter of Massachusetts was more restrictive and bore a greater resemblance to that of a royal colony than to those of its chartered neighbors.)

In any case, although the king remained the ultimate authority in Pennsylvania, Delaware, and Maryland, as in all the colonies, in practice a near-feudal system was at work in the proprietorships: the noble families, or proprietors, to whom the lands had been granted appointed the governor and the various administrative officials. Any legislation adopted by the elected assemblies in any of the colonies was ultimately only advisory, but in the case of the proprietary colonies, it was decidedly so. It was a delicate landscape that Franklin had to maneuver through, then, and his chief powers were those of persuasion and attempts to convince the peers of the Penn family to listen to reason. While in London, Franklin naturally became increasingly interested in progressive politics and gradually came to align himself with Whigs, most of whom were sympathetic to the colonists' interests.

Franklin returned to Pennsylvania for a time in 1762, only to become further embroiled in Penn-related disputes when a group of colonists known as the Paxton Boys slaughtered twenty peaceful Conestoga Indians as a form of protest over what they considered the Penn family's preferential treatment of the natives. Though Franklin publicly condemned the massacre, he, as a member of the Pennsylvania Assembly, was mindful of the widespread public discontent with the out-of-touch Penn family.

It is suspected that Franklin—a pragmatist at heart—actually helped the Paxtons lay out their complaints in a document titled "Declaration and Remonstrance," which he proposed they circulate as an alternative to further violence and a more logical way of attracting support for their cause. Franklin then used the document in his own campaign, attempting to unseat the Penn family as proprietors of the Pennsylvania colony and replace them with a governor appointed by the king. It is a telling indicator that in 1764 even as astute a statesman as Franklin still considered the king of England benevolent. His support of a royal replacement for the Penns did not find favor among his constituency, however, and the miscalculation cost Franklin his seat in the Pennsylvania legislature.

His former peers in the Pennsylvania Assembly were undaunted by the results of the election and quickly voted among themselves to return Franklin as their emissary to London, where they hoped he would be successful once and for all in convincing Parliament to end the proprietary rule over their colony. Back in London in 1764, Franklin made his proposal to Parliament, which promptly declined it.

Of more interest to the members of that body at the time than turning against their well-positioned landholding cronies was the question of where the country would come up with the funds necessary to pay off the considerable debt run up during the war against the French. The new prime minister, George Grenville, lamented that the Seven Years' War had left the country with a national debt of more than £130 million (nearly double that of 1754), and as the previous chancellor of the Exchequer he was also aware that the cost of maintaining troops and administrative officials in the colonies had escalated from £70,000 in 1748 to more than £350,000 in 1763.

One of the problems in appreciating the magnitude of such sums vexes modern historians writing of any previous era: how much is that in current dollars? Some commentators feel that the question cannot be answered—in the colonies, for instance, since most people were self-employed, it is very difficult to talk about "wage scales." And even if we know that a certain schoolmaster of the time might have earned £60 in a year or that a good saddle might have cost about £2, it is difficult to translate that information into twenty-first-century terms. One index calls for the comparison of such sums as saddles or schoolteachers' wages with the gross national product of a country in a given era. Which would be fine, were there the slightest agreement as to what the GNP of the colonies might have been in 1760.

Still, historical economists do their best to provide answers. Estimates of the current value of the pound sterling of 1760 vary anywhere from $40 to $90 or more, so if it is enlightening to think that our schoolteacher might have made the equivalent of $4,000 or $5,000 in a given year, readers should feel secure with the assumption. Perhaps it would be more enlightening to ask whether the young man would have spent £2 of his total of £60 to buy that saddle, though. Possibly he would have, but then again, since a good horse to put it on would have cost £15 to £20, very possibly not.

We can doubt that our teacher would have spent the £1.50 it would have cost him for a wig but not that he laid out 4 pence ($1.50) for a pound of butter or the 4 shillings ($18) it would have cost for a bushel of salt to preserve his foodstuffs. On and on it goes, but where schoolmasters were able to find employment at £60 per annum, they were clearly far more fortunate than a common laborer, who might command little more than £2 to £3 for his whole year's work.

So when Grenville suggested that his country's national debt stood now at the equivalent of $13 billion, it may not seem all that much to a modern reader accustomed to hearing that the U.S. debt surpassed that figure in *trillions* early in the new millennium. But certainly at a time when a common workingman earned the equivalent of $100 to $150 a year, such an announcement would have surely caught the attention of Parliament. Furthermore, with the British economy in a downward spiral and the populace restless, the prospect of raising taxes at home was out of the question. Turning to the colonies for help seemed expedient.

❖❖❖❖❖❖❖❖❖❖❖❖❖❖❖❖❖❖❖

2

MEASURES ILLEGAL, UNCONSTITUTIONAL, AND OPPRESSIVE

T hough the mother country had never levied any tax directly on its American dependency, various trade duties had been applied over the years. Earlier in 1764, in fact, Grenville had pressed for passage of the Sugar Act, a modification of a piece of 1733 legislation imposing a duty on molasses imported into the colonies from Britain. The new Sugar Act actually reduced the levy on molasses from 6 pence to 3 pence per gallon, a tactical move that Grenville hoped would find favor among colonists who had responded to the original act by smuggling most of their molasses past British customs agents—those few they were unable to bribe, that is.

The "new" tax was roundly decried as onerous by the colonists, how-ever, as their own economy suffered in direct proportion to the down-turn in Great Britain. Trade with the distressed mother country was down, and with the war over and its associated free spending dried up, prospects were grim. Moreover, a theoretical objection was also raised by opponents to the measure when it was noted that the British Constitution excepted its subjects from "taxation without representa-tion." Previous revenue-producing measures imposed by the British had been cloaked in the rhetoric of "trade regulation," but colonists argued that the Sugar Act was a bald-faced tax. And although the citizens of England might rightly be themselves taxed by the members of a Par-liament that they themselves had elected, the colonists had no represen-tatives in that body.

Each of the thirteen colonies employed a liaison to Parliament, an envoy—as was Franklin—sent across the Atlantic to lobby for its part of thirteen different sets of interests, but that was not the same thing as having a properly apportioned voting membership on the floor. "No taxation without representation" would of course become a rallying cry for the colonists, justifying a wide range of future actions. But whether it was the 3-penny sugar tax itself or the principle of the thing that sent the colonists inching down the road toward rebellion is an issue that has had historians wrangling ever since.

In any case, at the same time that Parliament approved the Sugar Act (which also added other duties and allocated funds for the upgrading of the British customs service), Grenville warned that there might be further measures proposed in the following session of Parliament, among them a tax for appending an official stamp on most legal documents, newspapers, and magazines used in the colonies. Such a tax, in Grenville's eyes, was nonregressive and would affect no specific group unduly. Furthermore, a number of such taxes had been levied by Parliament upon its citizens to no particular uproar.

To Franklin and a number of his fellow colonial envoys, the prospect of some tax being levied seemed inescapable. After all, the recent rebellion of tribesmen led by Chief Pontiac in the just-acquired territories of New France had reminded most responsible officials on both sides of the divide that *someone* would need to pay for maintaining a peacekeeping force on the colonial frontier. One knotty question remained, however: who?

Part of the colonists' antipathy to the revenue-boosting measures was attributable to a growing distrust of those who were sent from England to handle their principal affairs. As one American who had been living in London for a time wrote in a 1758 letter, "most of the places in the gift of the Crown have been filled out with broken Members of Parliament, of bad if any principles, pimps, *valets de chambre*, electioneering scoundrels, and even livery servants. In one word, America has been for many years made the hospital of Great Britain for her decayed courtiers, and abandoned, worn-out dependents." Paying for necessary services was bad enough, but the prospect of turning over one's hard-earned pennies to schemers and incompetents was to most colonists simply beyond the pale.

Likewise, the concept of paying for a permanent garrison of 10,000 British troops on the borders of Canada and the bayous of New France raised hackles among many. The prevailing sentiment was that colonial militiamen, among them a certain George Washington, had proved themselves to be as able as, if not more able than, the king's troops in the sort of irregular actions that had characterized much of the fighting on the frontier during the French and Indian War. Yet for all the ability of the colonial fighters, it was nearly impossible for a colonial militiaman to obtain a commission in the king's army.

From the opposite standpoint, few Britons gave the colonies much thought at all. The primary political concern of the nation was outmaneuvering its traditional rivals: Holland, France, Spain, Prussia, Germany, and Russia. Where the colonies registered at all, it was primarily among the merchant class. There was a fair amount of profitable trade with the colonies, though the perception was that the colonies were certainly on the receiving end, there only to be profited *from*. In short, in the minds of most Britons, the colonies existed primarily for the benefit of the mother country, and the colonists who went there should be pleased at whatever benefits they might accrue from association with the most powerful nation in the world.

As for the notion of providing the colonists with representation in Britain's Parliament, most on the eastern side of the Atlantic found the idea downright comical. One commentator described American colonists as a "crabbed race not very unlike their half-brothers, the Indians, for unsociable principles and an unrelenting cruelty." And others scoffed that any benighted New Englanders elected to Parliament would soon be spending their time outside the halls, building pyres for witches and scaffolds for the correction of Quakers.

Of course, some more thoughtful commentators opined that such patronizing attitudes would come back to haunt the British. Without the participation of Ireland and the colonies and a move toward free trade, the empire would ultimately collapse, an argument that Adam Smith would repeat in his influential *Wealth of Nations* (1776). In comparing the British colonies with those of Greece and Rome, Smith pointed out that those earlier empires had taken a more enlightened approach: "The mother city, though she considered the colony as a child, at all times entitled to great favour and assistance, and owing in return much gratitude and respect, yet considered it as an emancipated child over whom she pretended to claim no direct authority or jurisdiction. The colony settled its own form of government, enacted its own laws, elected its own magistrates, and made peace or war with its neighbours as an independent state, which had no occasion to wait for the approbation or consent of the mother city. Nothing can be more plain and distinct than the interest which directed every such establishment."

And Edmund Burke spoke of the idea of colonists participating in Parliament as a "visionary" one, though he worried that the enterprising new members might seek to align themselves with the king at the expense of the elected representatives of Britons. William Pitt, the "Great Commoner" and brilliant tactician who had guided his country to success against the French, was also among the more farsighted Britons who rose in Parliament to warn against climbing up the backs of the colonists: "I will be bold to affirm, that the profits to Great Britain from the trade of the colonies, through all its branches, is two millions a year. This is the fund that carried you triumphantly through the last war. . . . And shall a miserable financier come with a boast, that he can bring a pepper-corn into the exchequer, to the loss of millions to the nation?"

Such liberal thinking held little sway in practical British politics of the mid-1760s, however. Money was needed, and although no member of Parliament was willing to risk rioting in the streets of England by taxing his constituents, most were convinced that the colonies would cave in or pitch in when the matter was pressed. After all, Franklin's failure to convince the disparate colonies to unite at Albany in 1754 augured that there would be no concerted resistance to whatever measures were enacted—the colonies were simply too divided, geographically and politically. Grenville presented his ultimate argument for the Stamp Act this way: "If the Americans dislike it, and prefer any other method of raising the money themselves, I shall be content."

At a meeting with Franklin and a number of other American agents just prior to his introduction of the bill on February 2, 1765, Grenville repeated his challenge that this esteemed group of Americans propose a better idea for coming up with the necessary funds. Franklin, fifty-nine at the time, was wise enough to understand that there would be no dodging Grenville's insistence that the colonies pay for what he considered valuable and necessary services rendered. But Franklin was also a seasoned politician, and even 250 years ago any politician understood the impact of the ultimate three-letter word upon a constituency. Echoing the sentiments of the Pennsylvania Assembly and eager for anything other than a "tax" to be proposed, he suggested that Grenville simply draft a requisition to each colony in a specified amount.

Grenville nodded as if he took the suggestion seriously, then glanced around the room. "Can you," he asked, "agree on the proportions each colony should raise?"

There was an uncomfortable silence before Grenville gave an "I thought not" nod. The meeting was at an end.

On February 6, 1765, Grenville introduced the Stamp Bill in Parliament, where the House of Commons passed it by a vote of 245 to 49 on February 17. The House of Lords added its unanimous approval on March 8, and on March 22, King George III decreed that on November 1 would take effect the following: "AN ACT for granting and applying certain stamp duties, and other duties, in the British colonies and plantations in America, towards further defraying the expenses of defending, protecting, and securing the same."

Among its fifty-five provisions, the bill established a duty of anywhere from 3 pence to 20 shillings on virtually every legal document in common use. A will, for instance, was to be taxed at 6 pence, and a diploma was taxed at £2. As previously mentioned, it is difficult to give a modern equivalent of the sums (there are 12 pence in a shilling and 20 shillings to a pound)—and another of the prevailing economic issues

plaguing trade relationships with the colonies was the lack of a standard currency on the westward side of the Atlantic. But the eventual
establishment of the American dollar and of the exchange rate that prevailed more or less steadily for much of the next two centuries provides
something of a measure: while some of the fees could be measured in
pennies, the prospect of a tax of roughly $10, at base rate, on one's col-
lege diploma in 1764 would not have seemed insignificant.

A license to sell liquor would cost 10 shillings, while one to trade in
wine was £4. Any grant or license requiring the signature of a governor,
colony proprietor, or public governing body was to cost £6. Rates for
contracts of employment, deeds, land surveys, secured notes, and audits
were also carefully laid out, and provision number 41 attempted to lay
claim to anything inadvertently overlooked: "For every skin or piece
of vellum or parchment, or sheet or piece of paper, on which shall be
engrossed, written, or printed, any register, entry, or enrollment of any
grant, deed, or other instrument whatsoever, not herein before charged,
within the said colonies and plantations, a stamp duty of *two shillings*."

Also liable to the tax were playing cards (1 shilling), dice (10 shillings), broadsides (a penny), newspapers and pamphlets (1 shilling), and
advertisements in those papers and pamphlets (2 shillings). Almanacs
and calendars would be taxed at 2 to 4 pence depending on their length,
and any documents published in a foreign language would be assessed
at twice the rate of those composed in the king's tongue. Even documents of apprenticeship would be taxed, at 6 pence for every 20 shillings offered for the post.

The process was to be overseen by the commissioners responsible for
collecting similar taxes in England, though deputies responsible for collecting the duties would have to be appointed throughout the colonies.
The act stipulated that all monies would be deposited into a distinct
account maintained by the chancellor of the Exchequer, and that they
"shall be there reserved to be from time to time disposed of by Parliament, towards further defraying the necessary expenses of defending,
protecting, and securing, the said colonies and plantations."

If a colonist were not dismayed by the very length and breadth of the listings, the final codicil would clarify the gravity of the matter: any "offenses" relating to the legislation would be "prosecuted, sued for, and recovered, in any court of record, or in any court of admiralty, in the respective colony or plantation where the offense shall be committed, or in any court of vice admiralty appointed or to be appointed, and which shall have jurisdiction within such colony, plantation, or place." In other words, the provisions of the Stamp Act were not suggestions—violators could be hauled into courts administered not by locals but by the Crown.

As noted, it was not as if there had been no "taxes" levied on colonists before. Local assemblies assessed various fees as a means of raising revenues for law enforcement, firefighting, road building, and other governmental activities. In his extended study of the Sons of Liberty in Charleston, historian Richard Walsh points out that Charlestonians felt that they, for one, were simply taxed out: in that colony, for instance, residents paid a tax of 35 shillings for each slave; 17½ shillings per hundred pounds' value on lots, wharves, and buildings; 17½ shillings per hundred pounds on interest-bearing notes; 17½ shillings per hundred pounds on profits from professional activities, manufacturing, and trade; and on and on. The Stamp Act added especially to the burden of attorneys, but also to that of anyone doing business handled by an attorney. It also seriously affected skilled labor, with the taxes on apprenticeship agreements amounting to more than half the weekly wage for an average master craftsman. The most galling feature of the Stamp Act, however, was that it had originated not in local government but in Parliament.

While a liberal-minded Congregationalist minister named Jonathan Mayhew is sometimes credited with having decried the practice of "taxation without representation" in a noted sermon published in 1750, the truth is a bit more complicated. In his *Discourse Concerning Unlimited Submission and Non-Resistance to the Higher Powers*, Mayhew does lay out a compelling justification for civil disobedience, but the main point of that sermon was to justify the execution of King Charles I by the Puritans a hundred years or so before. As close as

Mayhew got to the issue of "taxation" in his 1750 address was a complaint that Charles I had "levied many taxes upon the people without consent of parliament."

One dedicated blog writer and historian (J. L. Bell, *Boston 1775*) cites the first literal colonist's use of the phrase as occurring in a pamphlet—*An Humble Enquiry into the Nature of the Dependencies of the American Colonies*—published by a Savannah minister named John Joachim Zubly in 1769: "In *England* there can be no taxation without representation, and no representation without election; but it is undeniable that the representatives of *Great-Britain* are not elected by nor for the *Americans*, and therefore cannot represent them."

However, the concept of the basic unfairness of being taxed without the consent of one's elected representatives had certainly been eloquently expressed by the Boston assemblyman and attorney James Otis, Jr., as early as 1764 in a pamphlet of protest, *The Rights of the British Colonies Asserted and Proved*. Otis framed his argument by asking, "Can there be any liberty where property is taken away without consent?" Then he began his answer with a second question: "Is there the least difference as to the consent of the colonists whether taxes and impositions are laid on their trade and other property by the crown alone or by the Parliament?"

For Otis, it was a simple matter, though he made his case with passion: "I can see no reason to doubt but the imposition of taxes, whether on trade, or on land, or houses, or ships, on real or personal, fixed or floating property, in the colonies is absolutely irreconcilable with the rights of the colonists as British subjects and as men . . . for in a state of nature no man can take my property from me without my consent: if he does, he deprives me of my liberty and makes me a slave. If such a proceeding is a breach of the law of nature, no law of society can make it just. *The very act of taxing exercised over those who are not represented* [emphasis added] appears to me to be depriving them of one of their most essential rights as freemen, and if continued seems to be in effect an entire disfranchisement of every civil right."

It was in essence the same complaint that Irishmen were voicing about their treatment by the British for a century, but the modern reader can see a certain ingenuousness in the tenor of Otis's prose. "His Majesty *George III* is rightful King and sovereign, and, with his *Parliament*, the supreme legislative of Great Britain, France, and Ireland, and the dominions thereto belonging; that this constitution is the most free one and by far the best now existing on earth; that by this constitution every man in the dominions is a free man; that *no parts of His Majesty's dominions can be taxed without their consent* [emphasis added]; that every part has a right to be represented in the supreme or some subordinate legislature; [and] that the refusal of this would seem to be a contradiction in practice to the theory of the constitution."

How could anyone fault such logic? The reader might be forgiven for asking in the wake of Otis's stirring statement. And in truth, there were quite a few in the colonies who found the argument compelling, even if Otis himself stopped short of advising outright rebellion at the time. Even if the prospect of stamp taxes was unjust, Otis counseled moderation: "As it is agreed on all hands the crown alone cannot impose them, we should be justifiable in refusing to pay them, but must and ought to yield obedience to an act of Parliament, though erroneous, till repealed."

If Otis was calling for colonists to boycott the tax, however, shortly after the act's passage the British were taking steps to see that the desperately needed funds would in fact begin flowing into the national coffers. Even Benjamin Franklin miscalculated the depth of passions loosed in the colonies, it seemed, for he went so far as to nominate a Philadelphia friend, John Hughes, to serve as stamps distributor for Pennsylvania. It was only when word reached Franklin that an angry mob had surrounded Hughes to prevent him from assuming his duties and another had marched on Franklin's own home, threatening to burn it down, that the envoy began to understand that a profound shift in Anglo-American affairs had taken place.

Further proof that a tipping point had been reached came in the form of the widespread and independent nature of actions taken to protest the tax. News did not travel to, from, or through the colonies at the speed of light as it does today, of course. It could take six to eight weeks for a ship to carry mail and newspapers the five thousand miles from London to Boston (it was Franklin, ironically, who first called popular attention to the fact of the Gulf Stream, which could retard a westward-bound ship by as many as two extra weeks). And it took the better part of a week to travel the 250 miles from Boston to New York by land (though only two days by sea).

Colonial legislatures were convened once a year and for limited periods for very practical reasons. Travel was not so much broadening in those days as it was deadening. Roads were rutted and either dust-plagued or mud-mired in summer; in winter most were simply impassable. For that very reason, every major city that developed in the colonies was a seaport, and nine out of ten colonists lived within fifty miles of the Atlantic.

Albany itself had come into existence because of its place on the navigable portion of the Hudson River. As a gateway for the lucrative fur trade between the port of New York and the western frontier, Albany was serviced largely by a fleet of single-masted wooden sloops that generally took two or three days to travel the 135 miles or so between the two cities. There was no real hurry and no such thing as regularly scheduled passenger service, though many of the boats did have staterooms and could accommodate as many as thirty-five or forty in addition to the crew. A ship, however, sailed when its cargo hold was full and when there was a reasonable expectation that there would be some set of goods waiting to be loaded up at the other end. "Information transfer" was important, of course, but it was a decidedly secondary consideration under ordinary circumstances.

In the Albany of January 1766, things had indeed begun to trend away from the ordinary, but it was a fact of which the newly appointed stamp deputy Henry Van Schaack was only dimly aware as he was ushered into that steaming tavern on a dark night shortly after the arrival of the New Year.

3

THE SONS ARE BORN

When John Lansing, the spokesman for the gathering, angrily accused Van Schaack of having sought appointment as the local tax collector for Parliament, the postmaster tried to talk his way out of it: "I assured them that I never had made any Such application, and begged they would do me the justice and let me know who was my informer that I might clear myself upon the spot."

But it was to no avail. In response, John Vishher, a member of the crowd, stepped forward with a demand. It was all well and good that Van Schaack swore he had not sought the despised position. If that was his claim, then so be it.

All that the group wanted from him on this night was his solemn oath that he would never take the job. The reasoning of the assembly was simple: if they identified the members of the Albany citizenry who were even remotely qualified for the post of tax collector and "convinced" each of them to pledge not to accept the appointment, how could the Stamp Tax ever function?

In fact, four stalwarts of Albany—men well known to Van Schaack—had already applied for the position, but after consultation with the group that Van Schaack now faced, each had decided to remove himself from consideration. In Van Schaack, however, the group confronted an individual whose stubbornness and sense of independence would prove as strong as their own. Of course, he might have reasoned that signing such a public oath might also result in the loss of his other public position as postmaster, but hardheadedness and individuality were the hallmarks of many a man who left the confines of the highly stratified and static social system in Europe for the relative freedom of life in the American colonies.

"I attempted Several times to argue with those people about the unreasonableness of their demand," Van Schaack said, "but all to no purpose."

As a result, and in the words of one commentator, "Thereupon trouble ensued."

"Finding myself Surrounded by a Set of Men unable to reason and Determined upon measures against me that appeared illegal, unconstitutional and oppressive, I resolved to leave the room," said Van Schaack. But as he turned to go, John Vishher caught him by his sleeve.

By God, he would sign an oath never to serve as tax collector, Vishher told Van Schaack, or he would not leave the room.

"Has every man among you signed such an oath?" Van Schaack shouted back, wresting himself free from Vishher. "Has every Freeholder in Albany done so?"

There was an uneasy silence in answer to Van Schaack's bold questions. "I've sworn to you that I have not sought this position," he repeated, "and that's all you'll get from me."

Faced with the sort of bravado that prompted them along their own collision course with authority, the group seemed to relent. The group's leader, Lansing, motioned for Vishher to step out of Van Schaack's path, and the postmaster took his leave.

It was hardly the end of the matter, however. As soon as he left Williams's Inn, Van Schaack went to the home of his friend and counselor Richard Cartwright, where he set down his declarations to the ad hoc assembly in writing: he had never sought the post of tax collector in Albany, he repeated, but he thought it particularly unjust of the group to demand that he remove himself from consideration for a post that any of them were perfectly free to accept.

Though the message was delivered, Van Schaack's appeals to the group's sense of justice produced little effect. As a reporter for the *New York Mercury* put it, the group answered Van Schaack that they could no longer regard him as "on equal footing with themselves," for his refusal to disqualify himself "argued with some Degree of Inclination, the minutest Part of which was utterly inconsistent with their Sense of Liberty, and utter Abhorrence of any Post how profitable soever, so subversive of the very Foundation of human Happiness."

Van Schaack was resolute, however. "I had no notion that a Mob or any druncken Set of men had a right to make me Swear in that illegal way," he said, and made his way on home.

On Sunday morning, a friend came by Van Schaack's house to let him know that he had overhead some disturbing talk: some of those who had been in attendance at Williams's Inn the night before were not about to let the matter of Van Schaack's refusal rest. What he heard next led Van Schaack to write out a petition to the city's mayor in which he described the events of the previous evening and stated his fears that certain of the men who had confronted him now planned to "assemble to destroy me and my property." Van Schaack added the names of at least thirty of the individuals who had been arrayed against him the night before, and delivered his document, pleading for protection, to the mayor's home late Sunday evening.

For his part, Mayor Volkert Douw agreed to call the city's magistrates to a hearing on the matter on Monday afternoon, January 6. There Van Schaack repeated the demands of the assembly at Williams's and also reiterated his claim that he had never thought of applying for the post of tax collector.

The magistrates listened patiently, conferred among themselves, then turned to ask Van Schaack a question: since he had stated that he had never applied for this post and claimed that he never had intended to apply for it, what would be the harm in simply adding that he never would?

By now, staring at these magistrates with surnames such as Ten Eyck and Ten Broeck, Switts and Lansing, and others identical with those of the mob he had confronted at Williams's on Saturday night, Van Schaack was surely getting the picture. Still he was resolute: he would sign any oath or lawful instrument that all of his fellow citizens agreed to sign, and that was all.

The magistrates took this in; then one leaned forward to ask, "Just what sort of protection do you expect from us, Van Schaack?"

The protection afforded any citizen by the law, Van Schaack answered. After a glance at his pocket watch, he closed with the observation that the very people who had threatened him were likely meeting at that moment at the inn of Thomas Williams "& that it was probable they would in that meeting fall upon measures for my destruction."

According to Van Schaack, he had no doubt that the magistrates, now that he had warned them, would put a stop to any attempts upon his person or his property. "So fully was I convinced of this that I spent that evening abroad," he would say later.

Whether his reasons for absenting himself from his home are to be fully believed, what happened next does bear out that Van Schaack had reason for his warning to the magistrates. "About 8 O'Clock at Night I heard a great noise at my house," he would later write. "Being apprehensive the Mob was pulling it down and destroying my effects, I sent a trusty man to the Mayor." Unfortunately, Van Schaack's messenger was unable to get through, and, fearing for his life, Van Schaack fled to the British garrison in Albany for safe harbor.

Meantime, as was reported in the *New York Mercury*, a group of nearly four hundred citizens of Albany made their way to Van Schaack's home, "in very regular order," only to be informed by servants that the master was not at home. "The Boys searched the House in every Room," the correspondent wrote, "and not finding him, no Intreaties could prevent their committing some Outrages on the Furniture, Windows, and Balcony; which latter, tho' a very elegant Piece of Work, was entirely demolished."

From there, the group marched out into the night in search of their quarry, "drawing Mr. Van Schaack's pleasure Sleigh along with them, demolishing it piece meal, till they came to Captain Bradts, where they got Hay and Wood, and setting Fire to it, went with it blazing to Town."

In the morning Van Schaack ventured cautiously out from the garrison and along the quiet Albany streets. At the Dutch church, he found a notice hammered to the doors proclaiming that Van Schaack had "by great imprudence and unequaled obstinacy drawn upon himself the resentment of his Fellow Citizens to his considerable damage already." Further, the notice advised, Van Schaack might well present himself at Williams's Inn at ten a.m. on the following day to meet with the body that had posted this notice—that is, if he wished to "prevent worse consequences."

There was a less-than-heartening postscript added: "Damn you, Van Schaack, take care." A second paper tacked beside the first featured a drawing of a man hanging from a gallows. "Henry Van Schaack" was the legend scrawled atop the drawing. "The just fate of a traytor" was added below.

It is a testament either to his courage or to his obtuse nature that Van Schaack's immediate response was to sit down and pen a letter to the group that had threatened him with a lynching, once again offering to sign only such documents as all his fellow citizens would be required to sign as well. At the same time, he dashed off an appeal to James McEvers, a New York City merchant who had actually accepted a post as a stamp distributor in that city. Van Schaack had discovered that his accusers suspected him of having applied to McEvers, he explained, and he implored McEvers to "clear me of this imputation . . . in the most full, ample and publick manner you can. . . . You, I dare say, will easily conceive that the speedier your answer reaches me the better."

There is no record that McEvers ever replied to that note, but if he did, he would surely have told Van Schaack of his own experience in such matters. In fact, McEvers had already posted a public notice of his resignation as a tax collector and also circulated a pledge to never again seek such employment.

As the time for Van Schaack's appearance at Williams's grew near, friends came to implore him to relent. He would be ruined if he did not, they told him. Why continue this obstinacy?

"These arguments, with My own mortifying reflections that others would Suffer by my ruin," wrote Van Schaack, finally penetrated his resolve. Ultimately he appeared before the group, and despite his continued protest that it was "illegal, arbitrary and oppressive," he signed the oath. He had never sought the post of stamp collector for the British, he swore; and he swore that he never would.

For the men who had pummeled Van Schaack into submission, it was not so much a triumph over their fellow citizen—a former friend and colleague—as a blow against the British Parliament, that vast and predatory force intent, in their eyes, upon the continued oppression of every freedom-loving citizen in the colonies. It was hardly that in Van Schaack's eyes, of course. He even came up with a name for the group of men who had so persecuted him these several days: the Sons of Tyranny and Ignorance, he called them.

But over the course of their trials with Van Schaack, these men had come up with their own designation for themselves, and they could only hope that in time their methods and their aims would find favor in the hearts of their fellow citizens and inspire others to stand up to the abuses of the British lords.

Sons of Liberty, they now called themselves, and they were certain that they fought for right.

4

STORM BEFORE THE CALM

In the United States, it is a schoolchild's commonplace that the American Revolution, the event that so profoundly altered the political landscape of the modern world, was an exercise in ideology, distilled and conveyed over ensuing centuries in such stirring proclamations at that of Patrick Henry, "Give me liberty or give me death." Yet this view of history has proved controversial, at least within the realm of serious scholarship.

As early as 1913, Columbia University professor Charles A. Beard, at the time one of the country's most respected historians, published *An Economic Interpretation of the Constitution of the United States*, in which he laid out a careful analysis of how the economic interests of the members of the Constitutional Convention had affected their votes and the ultimate wording of that document. The book set off a firestorm of debate within academic circles, Beard's contentions raising serious doubt about the prevailing attitudes as to the "purity" of the American colonists' motives.

In 1967, Harvard professor Bernard Bailyn published the next major academic counterpunch in the debate. *The Ideological Origins of the American Revolution* appeared as a carefully reasoned and persuasive analysis that, in the minds of some critics, reduced the theoretical edifice erected by Beard a half century before to ruins. "What was once the grandest house in the province," said Richard Hofstadter in characterizing Beard's once authoritative work, "is now a ravaged survival."

But despite the fact that traditionalists (to this day) have rallied around Bailyn's work, his was hardly the last word. Ronald W. Michener, a University of Virginia professor, and his colleague Robert W.

Wright, a financial historian at New York University, have worked for several years on a treatise that harks back to Beard. "I think there's reason to doubt the Revolution would have happened as it did if it weren't for these economic conditions," says Michener. In their view, had the British been less eager to recoup the costs of fighting the French and the Indians by taxing the colonists, and had the deep recession plaguing the colonies been less severe and less protracted, the course of the United States' journey to independence might have followed the mild-mannered path of Canada's.

Such daring analysis does not go unnoticed in the halls of contemporary academe, of course. Gordon S. Wood, an eminent historian from Brown University, says, "There was a great deal of instability, but that is hardly an explanation for the Revolution. I don't think you can make a strong argument for an economic interpretation of the Revolution."

What can be deduced from such back-and-forth is that—at least among serious historians—the issue is a provocative one and, furthermore, is likely to be debated endlessly, for the simple reason that the seeming contradiction is ingrained irrevocably in the collective national consciousness. Surely, many Americans—when they are in a philosophical mood, that is—define themselves in terms of their allegiance to the concepts of individual liberty and freedom. That is one reason why so many tomes extolling the virtues of the founding fathers have been so popular in recent years. However, those same Americans have also been quick to "vote their pocketbooks" in the wake of the worst economic downturn since the crash of 1929. Woe indeed to any incumbent, regardless of party affiliation, who would dare to suggest that just possibly a few new taxes might be a good thing.

In recent years, budget deficit critics, taxation opponents, and far-right conservatives have found common ground under the banner of modern-day "tea parties" of one stripe or another, railing against big government and claiming to trace their lineage and their authority back to the patriots who opposed the British over tax issues in the 1760s. Opponents of the conservative groups scoff at such claims, pointing out that in contrast to the colonists of 1765, all modern-day Americans have representation in Congress. Members of the modern Tea Party movement might not *like* certain of those representatives, but they nonetheless have been elected by the populace.

Rather than pick a side, however, this volume might frame the matter differently. In truth, the best narratives intertwine the physical and the psychological to create a sense of substance as they progress toward an inevitable end, as romantic or tragic as it might be.

Thus, what better way to reframe the debate regarding the onset, struggle, and outcome of the American Revolution? Consider those who set the stage for rebellion then—the Sons of Liberty, individually and collectively—as protagonists, perplexed, confounded, and infuriated by a series of economic setbacks dealt them by the antagonistic, faraway British Parliament. At the same time, the Sons were conditioned in their thinking by 150 years or so of distance from and relative independence of the Crown to think of themselves as the possessors of certain unalienable rights, among them life, liberty, and the pursuit of happiness.

Without such psychic certainty, they would have been ill equipped to carry out the physical struggles that lay ahead. The so-called contradiction, then, is truly to be understood as a synergy, in the same way that the great civil rights struggles of the twentieth century were grounded in moral principle but prompted by any number of very real and intolerable actions.

One of the most significant things for the contemporary reader to understand about the American Revolution is that it took place in a setting that was nothing like the United States that we know today. In 1760, there were no more than 1.6 million inhabitants in the American colonies, nearly a quarter of them Negro slaves (as a measuring stick, consider that Phoenix, Arizona, tallied about 1.6 million in the 2010 census, all by itself). Slavery was practiced in all thirteen colonies, with most slaves in the North employed as household servants and most in Maryland, Virginia, and other southern colonies as agricultural workers on the great plantations. Wherever they were and whatever they were doing, the fact of their slavery was lamented by relatively few, accounting for the fact that such illustrious founders as John Hancock, Thomas Jefferson, and George Washington were slave owners. Though some opposed slavery on economic grounds, the moral issues surrounding the practice would have to wait until after the American Revolution for serious and widespread debate.

Most of the colonists came from England and Scotland, along with a significant number from Germany. New York had been settled by the Dutch, who were still substantial in number and influence there. The total population of the colonies was divided roughly equally north and south of the Mason-Dixon Line. Virginia was the largest of the colonies, with about 340,000 inhabitants, nearly half of whom were Negro slaves. Second largest was Massachusetts, with about 200,000 persons, and third was Pennsylvania, with 184,000. New York was sixth, with a total of 117,000 inhabitants, about the same as North Carolina, which counted 110,000.

Philadelphia was the largest city in the colonies, with some 20,000 citizens. Boston had 16,000 and New York City about 14,000. The only other city with more than 5,000 inhabitants was Charleston, South Carolina, with 8,000, though Salem and Marblehead, Massachusetts, flanking their own seaport about 20 miles north of Boston, had nearly 10,000 citizens between them.

Nor were dark-skinned Africans and West Indians the only virtual slaves in the American colonies. There were a significant number of indentured servants at work there at well, including a number of convicted criminals who had escaped execution or prison in England in exchange for a certain period of bound slavery in the colonies. Estimates are that England sent as many as 50,000 convicts to the colonies in the half century leading up to the Revolution.

Other white indentured servants were sold to slave traders by their impoverished parents or were simply snatched off the streets and tossed into the holds of ships to be transported and sold to the highest bidders in America. In addition, a number of impoverished Brits, Scots, and Irish looking for a fresh start (an unskilled laborer in England might make £2 for a year of carrying hod or guiding an ox across a field) voluntarily sold themselves into servitude in exchange for the high cost of passage—anywhere from £6 to £10—to the New World.

Estimates by the U.S. Department of Labor suggest that as many as 80 percent of the total European emigration to the colonies consisted of voluntary "redemptioners," who typically spent anywhere from three to seven years working off their obligations. These included scullery maids and manual laborers, of course, but in addition, there were bricklayers, carpenters, watch- and shoemakers, barrel makers, blacksmiths, and skilled artisans of many types who regularly advertised in newspapers as available "for sale."

In addition to those arriving as slaves were the many bound apprentices laboring in the colonies. These were orphans or children of impoverished parents who were willing to give up offspring they could not support. An apprentice typically gained freedom at age twenty-one, becoming a journeyman, free to seek paid employment within the craft he or she had learned (women, by and large, were apprenticed to learn "housewifery").

While the practice might seem brutish to the modern reader, apprenticeship at least offered the promise of upward mobility to an otherwise prospectless young person. One study suggests that there were about five hundred bound apprentices registered in Philadelphia in the mid-1750s. The Boston-born Benjamin Franklin was himself an apprentice (as a printer, to his own newspaper-owning brother), though he fled from his master before his term was up and would come to embody the original Horatio Alger, up-by-his-own-bootstraps success story.

At the other end of the American social spectrum was the class from which "rulers"—given the limitations of the term in the British-bound colonies—were drawn. They included the landed gentry—in both North and South—and wealthy traders and merchants, as well as attorneys, clergymen, judges, and college professors.

In between were the majority of the citizenry: small shopkeepers, farmers, artisans, printers, and skilled workmen, or mechanics, many of them only recently removed from bound labor of some type and

distinctly aware of the difficulties of daily life. In that regard, statistics
sometimes suggest that the average life expectancy of the time (in England as well as the United States) fluctuated between twenty-five and
forty years, shocking numbers for contemporary Americans who expect
to live to sixty-seven or sixty-eight at a minimum. However, such figures are greatly skewed by the inordinately higher rate of infant mor-
tality of the time, which hovered at roughly 50 percent. Recent studies
have shown that a person who reached the age of twenty-one in the
colonies of 1765 might expect forty more years of life.

However long they lived, distinctions between the social classes of
those carrying on an existence in the colonies were clearly kept. In fact,
some made it law that no person was "to dress above his degree." Seat-
ing in churches and colleges was allocated according to rank, and families of station were careful to ensure that their children understood the
importance of maintaining the bloodline—there was to be no marrying
any mate less than a social equal. Still, there was nothing to stop an
enterprising young man of the ilk of Franklin or Andrew Johnson, an
apprenticed youngster who would eventually become president, from
bettering himself.

There were only seven colleges in the colonies at the time of the Stamp
Act: Harvard, the College of William and Mary, Yale, Princeton, Columbia, the University of Pennsylvania, and Brown. Most young men
did not think of going to college unless they intended to join the clergy.
And although secondary education was also a rarity, most towns in the
North maintained an elementary school. Several studies show that the
literacy rate in the colonies of the time reached 70 percent or higher,
actually outstripping that in England, where the rate is estimated variously at 50 to 70 percent. Reading—especially of prayer books and the
Bible—was encouraged in most homes, and the ability to write was
valued as a practical path to upward mobility: carrying on a business
or a trade.

Though life for the privileged few might have included travel
and exploration, riding, sailing, hunting, reading, and religious and

philosophical study, most colonists worked hard, six days a week. Leisure for most was confined to Sunday gatherings with family and friends and was often organized around the church. Children rolled hoops, tossed balls, and played variants of the hiding-and-seeking games that children have always played. Adults sang, played instruments, indulged in variants of bridge and rummy, and read aloud to each other. Courtship was carefully regulated in all aspects, and most married women, whether of means or no, stayed home to cook, can, gather honey, make candles from animal fat, sew, and raise children.

Men, when they were not working, did gather outside the home to gamble at dice, cards, and cockfighting. They frequented taverns to participate in those activities as well as to debate and to fight when words seemed inadequate to make a point.

Given the difficulty of making ends meet for the common man and the fact that a fair number of criminals had been sent over from England, crime—particularly theft—was not uncommon. Crime was punished variously: by hanging (which even a bit of forgery or counterfeiting could get a person), whipping, ducking in a local stream or pond, or a period of painful exposure in the pillory and the stocks of the public square, where a transgressor's ears might be nailed fast to the wood frame clamped about his or her neck and arms or his or her nostrils slit for good measure. There were few prisons, given the expense of maintaining them, so that criminals who hadn't been hanged were sent back to the streets, even if many were permanently branded—as Hester Prynne in Nathaniel Hawthorne's novel *The Scarlet Letter* nearly was—according to their sins on the forehead, cheeks, arms, or hands (B for burglary, T for thief, R for rogue, and so on.)

Modern social scientists have made much of the unlikely collaboration among American blacks, college students, intellectuals, and liberal politicians that fueled the civil rights uprisings of the 1960s, but a glance at the demographics of colonial America suggests a remarkably similar pattern. Some analysis of prerevolutionary protest holds that a small minority of privileged colonials manipulated a largely uneducated mob of workingmen to further their own economic or political ends.

But that sounds suspiciously like the kind of criticism that faulted only entitled "eggheads" and "liberals" for encouraging the protests against racism and the Vietnam War.

It was indeed a very different but equally diverse populace that combined to set the American Revolution into motion. Which constituency was primarily responsible for the outcome remains a matter of debate, even if the results were unmistakable.

Some in England complained at the time that much of the unrest concerning the stamp duties was fomented by merchants who simply wanted to avoid paying their fair share of the freight. They were attempting to duck out on part of the "cost of doing business," so to speak. But as most accounts of the conflict suggest, it was the common man as well as the more privileged who believed that any burden to trade and to the unfettered conduct of business would harm everyone in the colonies.

5

NOURISHED BY INDULGENCE

J ust as it is difficult to pin down the first usage of "taxation without representation," so is it something of a chore to determine just when the term "Sons of Liberty" was coined. The former embodied a concept that was in some ways as old as that of representative government itself, just as the latter phrase was something of a familiar catch-all prior to the events of 1765.

As the Stamp Act was being debated in the House of Commons, one member, Charles Townshend, stood to exclaim in rhetorical wonder, "Will these Americans, children planted by our care, nourished up by our Indulgence until they are grown to a degree of strength and opulence, and protected by our arms, will they grudge to contribute their mite to relieve us from heavy weight of the burden which we lie under?"

Townshend's statement prompted a passionate reply, one widely disseminated in the colonies, by Colonel Isaac Barré, a veteran of the French and Indian War and a proponent of the concept that the colonists should come up with their own way to contribute toward the costs of maintaining troops and paying down the war debt. "They planted by your care?" Barré responded indignantly to Townshend.

"No! Your oppression planted 'em in America. They fled from your tyranny to a then uncultivated and unhospitable country where they exposed themselves to almost all the hardships to which human nature is liable, and among others to the cruelties of a savage foe, the most subtle, and I take upon me to say, the most formidable of any people upon the face of God's earth."

Modern readers can only wonder if Townshend expected all this from one of his own, but Barré was just warming up: "They nourished by your indulgence? They grew by your neglect of 'em. As soon as you began to care about 'em, that care was exercised in sending persons to rule over 'em, in one department and another, who were perhaps the deputies of deputies to some member of this house, sent to spy out their liberty, to misrepresent their actions and to prey upon 'em; men whose behaviour on many occasions has caused the blood of those sons of liberty to recoil within them."

Barré closed with a passionate flourish that would certainly endear him to the colonists, even if his sentiment failed to win over his fellow parliamentarians: "They protected by your arms? They have nobly taken up arms in your defence, have exerted a valour amidst their constant and laborious industry for the defence of a country whose frontier, while drenched in blood, its interior parts have yielded all its little savings to your emolument. . . . The people I believe are as truly loyal as any subjects the king has, but a people jealous of their liberties and who will vindicate them if ever they should be violated; but the subject is too delicate and I will say no more."

In context, Barré's characterization of the many "sons of liberty" forced to submit to one incompetent British functionary after the next seems a casual rhetorical touch. But his assessment of the mood of many colonists was accurate, and whether the most passionate of them picked the phrase from Barré's remarks is immaterial. The concept of sore injustice was crystallized, and the reaction in the colonies would go far beyond mere words.

The passage of the Sugar Act in 1764 stirred a number of the colonies to establish what were called Committees of Correspondence, unofficial groups made up of influential citizens formed to share information regarding the actions of Parliament and discuss possible strategies to be adopted in response. The formation of such bodies would lay the initial foundation for revolution, but at the time any thought of outright divorce from the mother country was not on the table. What the committees initially facilitated was dissemination of sensitive information and the opportunity to build a sense of common resolve out of sight of the British. Implicit in all of these activities was the hope that Parliament could be reasoned with.

At the same time, some colonists were openly disputing the authority of Parliament in disguising taxes as regulation. In May 1764, Samuel Adams was appointed by the Boston Town Assembly to write out a set of "instructions" that would guide that body's set of representatives to the Massachusetts Assembly. (The body is properly identified as the Boston Assembly. The terms "Boston Town Assembly," "Boston Town Council," and "Boston Town Meeting" were also used interchangeably.)

In those instructions, Adams would reason, "If our Trade may be taxed why not our Lands? Why not the Produce of our Lands & every thing we possess or make use of? This we apprehend annihilates our Charter Right to govern & tax ourselves—It strikes our British Privileges, which as we have never forfeited them, we hold in common with our Fellow Subjects who are Natives of Britain: If Taxes are laid upon us in any shape without our having a legal Representation where they are laid, are we not reduced from the Character of free Subjects to the miserable State of tributary Slaves?"

By October 1764, Rhode Island formed its own Committee of Correspondence, and in December, the Virginia House of Burgesses sent a formal protest to London, arguing that it did not possess the hard currency that would be required to pay the proposed Stamp Tax. Massachusetts, New York, New Jersey, Rhode Island, and Connecticut also sent similar letters of protest, all emphasizing that taxation of the colonies without the colonists' assent was a violation of their rights.

No amount of aggrieved letter writing from the colonies or passionate argument by partisans in the Houses of Parliament would alter the course that Prime Minister Grenville had set, however. Though the Stamp Act was decreed as law in late March, word did not reach the colonies until May. When it did arrive, the sense of betrayal among the colonists was palpable. Most historians agree that no other action on the part of the British government was as effective a blow against its relations with the colonies.

Even had there not been the passage of a Stamp Act, what transpired over the course of the fateful decade to follow suggests that something else might have taken its place, of course, but the fact remains that no one on the eastern side of the Atlantic—not even Benjamin Franklin— seems to have gauged how provocative this action would be. As William Smith, Jr., an influential young lawyer and assemblyman from New York City, wrote to a friend in England, "This single stroke has lost Great Britain the affection of all her Colonies."

It may be difficult for a modern reader to appreciate the depth of feeling expressed in the colonists' reactions to the Stamp Act. Single legislative acts—the health care reform bill and the debt ceiling debates are recent cases in point—have certainly provoked acrimonious wrangling in Washington and hardened the lines between liberals and conservatives, but even in such litmus-test matters as those, the sense of anguished betrayal felt by the colonists in 1765 is generally absent. For one thing, the nation has experienced nearly two and a half centuries of political debate, and although there is no shortage of passion to be found when Republicans and Democrats (or splinter factions within either party) go toe to toe over important issues, at least the struggles take place on a field of contest far more level than that of 1765.

When the colonists sent their appeals concerning the Stamp Act to England, the route was not only *across* the Atlantic but considerably *upward* as well. The colonies were not viewed there as of equal status; as any number of Britons were happy to remind them, they were not called *colonies* for nothing. From the time of their creation, the colonies had been in large part dependent upon the benevolence of their caretakers for well-being. And when that benevolence was withheld, or unfair treatment dispensed, in spite of all that seemed logical and just, dismay and resentment began to set in. No son or daughter, hearing a father decree an unjust punishment, could have felt greater pain than did many colonists, who felt rebuked by the "mother" country.

The November 14, 1765, issue of the *Pennsylvania Journal* carried a letter written by an American to a British friend stating, "This shocking Act . . . filled all British America from one End to the other, with Astonishment and Grief. . . . We saw that we, and our Posterity were sold for Slaves." Typical of the letters sent to the editors of various papers was one from a Boston resident reminding the British of the many times that colonials had pitched in during a number of military campaigns of the 1700s. "Tis true you took Quebec," the writer said, but pointed out that it was taken "in Conjunction with the Royal Americans, who during the War, had above 15,000 Men in the Field. Now you, on your Side of the Water, make a Merit of taking Canada for our Sakes—but you know better—and that it was for your own Sakes. For the above-mentioned Services, you have rewarded us with insupportable Taxes, and even infernal ones, Stamp-Duty, etc.—And that you, our tender Parent, who Mr. Grenville says, has nursed us in our Infancy, should not be wanting in Acts of Kindness to us."

Nor were the reactions confined to the realm of the subjective. By July, the *Boston News-Letter* reported, "It is said that the Prospect of the Stamp-Act has put a Stop to three Gazettes already on this Continent, viz. Virginia, Providence, and one of the New York. It is also said, the *Maryland Gazette* is in a very ill State . . . and it is thought [it] cannot possibly survive the Month of October next."

It is interesting, in fact, to note that in the years leading up to the proposal of the Stamp Act, there were a total of twenty-four newspapers operating in the colonies. New England publications included the *New-Hampshire Gazette* (Portsmouth), the *Boston Evening-Post*, the *Boston Gazette*, the *Massachusetts Gazette and Boston News-Letter*, the *Boston Post-Boy*, the *Newport Mercury*, the *Providence Gazette*, the *New London Gazette*, and the *Connecticut Gazette* (New Haven), though the last suspended operations in April 1764. In the middle colonies were the *New-York Gazette*, the weekly *Post-Boy*, the *New York Mercury*, and the Philadelphia papers, the *Pennsylvania Gazette* and the *Pennsylvania Journal,* along with the *Wochentliche Philadelphische Staatsbote* and the *Germantowner Zeitung.* In the southern colonies were the *Maryland Gazette* (Annapolis), the *Virginia Gazette* (Williamsburg), the irregularly published *South-Carolina Gazette* of Charleston, the *South-Carolina and American General Gazette,* also of Charleston, and the *Georgia Gazette* (Savannah). Three fresh papers established in 1764 were the *North-Carolina Magazine* (New Bern), the *Connecticut Courant* (Hartford), and the *North-Carolina Gazette*, of Wilmington.

While a number of editors were strident in their condemnation of a tax they feared would put them out of business, others chose to ignore the matter entirely. Among the earliest public reactions came one from the Virginia House of Burgesses, when word of the Stamp Act's passage reached its chambers in late May, after many members of that body, including George Washington, had already left Williamsburg for the summer and business was winding down. As the historians Edmund and Helen Morgan write in their thoroughgoing treatment, *The Stamp Act Crisis*, it is difficult to pin down exactly what happened on the day that the newly appointed representative Patrick Henry (he'd held office for only nine days) rose to introduce a number of resolutions. No secretary took notes, and no reporter was in attendance—the publisher of the Williamsburg paper being apparently indifferent to what the burgesses might have been debating that day.

Thus, although the twenty-two-year-old Thomas Jefferson watched the proceedings from the lobby on that day and would some forty years later do his best to reconstruct exactly what had happened, the words of an anonymous Frenchman in a letter discovered a century and a half later provide the most reliable account of the momentous proceedings.

Legend has it that Henry stood encased in a bastion of oratory as others among the burgesses tried to stop him with shouts of "Treason!" While it is likely that Henry, even though a novice, owned the good sense to wait until a number of the more conservative members decamped from the chambers for home precisely so that some of the since-reported drama did not take place, there can be no doubt as to the content of the resolutions that the roughly one-third of his fellow assemblymen did pass.

The first stipulated that all the original settlers of the colonies brought with them and passed down to their present heirs "all the liberties, privileges, franchises, and immunities that have at any time been held, enjoyed, and possessed by the people of Great Britain."

The second reiterated the terms of the royal charters of King James

I, stipulating that the colonists were "entitled to all liberties, privileges, and immunities . . . as if they had been abiding and born within the Realm of England."

The third stated that "the taxation of the people by themselves, or by persons chosen by themselves to represent them, who can only know what taxes the people are able to bear, or the easiest method of raising them, and must themselves be affected by every tax laid on the people, is the only security against a burdensome taxation," closing with the insistence that such a principle was "the distinguishing characteristic of British freedom."

In the fourth, Henry asked for agreement that until the recent imposition, colonists "without interruption enjoyed the inestimable right of being governed by such laws, respecting their internal policy and taxation, as are derived from their own consent, with the approbation of their sovereign, or his substitute; and that the same has never been forfeited or yielded up, but has been constantly recognized by the kings and people of Great Britain."

All of that was mild enough. However, it was the fifth of the resolutions that began an uproar. In it, Henry asked for his colleagues' agreement "that the General Assembly of this Colony have the only and exclusive Right and Power to lay Taxes and Impositions upon the inhabitants of this Colony and that every Attempt to vest such Power in any person or persons whatsoever other than the General Assembly aforesaid has a manifest Tendency to destroy British as well as American Freedom."

In essence, in this resolution, not only was Henry insisting that it was the sole province of the Virginia assembly to tax Virginians, but he was also calling those who passed the Stamp Act enemies of liberty—and it was there that he had gone too far for several of his peers.

Though Henry had of course written down the resolutions themselves, he did not do the same with the excited rhetoric he used to frame his introduction of them. However, it is generally agreed that at one point he went so far as to suggest that there would be dire consequences to a king who allowed such legislation as the Stamp Act to

stand, referring to other imperious rulers, including Julius Caesar and
Charles I, who had been brought low by agitated subjects offended by
their actions (Brutus, Cromwell, and so on). Such a threat, history tells
us, brought Henry's opponents to their feet, crying, "Treason!"

There are garbled and conflicting accounts of the exchange contained
in subsequent letters and distant newspaper accounts of the time, and
more eloquent accounts would appear in histories penned on both sides
of the Atlantic in the immediate aftermath of the Revolution. One of
the most stirring is found in William Wirt's *Sketches of the Life and
Character of Patrick Henry*, published in Philadelphia in 1816:

> It was in the midst of this magnificent debate, while he was des-
> canting on the tyranny of the obnoxious act, that he exclaimed,
> in a voice of thunder, and with the look of a god, "Caesar had his
> Brutus—Charles the first, his Cromwell, and George the third"—
> ("Treason!" cried the speaker—"treason, treason," echoed from
> every part of the house. It was one of those trying moments which
> is decisive of character. Henry faltered not an instant; but ris-
> ing to a loftier attitude, and fixing on the speaker an eye of the
> most determined fire, he finished his sentence with the firmest
> emphasis)—[we] may profit by their example. If *this* be treason,
> make the most of it.

The very ring of such a concluding phrase (the italics have been
added) is the stuff of which legends are made. And were it not for the
chance discovery, more than a century and a half later, of the account
of an anonymous Frenchman's travels through the colonies, who would
ever be the wiser as to the truth?

"Mr. Abel Doysie, searching Paris archives under the general direction of Mr. Waldo G. Leland, of the Carnegie Institution of Washington, was so fortunate as to discover the following journal in the archives
of the *Service Hydrographique de la Marine*," began an article in the
American Historical Review of 1921, "and, immediately appreciating

its interest and importance, has placed it at the disposal of the Review."

The editors of the review go on to theorize as to who the author of this letter found in history's bottle might be:

> The writer was a Catholic, and apparently a Frenchman, indeed apparently an agent of the French government; but all efforts to identify him, both by careful investigations in the French archives and by consultation of books and manuscripts in this country, have thus far been unsuccessful. . . . He seems to use English and French with nearly equal freedom, at any rate spells both about equally well. The manuscript is in the same hand throughout, with the same peculiarities of execution, such as the almost constant capitalizing of C, D, and E.

Of more interest than our agent's identity, however, is the keen eye for detail that he displays, not to mention his lack of vested interest in the fabled scene in 1765 that he describes:

> Set out Early from halfway house in the Chair and broke fast at York, arived at williamsburg at 12, where I saw three Negroes hanging at the galous for haveing robed Mr. Waltho of 300 ps. I went imediately to the assembly which was seting, where I was entertained with very strong Debates Concerning Dutys that the parlement wants to lay on the american Colonys, which they Call or Stile stamp Dutys. Shortly after I Came in one of the members stood up and said he had read that in former times tarquin and Julus had their Brutus, Charles had his Cromwell, and he Did not Doubt but some good american would stand up, in favour of his Country, but (says he) in a more moderate manner, and was going to Continue, when the speaker of the house rose and Said, he, the last that stood up had spoke traison, and was sorey to see that not one of the members of the house was loyal Enough to stop him, before he had gone so far. upon which the Same member stood

up again (his name is henery) and said that if he had afronted the
speaker, or the house, he was ready to ask pardon, and he would
shew his loyalty to his majesty King G. the third, at the Expence
of the last Drop of his blood, but what he had said must be atrib-
uted to the Interest of his Countrys Dying liberty which he had
at heart, and the heat of passion might have lead him to have
said something more than he intended, but, again, if he said any
thing wrong, he beged the speaker and the houses pardon. some
other Members stood up and backed him, on which that afaire
was droped.

From "If that be treason, make the most of it" to pledging a blood-
oath loyalty to King George III and begging pardon from one and all,
thank you very much. What is a student of history to believe?
   Whatever one chooses to believe in the end, our anonymous Frenchman proves at least some of his observations to be in accord with known
fact, for he would return to the House of Burgesses for more on the following day:

May the 31th. I returned to the assembly today, and heard very
hot Debates stil about the Stamp Dutys. the whole house was for
Entering resolves on the records but they Differed much with regard the Contents or purport therof. some were for shewing their
resentment to the highest. one of the resolves that these proposed,
was that any person that would offer to sustain that the parlement
of Engl'd had a right to impose or lay any tax or Dutys whats'r
on the american Colonys, without the Consent of the inhabitants
therof, Should be looked upon as a traitor, and Deemed an Enemy
to his Country. there were some others to the same purpose, and
the majority was for Entring these resolves, upon which the Governor Disolved the assembly, which hinderd their proceeding.

In fact, the House of Burgesses did reconvene the following day and
the matter of Henry's resolutions was brought back for reconsideration

by that body. After considerable debate, the inflammatory fifth resolution was excised from the formal list. But that formality mattered little. Newspapers throughout the colony already were in possession of their copies of Patrick Henry's original declarations, and they would be published in the original form, the first shots fired of what would become a fearsome volley.

6

UNLEASHED

The Virginia Resolves, as the resolutions introduced by Patrick Henry came to be called, would influence a number of other colonial assemblies to issue similar statements in short order. Furthermore, those subsequent reiterations often included Henry's unsuccessful fifth resolution, as well as two others that he apparently intended to include, depending—one supposes—on the reception of his colleagues to the others as he introduced them (keep going until they flinch, as some pols like to put it).

While it is unclear whether the sixth and seventh resolutions were actually debated on the floor, one can imagine that if some of Henry's colleagues were merely hissing over the first five stipulations, the final two would have brought out shouts. The sixth resolution stated that "the inhabitants of this colony, are not bound to yield obedience to any law or ordinance whatever, designed to impose any taxation whatsoever upon them, other than the laws or ordinances of the General Assembly aforesaid." And the last provided that anyone who denied the assembly's exclusive power of taxation "shall be deemed an Enemy to this his Majesty's Colony." Parliament, it was clear, was the devil incarnate in Patrick Henry's eyes.

The first newspaper account of the resolves came in the *Newport Mercury,* identified as having been sent in a letter of June 18, 1765, "from a gentleman in Philadelphia, to a Friend in this Town." The anonymous letter writer said that as soon as the governor of Virginia, Sir William Berkeley, had laid eyes on the document, he had informed the burgesses that he would dissolve the resolutions, "and that minute they were dissolved." However, the writer continues, he was sending them along anyway: "As they are of an extraordinary nature, though they might not be disagreeable."

With the publication of such accounts, historians of the likes of Arthur Schlesinger argue, newspaper publishers began to sense that perhaps the bill they worried would kill them might actually bring added revenue to their coffers. Now, in addition to news of local thefts and the occasional necessary hanging, the odd bit of months-old stuff from far-off Europe, and a recitation of newly arrived goods at local stores, readers could find themselves galvanized by controversy surrounding the deviousness of the British and their local agents. As the publishers began to realize, nothing could sell newspapers like such trouble.

Meanwhile, in September 1765, the Rhode Island Assembly passed its own version of the Virginia Resolves, essentially copying three of the milder resolves passed by the burgesses, as well as two of the more inflammatory resolutions reported in the *Mercury* and adding a rather incendiary sixth clause of its own, asking that Rhode Island officials simply refuse to enforce the Stamp Act. The colony had a popularly elected governor, Samuel Ward, who wrote to British authorities to explain why the matter was so troubling. The issue was a simple one, he said: the duties and taxes had been laid upon his constituents without their knowledge or consent.

The Maryland Assembly passed its set of resolutions in late September, though, as the historian Edmund Morgan points out, a subtle distinction was incorporated into their protest. Maryland allowed that the Crown might have the authority to levy an excise duty on trade, but as to "internal" taxation—i.e., on the conduct of business within the colonies—such rights should be reserved to the colonies themselves. Such points seemed sophistries to any number of politicians in Great Britain—what was the difference between "internal" and "external" taxes? Just pay your fair share of the burden and stop the quibbling.

To Americans, however, the "petty" distinction was at the very heart of the matter. Being asked to pay a bill was one thing; having a hand stuck into one's pocket was something else altogether. At the very least, the distinction allowed the colonies to justify their outrage in logical terms, and at that point in the contest it was believed that logic would surely prevail.

Before the end of the year, the assemblies of Massachusetts, Connecticut, New Hampshire, New Jersey, New York, and South Carolina would publish similar sets of resolutions or dispatch revised letters of protest to King George and members of Parliament. And at the same time, the day of implementation of the Stamp Act—November 1, 1765—was drawing near.

Fourteen boxes of stamped paper arrived in Boston harbor in late September and were transferred to the British garrison in the city. Stamps intended for New Hampshire and Rhode Island also arrived but remained on board a ship guarded by British navy vessels. Other stamps arrived in Philadelphia and in New York. As the biographer Harlow Unger notes, the influential Boston merchant John Hancock pressed associates in London to prevail upon Parliament or the king to reverse themselves before catastrophe struck. The consequences of the Stamp Act "will be bad, & I believe I may say more fatal to you than to us," he said. "For God's sake use your Interest to relieve us. I dread the Event."

As early as June, the Maryland Committee of Correspondence circulated a call to all the other colonial assemblies that a congress be assembled in which representatives might "consult together on the present circumstances." Nine of the thirteen colonies (Georgia, Virginia, North Carolina, and New Hampshire did not participate) would appoint a total of twenty-seven distinguished and influential delegates to attend the meeting, set for New York, on October 19.

At the same time as such reasoned responses to the loathsome tax were being formulated, however, the situation on the streets was fast deteriorating. On August 14, matters in Boston would spiral completely out of control. "My Lords, I am extremely concerned," began a letter from Massachusetts governor Francis Bernard to his superiors across the Atlantic on the following day. Bernard, before going into detail as to what had taken place, warned that the news would "reflect disgrace upon this Province, and bring the Town of Boston under great difficulties."

As he continued his preamble, Bernard disclosed that he, like most of his colleagues, had completely miscalculated the mood of his constituents: "Two or three months ago, I thought that this People would have submitted to the Stamp Act without actual Opposition. Murmurs indeed were continually heard, but they seemed to be such as would in time die away."

One of course imagines bewigged British ministers casting apprehensive glances at each other as they bent over this missive brought fresh from the docks. *What on earth is the man driving at?*

Bernard went on to explain. It was all the fault of the burgesses, he declared, and the damnable insistence of the vile *newspapers* in reprinting their frivolous notions: "The publishing of the Virginia Resolves proved an Alarm bell to the disaffected. From that time an infamous weekly Paper, which is printed here, has swarmed with libels of the most atrocious kind."

Here, Bernard was bemoaning the actions of the *Boston Gazette*, which was carrying continuing installments of "A Letter to a Noble Lord." Covering the entirety of the paper's front page, for instance, the installment of August 12 began, "Can anyone tell me why trade, commerce, sciences, and manufactures should not be as free for an American as for a European?"; then it went on to decry at great length the insidious tactics of the British in offering the newly created tax collector posts to colonists. It was a shameless appeal to desperate citizens, the writer complained; furthermore, the writer had no doubt that the British intended it only as a temporary practice. Soon the new ministry would be back to business as usual, installing loyalists and lackeys into the posts.

Moreover, Governor Bernard said, he was reconsidering the seriousness of these portents: "These have been urged with so much Vehemence and so industriously repeated, that I have considered them as preludes to Action. But I did not think, that it would have commenced so early, or be carried to such Lengths, as it has been."

At that point, one might imagine an impatient lord snatching Bernard's letter from a stuttering minion so that he could read for himself:

"Yesterday Morning," Bernard went on, finally getting to the point, "at break of day was discovered hanging upon a Tree in a Street of the Town an Effigy, with inscriptions, shewing that it was intended to represent Mr. Oliver, the Secretary, who had lately accepted the Office of Stamp Distributor. Some of the Neighbours offered to take it down, but they were given to know, that would not be permitted."

The hanging of an effigy of Boston's newly appointed stamp master (the oak from which it dangled was the one that would come to be known as the "liberty tree") might in itself have passed without the need for a distressed letter from the governor to his superiors, but Bernard explained that the matter scarcely ended there. "Many Gentlemen, especially some of the Council, treated it as a boyish sport, that did not deserve the Notice of the Governor and Council," he continued. "But I did not think so however. I contented myself with the Lt. Governor, as Chief Justice, directing the Sheriff to order his Officers to take down the Effigy; and I appointed a Council to meet in the Afternoon to consider what should be done, if the Sheriff's Officers were obstructed in removing the Effigy."

Readers will probably not be surprised to learn that while Bernard was still closeted with his advisers, the sheriff returned with alarming news. "His Officers had endeavoured to take down the Effigy," Bernard reported, "but could not do it without imminent danger of their lives."

Bernard reported the matter to the councilmen and shared his fears that it was only the beginning of, as he put it, "much greater Commotions." The question that the governor next posed marked him as something less than a despot. "I desired their Advice," he says, "what I should do upon this Occasion."

As Bernard described it, the response reveals the committee system functioning at its fullest:

A Majority of the Council spoke in form against doing anything but upon very different Principles: some said, that it was trifling Business, which, if let alone, would subside of itself, but, if taken notice of would become a serious Affair. Others said, that it was

a serous Affair already; that it was a preconcerted Business, in
which the greatest Part of the Town was engaged; that we had no
force to oppose to it, and making an Opposition to it, without a
power to support the Opposition, would only inflame the People;
and be a means of extending the mischief to persons not at present
the Objects of it.

If Bernard held any misperceptions as to where the buck would finally stop, his advisers were quick to correct him:

Tho' the Council were almost unanimous in advising, that nothing should be done, they were averse to having such advice entered upon the Council Book. But I insisted upon their giving me
an Answer to my Question, and that it should be entered in the
Book; when, after a long altercation, it was avoided by their advising me to order the Sheriff to assemble the Peace Officers and
preserve the peace which I immediately ordered, being a matter of
form rather than of real Significance.

If Bernard presented himself as something less than a martinet, and
if the councilmen behaved as any blame-dodging politician might in a
difficult situation, what is most interesting in the account is the sense
that no one in the government seems to have seen such a thing coming.
Polite dissent on a rural assembly floor, all well and good. Scurrilous
letters printed in an irresponsible Whig newspaper, to be expected. But
threatening a duly instructed sheriff and his men with their lives? No
one could misconstrue such threats.

Still, as Bernard recounted, matters grew even more dire:

It now grew dark when the Mob, which had been gathering all the
Afternoon, came down to the Town House, bringing the Effigy
with them, and knowing we were sitting in the Council Chamber,
they gave three Huzzas by way of defiance, and passed on. From
thence they went to a new Building, lately erected by Mr. Oliver

to let out for Shops, and not quite finished: this they called the Stamp Office, and pulled down to the Ground in five minutes. From thence they went to Mr. Oliver's House; before which they beheaded the Effigy; and broke all the Windows next the Street; then they carried the Effigy to Fort hill near Mr. Oliver's House, where they burnt the Effigy in a Bonfire made of the Timber they had pulled down from the Building.

As Bernard explained, Oliver sent his family from his home and was persuaded by friends to take his own leave, lest an effigy prove too insubstantial a fuel for the bonfire. When the mob discovered that Oliver's friends had remained behind to barricade the house, "they broke down the whole fence of the Garden towards fort hill, and coming on beat in all the doors and Windows of the Garden front, and entered the House, the Gentlemen there retiring."

As Bernard recounted, "As soon as they had got Possession, they searched about for Mr. Oliver, declaring they would kill him." When it became clear that Oliver had fled, the mob then poured out upon the two neighboring houses, "in one of which Mr. Oliver was."

It might have been the end for the stamp master, but, as Bernard puts it, "happily they were diverted from this pursuit by a Gentleman telling them, that Mr. Oliver was gone with the Governor to the Castle. Otherwise he would certainly have been murdered."

By then it was nearing midnight and the mob seemed to have lost some of its steam, according to Bernard. It was decided that Lieutenant Governor Thomas Hutchinson might venture, along with the sheriff, to Oliver's house, "to endeavour to perswade them to disperse."

The attempt did not go well, however: "As soon as they began to speak, a Ringleader cried out, The Governor and the Sheriff! To your Arms, my boys! Presently after a volley of Stones followed, and the two Gentlemen narrowly escaped thro' favour of the Night, not without some bruises."

It was essentially the end of the incident, though the governor added something of a telling postscript: "I should have mentioned before, that

I sent a written order to the Colonel of the Regiment of Militia, to beat an Alarm; he answered, that it would signify nothing, for as soon as the drum was heard, the drummer would be knocked down, and the drum broke; he added, that probably all the drummers of the Regiment were in the Mob."

In any event, Bernard concluded, "Nothing more being to be done, The Mob were left to disperse at their own Time, which they did about 12 o'clock."

The account of the incident as reported in the August 19 edition of the *Boston Gazette* differed little from the governor's except in some details. The reporter noted, for instance, that there was a sign hung around the neck of the effigy, "In Praise of Liberty," with a warning added: "He who takes this down is an enemy to his country."

It was also reported that the mob who had advanced on the house of Oliver (he who had been unwise enough to fulfill "a very unpopular office") had not only burned up the coach and stripped the garden's trees of their fruit but also made their way into the cellar of the house "and helped themselves to the liquor that they found there." Among other depredations, the mob had managed to shatter two mirrors, one said to be "the largest in North America."

According to the *Gazette*, Oliver sent letters to a number of individuals believed to be connected to the protesters, assuring them that he had not in fact taken the position of stamp master. It was not enough to prevent protesters from gathering again in the town square that next evening, whereupon the makings of a bonfire were piled high. Only when a proclamation sent by Oliver to disown any interest in the position was read aloud did the mob disperse, though some marched down to the residence of Lieutenant Governor Hutchinson to have a chat. Finding Hutchinson not at home, they concluded the evening by marching about the city, stopping here and there to read from Oliver's letter, a copy of which they were assured was already on its way to London via packet ship.

The story concluded with the writer sharing word that the crowds involved in the fracases had by no means been made up solely of residents of Boston but had been swelled by others from Charleston, Cambridge, and other nearby towns. The truth of these rumors, the reporter said, tongue firmly in cheek, would "possibly be hereafter discovered by the Vigilance, Industry, and Zeal of the Attorney-General."

As to the origin of the effigies, the reporter theorized that they had been constructed in Cambridge, as evidenced "from this remarkable Circumstance, that the very Breeches were seen upon a Gentleman of that Town on Commitment Day."

Bernard's fears that the events of August 12 and 13 were only the prelude to "much greater Commotions" proved to be prophetic. On the evening of August 26, Lieutenant Governor Hutchinson was sitting at dinner in his Boston home with his family when there came a frenzied pounding at his door. A mob was on its way and the family would have to flee, a friend explained to Hutchinson, who was disbelieving at first. There had been rumors that there was trouble afoot, but the word was that protesters intended to march to the home of Charles Paxton, an officer of the Vice Admiralty Court, as well as that of Benjamin Hallowell, the customs chief of Boston. The houses of admiralty officers might also be a target, Hutchinson's intelligence suggested, but he had been assured that he was no longer at risk. "The rabble were satisfied with the insult I had received and that I was become rather Popular," he told his friend Richard Jackson, the agent for the colony of Connecticut.

Hutchinson, who had already faced the mob once, might have been tempted to stand his ground, but putting his family at risk was out of the question. "I directed my children to fly to a secure place," he told Jackson, "and shut up my house as I had done before intending not to quit it but my eldest daughter repented her leaving me and hastened back and protested she would not quit the house unless I did. I could not stand against this and withdrew with her to a neighbouring house."

It was just as well that his daughter forced him to flee. They'd been gone only minutes, before, as Hutchinson put it, "the hellish crew fell upon my house with the rage of devils and in a moment with axes split down the doors." From the house next door, Hutchinson and his family listened in disbelief to the shouts of the men who had broken into his home.

"Damn him!" one cried. "He is upstairs. We'll have him."

Hutchinson peered through his neighbor's curtains, watching the shadows of men bustle past the windows of his home, even to the top of the house. The rooms downstairs, he saw, were jammed with mob members, so many that most of the crowd was forced to mill about the street outside.

"They'll be in here soon enough," the friends who'd raised the alarm told Hutchinson. He'd better get his family out to someplace safer.

Thus "I was obliged to retire thro yards and gardens to a house more remote," Hutchinson told Jackson. He and his family huddled there in fear until nearly 4 a.m., he said, "by which time one of the best finished houses in the Province had nothing remaining but the bare walls and floors."

"Not contented with tearing off all the wainscot and hangings and splitting the doors to pieces," he continued, "they beat down the Partition walls and altho that alone cost them near two hours they cut down the cupola or lanthern and they began to take the slate and boards from the roof and were prevented only by the approaching daylight from a total demolition of the building."

The sight to which Hutchinson and his family returned would have been evocative of a hurricane's passage: "The garden fence was laid flat and all my trees &c broke down to the ground," he said. "Such ruins were never seen in America. Besides my Plate and family Pictures household furniture of every kind, [and] my own my children and servants apparel, they carried off about £900 sterling in money and emptied the house of everything whatsoever except a part of the kitchen furniture, not leaving a single book or paper in it and have scattered or destroyed all the manuscripts and other papers I had been collecting for 30 years together besides a great number of Publick papers in my custody."

Indeed, it must have seemed to Hutchinson that the world was turned upside down. Only a few weeks before, he had been a comfortable and well-paid minister of the king, in charge of one of the most prosperous of the American colonies. And then one night a hundred men had burst into his home with the apparent aim of killing him.

He'd had to flee without so much as a coat. "The evening being warm I had undressed me and slipt on a thin camlet surtout over my wast-coat," he told Jackson. "The next morning the weather being changed I had not cloaths enough in my possession to defend me from the cold and was obliged to borrow from my host.

"Many articles of cloathing and good part of my Plate have since been picked up in different quarters of the town," he continued, "but the Furniture in general was cut to pieces before it was thrown out of the house and most of the beds cut open and the feathers thrown out of the windows."

Given the evidence of such fury, Hutchinson decided to spirit his children down to Milton, a southern suburb where he kept a second residence, but as they rode, hidden behind drawn curtains, two separate parties of men attempted to stop their coach. As the coach slowed a third time, Hutchinson heard his coachman mutter and drew the curtain aside. A group of men approached from the roadside and one called out, "There he is."

The driver yanked the reins and managed to turn the coach about, galloping them back the safety of the British garrison in Boston. "My daughters were terrified," Hutchinson told Jackson, "and said they should never be safe."

For all that he had gone through, Hutchinson told Jackson that it was his belief that others among the colonists had come forward with apologies that he seemed surprisingly willing to entertain: "The encouragers of the first mob never intended matters should go this length and the people in general express the utmost detestation of this unparalleled outrage and I wish they could be convinced what infinite hazard there is of the most terrible consequences from such daemons when they are let loose in a government where there is not constant authority at hand sufficient to suppress them."

He was further reassured that more responsible parties would make him financially whole: "I am told the government here will make me a compensation for my own and my family's loss which I think cannot be much less than £3000 sterling. I am not sure that they will. If they should not it will be too heavy for me and I must humbly apply to his Majesty in whose service I am a sufferer."

But for Hutchinson the matter clearly went far beyond monetary concerns. "This and a much greater sum would be an insufficient compensation for the constant distress and anxiety of mind I have felt for some time past and must feel for months to come," he explained. "You cannot conceive the wretched state we are in. Such is the resentment of the people against the stamp duty that there can be no dependence upon the general court to take any steps to enforce or rather advise the payment of it."

Hutchinson could not have been more blunt concerning the prospects of the Crown's insisting upon the enforcement of the tax: "Such will be the effects of not submitting to it that all trade must cease, all courts fall, and all authority be at an end."

Nor should the king and his ministers feel shamefaced, Hutchinson insisted. The fear that Parliament would lose its authority over the colonies if it backtracked on the Stamp Act was to be disregarded, he counseled. For if military force sufficient to ensure compliance were ever applied, it would mean the danger of "a total lasting alienation of affection" between the colonies and the Crown.

"Is there no alternative?" the shaken Hutchinson pleaded before closing. "May the infinitely wise God direct you."

7

STRONG DRINK IN PLENTY

ollowing the account of the events through Hutchinson's eyes may allow the modern reader to more fully appreciate the magnitude of the shift that was taking place in the colonies of 1765. Of course, the mob was convinced of the rectitude of its actions (or ceased to think too much at all after a certain point). And it is pointed out by more than one historian that Hutchinson and his governor were not exactly hail-fellow-well-met.

But it is difficult to find much beyond sheer astonishment in the account the lieutenant governor gives concerning his experience. How could matters have come to this? he seems sincere in asking. And what in God's name was to be done about it? What a monumental shift it must have seemed from the way things had always been.

As it turned out, Hutchinson's intelligence was partially correct. Before descending upon his house, the mob had indeed ransacked the homes of William Story, the deputy registrar of the Admiralty Court, and Benjamin Hallowell, the customs collector for the Port of Boston. On the following Monday, September 2, the front pages of both the *Boston Gazette* and the *Boston Post-Boy* carried vivid descriptions of those events.

Since Story was only a renter, accounts agreed, the mob had spared the building in which he lived and had been content to burn his papers and furniture. The damage to Hallowell's home was more severe—in addition, the rioters did "drink and destroy the Liquors in his Cellars, take away his Wearing-Apparel, break open his Desk and Trunks, and

take out all his Papers, and about Thirty Pound Sterling in Money."
Governor Bernard announced a reward of £100 for the identification
of anyone involved in the crimes and £300 "for the Discovery of the
Leader or Leaders of the aforesaid."

While Bernard waited in vain for someone to claim the reward,
other such disturbances were popping up spontaneously elsewhere in
the colonies. On August 27, in Newport, Rhode Island, demonstrators
carried the effigies of Augustus Johnston, their newly appointed stamp
commissioner, along with two other royal officials, to a gallows newly
erected in front of the town courthouse, where they were hanged. To
attract a larger crowd, organizers of the event promised "strong drink
in plenty with Cheshire cheese." As the *Newport Mercury* of September
2 reported, while Johnston and the other officials fled for safety to the
Cygnet, a British man-of-war anchored in Newport harbor, demonstrators punctuated their event by cutting down the effigies and tossing
them onto a bonfire.

The crowd then dispersed and the matter might have ended there,
had not Johnston and his associates come back ashore so soon. The
following afternoon, as they stepped off the docks, the group was accosted by a small party of men who had been among the rioters of the
day before. Words were exchanged, and one of the men put Johnston
in a headlock. Though the scuffle was broken up and Johnston and his
associates made away for their homes, the trouble did not end. Within
hours, the mob assembled again, and with faces painted in disguise and
sharpened axes raised, they made for the homes of Johnston and the
British ministers.

The actions taken were much the same as in Boston: doors were
kicked down, furnishings shattered, paintings slit, and—of course—
stocks of liquor consumed. Johnston and his friends had the good sense
to flee their homes, and no physical harm came to anyone, but the following morning Johnston's resignation of the post of stamp master was
read aloud in the town square to great huzzahs.

The *Mercury* offered an interesting postscript: scarcely was the resignation read when a man whom the paper identified as a young Irishman named Maffaniello stood up to identify himself as the leader of the depredations enacted over the previous days. According to the writer, Maffaniello was immediately arrested and taken aboard the *Cygnet* for safekeeping. This, however, raised a fresh outcry in the town, and the fearful authorities ordered Maffaniello released.

The next day found Maffaniello marching about the streets of Newport, boasting of his power and threatening to destroy the homes of all British officials in the town unless "they made him Presents agreeable to his demands." At this, former stamp master and still attorney general Johnston had heard enough. As it is reported, Johnston "heroically seized upon" Maffaniello, "and some Gentlemen running to his assistance, they carried him off to Jail."

"This proved effective," the reporter added. "Nobody appeared to rescue him, nor to say a Word in his Favour. He is now under Confinement;—the Town is again in Peace, and we sincerely wish it may continue so."

It was an understandable wish, but an unlikely one, for the discontent underlying the disturbances in Boston and Newport was incubating like a fever throughout the colonies. Newspapers played a role in fueling the fire of discontent, of course, but events that took place in Boston on August 26 would not be reported in Newport until a week later. When Rhode Islanders took to the streets the very next day, they had no idea what their counterparts seventy miles to the north had done. The juggernaut had begun to roll, independent of control.

In New York, Stamp Master James McEvers resigned his post shortly after word came of what had transpired in Boston, and the *New-York Gazette* published a letter congratulating him for the move. The letter, reprinted in a number of colonial papers in the weeks to follow, also contained a call addressed "To the Stamp Officers who have not yet resign'd."

"You have now an opportunity put into your hand of showing whether you are friends or enemies to your country," the writer said. "If we are enslaved, it will be thro' the helping hand you lend towards it; for if you do your duty to your country by a refusal, we shall undoubtedly preserve our rights and liberties—His Majesty and our brethren in England will hear our complaints, and redress our grievances."

On October 7, 1765, the first pan-colonial or "continental" congress opened in New York City, at the site that would eventually become known as Federal Hall. Though Virginia, New Hampshire, North Carolina, and Georgia were not represented, each sent word that it would go along with whatever the body decided.

After some debate as to whether certain delegates were authorized to vote or merely advise, the work began in earnest. In their words (*Journal of the First Congress of the American Colonies, in Opposition to the Tyrannical Acts of the British Parliament*), "The congress took into consideration the rights and privileges of the British American colonists, with the several inconveniencies and hardships to which they are, and must be subjected by the operation of several late acts of parliament, particularly the act called the stamp act."

For the next ten days (the body did not meet on Sundays) the various issues were debated, and on October 19 the seven voting members (Connecticut and South Carolina are not named) signed a Declaration of Rights, a document that might be properly thought of as the precursor to another declaration that would appear some eleven years later.

Following what was described as "mature deliberation," the members were agreed on certain rights and grievances of the colonists in America: "The members of this congress, sincerely devoted, with the warmest sentiments of affection and duty to His Majesty's person and government, inviolably attached to the present happy establishment of the Protestant succession, and with minds deeply impressed by a sense of the present and impending misfortunes of the British colonies on this continent," it began, "esteem it our indispensable duty to make the following declarations, of our humble opinions, respecting the most essential rights and liberties of the colonists, and of the grievances under which they labor, by reason of several late acts of Parliament."

The declarations were fourteen in all, many of them covering what by that time were familiar assertions:

1. That colonists were, like residents of Great Britain, subjects of the king and owed their loyalty as well to "that august body, the Parliament of Great Britain."

2. That colonists were also "entitled to all the inherent rights and privileges of his natural born subjects within the kingdom of Great Britain."

3. That it was "the undoubted rights of Englishmen, that no taxes should be imposed on them, but with their own consent, given personally, or by their representatives."

4. That the colonists were not, and "from their local circumstances" could not practically be, represented in Parliament.

5. That "the only representatives of the people of these colonies are persons chosen . . . by themselves," and that furthermore only taxes imposed by their own assemblies could be construed as constitutional.

6. That it was "unreasonable and inconsistent with the principles and spirit of the British constitution" for Parliament to extract monies from colonists for the benefit of the Crown.

7. That trial by a jury of one's peers (not admiralty officers) was the right of every resident in the colonies.

8. That the recent Stamp Act "and several other acts," by extending the jurisdiction of the courts of admiralty beyond its traditional limits subverted the rights and liberties of the colonists.

9. That the duties imposed by the Stamp Act and other "late acts of Parliament" would be burdensome, grievous, and "from the scarcity of specie" be impossible to pay.

10. That Great Britain profited greatly by trading with the colonies.

11. That duties and levies would seriously impair colonists' ability to purchase British products.

12. That "the increase, prosperity, and happiness" of the colonies was dependent upon "full and free enjoyment" of rights and liberties and an "affectionate" relationship with Great Britain.

13. That it was the unquestioned right of the colonists to petition "the king or either house of Parliament."

14. And, finally, that it was the indispensable duty to the king, the mother country, and themselves (with all due respect to both His Majesty and Parliament) "to procure the repeal of the act for granting and applying certain stamp duties, of all clauses of any other acts of Parliament whereby the jurisdiction of the admiralty is extended as aforesaid, and of the other late acts for the restriction of the American commerce."

Certainly all those notions had been conveyed to the mother country before, but this was the first time that all the colonies were speaking in a single voice. That they managed to so much as convene such a gathering, let alone reach agreement on those weighty matters, was remarkable.

But the truth is that even the British began to see the folly of their actions. In an article that attempts to explain the differences between colonial and British thinking on the limits of parliamentary power, historian Edmund Morgan points out that some two weeks prior to the New York gathering, Governor Bernard of Massachusetts had gone to far as to write a letter to Timothy Ruggles, one of the more conservative members of that colony's delegation, suggesting that he urge the congress to submit to the Stamp Act, given that it was very likely to be repealed.

Furthermore, Morgan argues, the colonists who were still hoping for a reasoned conclusion to the issues were putting a very fine point of logic into their declarations. The implication of declaring "subordination" to Parliament while denying its right to levy taxes might seem puzzling, but the argument essentially was that taxes were "internal" matters. Parliament could levy "external" duties having to do with trade regulation (though the language of the declarations seemed to decry the effects of the Sugar Levy as well), but taxes were the "free gift" of the common people and could be levied only by their own representatives.

Whatever the exact thinking of the men who drafted and debated those declarations of October 1765, it is clear that such shadings of meaning held little sway once passions were unleashed in public settings.

Debate among historians continues to this day as to the extent to which politicians willfully manipulated mob actions in order to further their own ends, but what happened on the streets of Boston, Providence, and elsewhere is unmistakable.

Even in distant Charleston, South Carolina, one of the principal shipbuilding centers of the colonies, the demonstrations took on a similar character. With their principal spokesman, Christopher Gadsden, away at the Stamp Act Congress in New York, a group of mechanics organized a spectacle similar to that in Boston. On the morning of October 19, Charlestonians awoke to find that a twenty-foot-high gallows had been erected at the busiest intersection in town, with the effigy of George Saxby, the newly appointed stamp commissioner, dangling from a noose and the likeness of the devil hanging by his side. "Liberty and no Stamp Act" was the legend emblazoned on the gallows.

Later in the evening, the figures were cut down and paraded through the streets by a crowd of two thousand. At one stop in their travels, the mob entered the home of Saxby but, finding neither the stamp master nor any papers inside, moved along to the town commons, where they burned the effigies, along with a coffin bearing a sign, "American Liberty." Before the week was out, Saxby and every other stamp agent in the colony resigned his post, at least until the king and Parliament could consider, in the resignees' words, "the repeal of an act that had created so much confusion." Worse yet for the loyalists, it was "confusion" that would only spread.

8

MURDERER OF RIGHTS
AND PRIVILEGES

On the moonless night of November 1, 1765, sentries at watch atop the walls of Fort George, the British garrison at the tip of New York Island, stared warily northward as a crowd of torch- and candle-bearing men moved down Broadway ever closer to their post. Church and meetinghouse bells in the city began to toll incessantly, and scraps of angry shouting drifted from the direction of the city commons, a mile away.

Though they were ignorant of the size of the group that was approaching, there were fifteen thousand or more residents in the square mile or so of inhabited land that lay at the end of the island, squeezed between what were then known as the North River and the East River. And even with their forces recently bolstered by the arrival of the 60th Regiment from Crown Point, there were only a hundred soldiers inside the fort. There had never been anything resembling a military action waged by colonists against an installation of the king, but the fort's defenders were well aware that there was trouble in the air.

When a figure stepped forward out of the darkness and moved quickly toward the sentry at the gates, more than one musket barrel would have followed the shadow as it went. But the moment when a finger might have tightened on a trigger passed. The figure arrived unharmed before the gate, handed a letter to the sentry with brief instructions, and was quickly gone.

The sentry passed the letter to a guard inside the gates, who took it quickly to the quarters of Lieutenant Governor Cadwallader Colden.

The seventy-seven-year-old Colden, a longtime servant of the king, was the acting governor of New York and, with the Stamp Act due to take effect on this day, had left his home for the safety of the fort, where the first stamped papers from London had been stored since their arrival on October 24.

Colden gave the guard a glance, then smoothed the letter on his table and lit a second candle to aid his aging eyes. "To the Honorable Cadwallader Colden, Esq., Lieut. Governor of the City of New York," the letter was addressed.

Sir,

The People of this City and Province of New York, have been inform'd that you bound yourself under an Oath to be the Chief Murderer of their Rights and Privileges, by acting as an Enemy to your King and Country . . . in the Inforcement of the Stamp-Act which we are unanimously determined shall never take Place among us, so long as a Man has Life to defend his injured Country. . . . We can with certainty assure you of your Fate if you do not this Night Solemnly make Oath before a Magistrate, and publish to the People, that you never will, directly or indirectly, by any Act of yours or any Person under your Influence, endeavor to introduce or execute the Stamp-Act, or any Part of it, that you will to the utmost of your Power prevent its taking Effect here, and endeavor to obtain a Repeal of it in England. So help you God.

That much might have been enough of an affront to the duly appointed governor, but what followed went well beyond the bounds of polite political debate:

We have heard of your Design or Menace to fire upon the Town, in Case of Disturbance, but assure yourself, that, if you dare to Perpetuate any Such murderous Act, you'll bring your grey Hairs with Sorrow to the Grave, You'll die a Martyr to

your own Villainy, and be Hang'd . . . upon a Sign-Post, as a
Memento to all wicked Governors, and that every Man, that
assists you Shall be, surely, put to Death.

New York

If there was any doubt as to the seriousness of the situation, it was now at an end.

Compared with that of other colonies, wrote the historian Carl Becker, the initial response to the Stamp Act in New York was relatively measured and moderate. There had been visible anti-British conflict in New York since 1732, when, Becker says, pro- and anti-British feeling had begun to coalesce around a few central issues not necessarily limited to that colony alone: (1) freedom of the press, (2) the independence of the judiciary, (3) authority of royal decrees, (4) the frequency of elections, (5) the appointment of the colony's agents to England, and (6) the degree to which the local assembly could control the raising of revenue and the administration of the laws.

New York had been successful in defending the first of those issues as far back as 1734, when John Peter Zenger, the editor of the *New York Weekly Journal,* had published an attack on then-governor William Cosby. Though Cosby had had Zenger jailed on charges of libel, Zenger had subsequently been tried and acquitted by a jury, thus establishing the principle of truth as a defense against such claims.

In addition, the New York Assembly was steadfast about maintaining its own authority over its internal affairs, often refusing to raise revenues at the request of the governor, refusing his lordship a life salary, and appointing its own agent to Parliament. There had been various shifting alliances over the past decades, with the proprietors of the large tracts of land up and down the Hudson tending toward the more conservative pro-British faction and the professionals and merchants aligning more toward an independent stance, but the prospect of the Stamp Act was of a much greater magnitude than anything that had ever intruded on New York politics before, an issue that would obliterate familiar party lines.

Though the state assembly in late 1764 formed its own committee of correspondence with reference to issues of "trade of the northern colonies," news of the passage of the Stamp Act escalated matters significantly. For the first time, the largely intermingled interests of the three classes that traditionally dominated how things were done in the colony were being challenged by men who previously had little influence over their colony's affairs. These were the farmers and "mechanics," or skilled workmen, and the laborers at the bottom of society's ladder, as Lieutenant Governor Cadwallader Colden described them in a report to the British lords of trade.

"Though the farmers hold their land in fee simple, they are, as to condition of life, in no way superior to the common farmers in England," he said, though he was not discounting their importance. "This last rank includes the bulk of the people and in them consists the strength of the province." In fact, this "last rank" would have a large part in actions that Becker said would "complete the formation of the Revolutionary parties" in the state.

In New York, there had been grumblings among Colden's constituency from the time of the announcement of the Sugar Act the year before, and earlier in 1765 there had been formed a society "For the Promotion of Arts, Agriculture, and Economy" that intended to promote local manufacturing and look into the boycotting of British goods. But Colden was not concerned at the time. A March issue of the *New-York Gazette*, the liberal rag that it was in the eyes of loyalists, assured readers that the thought that "the Colonies aim at an Independency, is so entirely senseless and ridiculous, as to be almost beneath a serious Refutation."

Yet following the announcement of the passage of the Stamp Act, the tone of articles in the press and of broadsides that appeared in such gathering spots as Burns's Tavern was far less restrained. A young attorney named John Morin Scott published several articles under the pen name "Freeman" that summer, ending one with the declaration "If, then, the interest of the mother country and her colonies cannot be made to coincide; if the same constitution may not take place in both; if the welfare of the mother country necessarily requires a sacrifice of the colonies' right of making their own laws, and disposing of their own property by representatives of their own choosing—if such is really the case between Great Britain and her colonies, then the connection between them ought to cease . . . it must inevitably cease."

In addition, the *Gazette* published its own rendition of the Virginia Resolves, along with accounts of the demonstrations in Boston, Providence, and elsewhere. Though Colden professed little concern publicly, he did write to General Thomas Gage, the commander of British forces in the colonies, suggesting that the forces at Fort George be bolstered "as may be sufficient to secure it against the Negroes or a Mob."

Things began to change, however, when the newly appointed stamp master, James McEvers, wrote to Colden on August 30 to resign a position that had scarcely been announced. McEvers, a local merchant, explained to Colden that threats he had received had convinced him that were he to keep the job, his "house would have been Pillag'd, my Person Abused and his Majestys Revenue Impair'd."

None of that deterred Colden, however. Perhaps motivated by his wish to shed the "Acting" portion of his title, he informed his friend Sir William Johnson, the British superintendent for Indian affairs, that he would prevail over the brigands who opposed the Stamp Act and interfered with the duties of public officials. "I expect to defeat all their Measures," he told Johnson. "The Stamps shall be delivered in proper time after their arrival. I shall not be intimidated."

Colden wrote again to General Gage, asking that reinforcements be sent to Fort George, then warned Captain Kennedy of the Royal Navy that the ship bearing the stamps for New York would need protection. Kennedy agreed to have a British man-of-war meet the good ship *Edward* at Sandy Hook and escort it into New York harbor.

Meanwhile, with news of what had happened in Providence and Boston now widely reported, the Connecticut stamp agent, Jared Ingersoll, wrote to Colden on September 9 suggesting that perhaps the

stamp papers bound for his office should be held in New York for a bit
upon their arrival from London. Less than a week later, Ingersoll told
Colden that he had been forced to pledge that he would have nothing
to do with the papers. What Colden decided to do with Connecticut's
stamps was up to him. On September 25, New Jersey governor William
Franklin advised Colden that he could find no person willing to assume
responsibility for his colony's stamps; when they arrived in New York,
Colden had better hang on to them.

Meanwhile, the stamp agent for Maryland, Zachariah Hood, fled his
home for New York, where he hoped to hide from his increasingly irate
fellow citizens. The protesters' counterparts in New York were advised
that Hood was now among them, however, and the panicked stamp
agent sent a note to Colden saying that a mob had "declared their intention to Attack" the hotel where he was staying and "destroy" him. One
might have presumed that all this would signal Colden that a change
in strategy was in order, but the resolute lieutenant governor sent word
to Hood that he should quit the King's Arms Hotel and take refuge at
Fort George.

Essentially, Colden was now responsible for the stamps of three colonies and was harboring the stamp master of a fourth. One could be
forgiven for passing off his actions as those of a doddering near octoge-
narian, but the energy that Colden applied to his duties suggests that
he was fully aware of what he was doing. Colden's own letter book
and other correspondence in the archives of the New-York Historical
Society show a voluminous correspondence during the period that also
reveals that he and his councilmen were barely on speaking terms by
the fall of 1765.

Scott, the notorious author of the "Freeman" articles in the *New-York
Gazette,* joined with two other young liberal lawyers in publishing the
Sentinel, a weekly devoted almost entirely to the excoriation of Colden
and his shortcomings. In addition, copies of a broadside titled the *Constitutional Courant,* which Colden said contained accusations too slan-
derous for even the likes of John Holt and the *New-York Gazette* to

reprint, made their way to New York City. The masthead of the sheet featured a rendering of a snake cut into pieces, representing the colonies. "Join or Die" was the motto.

Though the *Courant* has since been attributed to the work of William Goddard, a New Jersey activist, Colden's efforts to discover who was responsible for the popular sheet were fruitless. One vendor told an official that he picked up his copies at "Peter Hassenclever's ironworks," a witticism that sent the vendor and his fellows into hysterics as they watched Colden's minion hurry away in search of Hassenclever's mythical lair of sedition. Until shots rang out at Concord, defenders of liberty throughout the colonies would claim that their papers were printed by the nonexistent Hassenclever.

The impact of such publications on the colonial public might be hard to fathom for a contemporary observer, but just as a few populist newspapers such as the *Los Angeles Free Press* and the *Berkeley Barb* were of extreme importance for political activists of the 1960s, the papers and broadsheets of the mid-1760s were the principal means of information for ordinary citizens.

Copies were brought to taverns and read aloud, and when crowds had enough of shouting "Huzzah!" and "For shame!" they joined in the singing of popular ballads that were also printed and circulated by hand. One quoted by Henry Dawson, a nineteenth-century chronicler of the period, was titled "An Excellent New Song for the Sons of Liberty in America" and ran to thirteen stanzas with sentiments that made it the "We Shall Overcome" or "The Age of Aquarius" of its day:

> *With the Beasts of the Wood, we will ramble for Food,*
> *And lodge in wild Deserts and Caves.*
> *And live as Poor as Job, on the skirts of the Globe,*
> *Before we submit to be Slaves. . . .*

> *The Birthright we hold shall never be sold*
> *But sacred maintain'd to our Graves;*

Nay, and ere we'll Comply, We will gallantly die,
For we must not and will not be Slaves; Brave Boys,
We must not, and will not be Slaves.

Despite all this, however, Colden soldiered on. He called a meeting of his council to announce that indeed the stamps for New York were expected from London shortly, that men-of-war would escort the vessel into New York harbor, and that he intended to house the paper at Fort George. When he announced that he was petitioning General Gage for reinforcements, though, his advisers suggested that he was going too far. They believed there was little likelihood of citizens' storming one of His Majesty's garrisons and thought that the sight of troops marching through the streets would surely only fan further discontent.

Colden thanked the councilmen for their advice but continued down his own path. One ally, Indian Commissioner Johnson, wrote to reassure Colden that he was doing the right thing. Certainly, in Johnson's view, the British system of government would not be intimidated by mobs and rioters. General Gage went so far as to suggest to Colden that they consider arresting inflammatory publishers such as Holt and Scott, but the local magistrates talked them out of it.

Colden expressed his frustration concerning the situation in a letter home. Though he admitted that he had come to agree with his advisers that now was probably not the right time to begin hauling the press off to jail, it nonetheless galled him that his own attorney general "did not think himself safe" to press charges against such rabble-rousers. Worse yet, he said, he was fully convinced that the anonymous authors of some of the most inflammatory pieces were attorneys of stature and well known to the judges and others "of the highest trust in Government."

Colden complained further, "No man who converses generally and knows the characters of the Men doubts who the Authors are, but in the present circumstances, it is not practicable for me to obtain legal evidence." What modern reader who has seen Lyndon Johnson pictured at his desk with his bowed head held in his hands or Richard Nixon standing in jut-jawed defiance before reporters cannot have some inkling of what was going through Colden's mind?

Still the lieutenant governor set about bolstering the defenses at Fort George, aided by an eager artillery officer, Major Thomas James, and by Lieutenant John Montresor, a military engineer, whose careful journals of the period would become a valuable source for future historians. Montresor found that the walls and gate of the fort would have to be shored up and that more guns and ammunition would be needed. The men of the 60th Regiment arrived, and the warships *Garland* and *Hawke* were sent out to await the imminent arrival of the stamp ship— the *Garland* to the Narrows and the *Hawke* to Sandy Hook.

At the same time, the Stamp Act Congress was beginning its deliberations, and although Colden considered the meeting illegal, provocative, and at odds with the letter of the British Constitution, there was little he could do to obstruct it. When the results of the Congress were published, the basically respectful tone of the document roused no calls to arms. Much of what was contained had been said before, and with plans set for petitions to the House of Commons, the Lords, and the king appended to the resolutions, all seemed in order.

Artillery units arrived at the fort, and Montresor was almost finished with his repairs. Commissioner Johnson wrote again to Colden, congratulating him on the fine job he'd done of tamping down unrest. All that seemed likely to blow over now, Johnson opined—but then the stamps arrived.

On October 22, after a voyage of nine weeks from London, the *Edward* rounded Sandy Hook, and on October 23, accompanied by Captain Kennedy and the *Coventry* and the *Garland*, she dropped anchor in the waters just off the Battery. After a year and a half of prelude, an abstract concept was now undeniable reality. A few hundred feet from colonial shores floated a British ship, her hold containing a cargo that had inflamed a group of largely ordinary men as nothing else could. Two thousand men were gathered at the docks shouting defiance. Flags on the other ships at harbor lowered their flags to half-mast, as the *Gazette* reported, "to signify Mourning, Lamentation, and Woe."

Colden wisely waited out the immediate display of passion, knowing better than to try to tie up the ship and unload the papers at the dock. Better, he thought, to hire a sloop or two from the local yards and, when the time was right, have the papers taken directly from the *Edward* to the fort under the looming cannon on the ramparts.

Local boatmen were having none of that, however. Scarcely did the *Edward* drop anchor than placards were nailed up on street posts, office doors, and public houses throughout the city, from the docks to the northern fringes at Warren Street. "PRO PATRIA," declared one, with a message brief and to the point: "The first Man that either distributes or makes use of Stampt Paper, let him take Care of his House, Person, and Effects. We dare." The threat was signed by "Vox Populi." The effect was that not a sloop in all New York City found itself available for Colden's hire, not at any price.

Finally, after night fell on October 24, crews from the *Coventry* and the *Garland* boarded the *Edward* and took charge of the ten crates of stamped paper that had probably been carried as unmarked cargo by an unsuspecting merchant captain. The *Edward* was no government vessel, after all, and its captain—one William Davis—was a businessman whose other trade goods in his hold, and those on the dock that he hoped to carry back to England, were far more important to him. If he could have known precisely what he would be in for once he reached New York, it is quite likely he would have refused the consignment.

In any case, the papers were secured by the British sailors and transported quickly to the fort without incident. It was hardly the end of the matter, of course. David McEvers, the son of the recently resigned stamp master, went to Colden and announced that he would eagerly serve in his father's place. And Major James, perhaps emboldened by the two artillery units now in place at Fort George, made the unfortunate statement that he looked forward to cramming the stamps down the throats of New Yorkers "with the tip of his sword."

Furthermore, he attested, should there be any uprising of the people, he would "drive them all out of town, for a pack of rascals, with four and twenty men."

Such talk did nothing to calm the situation, and on the eve of the act's commencement, Colden wrote a note to the mayor of the city that an informant—a shoemaker named Ketchum—had come forward with news that a plot was under way "to bury Major James alive, this day or tomorrow." In the midst of all this, Colden was obliged—as was every colonial governor—to appear before his council on October 31, 1765, and publicly attest to the following: "You Swear that you shall do your utmost that all and every of the Clauses contained in an Act of Parliament of Great Britain, passed in the fifth Year of the Reign of our Sovereign Lord King George the Third . . . be punctually and bona fide observed according to the true intent and meaning therof, so far as appertains to you, So help you God."

On that day, wrote Lieutenant Montresor, the mood in the streets was that of a great day of mourning. The mood, said Montresor, "Descended even to the Bag-gammon Boxes" at the popular Merchants Coffee House at the corner of Water and Wall Streets near the docks. The games were shrouded in black, he said, and the very dice were wrapped up in crepe. There was a sense of sad resolve. Outright rebellion, it seemed, could not be avoided. The fort must necessarily be stormed and the offensive papers burned.

An issue of the *Gazette* appeared on the streets, and though it was not unusual for the paper to announce a funeral, the one featured on this day was noteworthy:

A FUNERAL LAMENTATION

On the Death of

LIBERTY

Who finally expires this

Thirty first of October,

In the Year of our Lord

M.DCC.LXV.

Also in the paper was news of a meeting of all the city's merchants to be held that day "in consternation over the new tax" at Burns's City Arms Tavern, located at Broadway and Thames Street, a few short blocks from the fort. Two hundred merchants met that afternoon, and after some debate "on the melancholy state of American commerce," they issued the following resolves: (1) that they would import no further goods or merchandise whatsoever until the Stamp Act should be repealed; (2) that orders already on the way to England were to be considered null and void and no merchandise should be shipped; (3) that they would sell no goods shipped from Britain after the following January 1; and (4) that those resolves should remain binding upon all until any future meeting at which amendment might be made.

Appended to notices of the merchants' resolves published in the city papers was a statement of support secured from the city's shopkeepers on that same day. Along with copies of those notices, the *New York Mercury* reprinted a letter from a "Principal House in London to a Gentleman of New York" that expressed the concern and support for the colonists' position from the merchants and tradesmen in England: "The present situation of the Colonies," the writer said, "is really alarming to every Person who has large Sums to come from them. . . . If the cursed Act is not repealed, we shall be great sufferers. . . . We dread the Consequences, and know not to what Fatality we are designed."

Of course, no one knew what would happen; observers knew only that something significant would. While the merchants and shopkeepers were shut up in Burns's City Arms Tavern, the stevedores, mechanics, and laborers gathered a few blocks northward on the common. A parade took shape, making its way down Broadway past Burns's and onward to the fort, but finally the group dispersed. The *Gazette* reported that smaller bands were heard tramping through the streets later on, breaking lamps and windows, shouting "Liberty," and promising that they'd be back the following night in greater numbers to "pull down houses," but the night passed without serious incident.

On the morning of November 1, Lieutenant Governor Colden sent off his missive to Mayor John Cruger, Jr., warning of the rumored plot against Major James and requesting that the mayor do everything in his power to help calm the populace. He next sent a deputation of troops to watch over Vaux Hall, the home of James, then turned his attention to the final preparations at Fort George.

In the city, little work was getting done, as men gathered in knots on street corners to speculate on what might happen next. In the Merchants Coffee House, someone tacked up a copy of the letter that would later be carried to Colden. Bulletin boards about the city were covered with notices, "Some of them in a good Stile," according to the *Gazette*, threatening woe to anyone who dared to "apply for, deliver out, receive, or use a Stamp or should delay the Execution of any customary public Business without them."

Meanwhile, the cannon at the fort were loaded with musket balls and turned from their customary position overlooking the harbor so that they now pointed at the city streets. A pair was positioned directly behind the gates, where any entry would probably be attempted. The cannon belonging to the merchants were ordered to be spiked (rods driven into the fuse holes) to prevent them from being used in an assault against the fort. Colden prevailed upon the navy to dispatch an additional contingent of marines to the fort, and sixteen artillerymen now stood guard at Major James's home. Now he could only wait and see.

As it grew dark, the crowd on the common grew steadily, and in distinction to the night before, a number of influential men caught up in the discussions with the merchants and shopkeepers at Burns's were there to lend some focus to the gathering. It was said to be an unusually calm night, with no wind to disturb the candles and the torches that lit the green. According to the *Gazette*, it was about 7 p.m. when a commotion rose up.

Men at the edge of the crowd turned to see a portable gallows being trundled toward them, and shouts of approval rang out as the contraption moved into the light. Dangling from the gallows noose was an effigy of Colden, "a Man who had been honoured by his Country with an elevated Station, but whose public Conduct . . . has unhappily drawn upon himself the general Resentment of his country." The figure

clutched a sheet of stamped paper in its hand, and a drum—alluding
to Colden's purported service as a drummer in a long-ago Scottish
battalion—was slung across its back. Beside the figure of Colden hung
a familiar form: that of the devil, meant to be whispering encouragement into the governor's ear.

While that striking arrangement was receiving cheers, a second
group arrived on the common bearing a seated effigy of Colden, and
soon the two groups were off on parade through "most of the streets
of the city." One group reached the home of the former stamp master,
McEvers, where they stopped to bellow out three cheers. By that time,
the church and meetinghouse bells had begun to toll, and someone
darted from the shadows to deliver the demand to Colden.

It could not have been long after the governor finished reading the
message when the commotion outside the fort began. The effigy of
Colden seated in a chair was paraded past the walls, while threats and
taunts were hurled at Major James. As the crowds jockeyed, someone
found that the doors of the governor's coach house had been left un-
locked.

In the next moment, they were thrown open, and the governor's coach
was pulled out. Someone vaulted into the coachman's seat and reached
down to haul the effigy of Colden up beside him. Others snatched up
the coach rails and began to trot off toward the common.

"Fire, damn you!" men shouted to the artillerymen stationed at the
the looming cannon above. But no shots came.

Back up Broadway to the common the surreal procession went, its
leaders now hard pressed to keep matters under control. No windows
should be broken, it was understood, no violent acts committed.

The sight of Colden's effigy mounted on the governor's own coach
threw the crowds at the common into a frenzy. It was decided without
debate that everyone would return to the fort with the devil and the
dangling rendition of Colden along for the ride.

This time the mob, said by Montresor to have swelled to two thousand
or more, surged against the gates, pounding, demanding admission, once

more daring the troops and Major James to fire. But if James heard, he had the good sense to keep his sword sheathed and his tongue tied.

Finally the group turned away from the fort and made its way to the nearby Bowling Green. There would be a bonfire now, it was decided, and a ready group of volunteers tore planks from the fort's fence, then added "a Chaise and two Sleys" from the yawning coach house to the pile. In short order, there was a roaring blaze to which the governor's coach and its silent passenger were added, followed shortly by the gallows and its twisting pair.

It might have seemed enough for a night's effort, but for some it was just a start. A sizable contingent—described by Montresor as "300 carpenters"—peeled away from the huzzahs at the bonfire and advanced upon Vaux Hall. Perhaps the major, they thought, had not deigned to greet them at the fort because he was hiding under his bed at home.

The major had better sense than that, of course: he'd long since removed his family to safety aboard the *Garland*. As for the sixteen noble artillerymen guarding the major's home, they took one glance at the advancing mob and immediately decamped. Within moments, according to the account of one bystander, the mob burst through the doors of James's richly furnished home and its members were wreaking havoc. They shattered "the windos and dores the Looking Glasses Mehogany Tables Silk Curtains A Libiry of Books all of the China and furniture," the account attests, any shortcomings in its grammar supplanted by its vigor. "The feather beds they cut and throo about the streets and burnt broke and tore the Garden."

Thirsty after such efforts, they "drank 3 or 4 Pipes of wine destroyed the Beef throo the butter about and at last burnt the whole." Not much was left, it seems: "Only one red Silk Curtain they kept for a Colour," our observer notes. And with that the night was done.

9

MORNING AFTER

Lieutenant Montresor reported his relief that Colden had ordered the troops to hold their fire despite the insults and depredations of the night, for the result, he said, "would have been a great slaughter." Certainly, that much is true, for the mob was armed largely with stones and clubs and fortified primarily by drink. A hail of musket and cannon fire would have been deadly and would have put a quick end to bonfires and home wrecking, but as to the long-term consequences, it is more difficult to say.

Colden, for all his bluster and fervent allegiance to his king, had no desire to be the one to set all hell loose. And though he and his men might have been able to repel the previous night's assault, they were in no position to withstand a lengthy siege. Even as the morning of November 2 dawned, there were fewer than two hundred troops inside the walls, and the fort, designed to keep watch over the waters of the harbor, was not positioned to withstand an attack from its own citizens.

Colden wrote to British secretary of state Henry Conway that he feared that future attempts to storm the fort might end less fortunately, as "a great part of the Mob consists of Men who have been Privateers and disbanded Soldiers whose view is to plunder the town." Furthermore, despite the efforts of Major James and Lieutenant Montresor, the fort's position was precarious, "arising principally from the want of proper cover within, and being commanded by the Circumjacent Buildings."

Though it was a Saturday, Colden decided to call a meeting of his council. Given the general ineffectiveness of that group, he could not have expected much, but at the very least he could say he had tried.

The response of his advisers was maddening. They were by no means military men, they told Colden, but it seemed that the fort was adequately prepared and defended. Meantime, several members were absent, owing to the fact that the call from Colden had come unexpectedly. The council would summon its absent members to confer again in the afternoon.

While Colden stewed, he tried Captain Kennedy on a different idea. Perhaps the stamps could be moved aboard one of the naval ships in the harbor, thereby diverting the attention of the rabble from the fort? Captain Kennedy responded adroitly: as the stamps were already ensconced in Fort George, "a place of security sufficient to protect them from any attempts the Mob can possibly make to destroy them," he could see no reason for displacing them. In fact, he said, "the very attempt to move them must be attended with much greater risque than they can possibly run while there." In other words, the scalding potato would remain in the lieutenant governor's hands.

Finally, the absent council members were rounded up and Colden wearily addressed the body. He was giving this vexing matter considerable thought, he told them. It was indeed his duty as governor to receive those stamps and to place them in the fort, where they would be safe. However, from that point forward, he said, was it not the duty of the master of the stamps to determine what disposition should be made of them? And owing to the fact that there no longer was a stamp master, how could anyone say?

Sir Henry Moore had been appointed as permanent governor and was at that very moment en route to the colony aboard one of His Majesty's ships. Perhaps they might let the matter rest until the new governor arrived, Colden suggested. If there was any spite hidden in the long-overlooked Colden's suggestion, no one seemed to detect it.

According to the minutes of the meeting, the governor's council was of the unanimous opinion that Colden's proposal was the very thing. "His Honour might publickly declare he would do nothing in relation to the Stamps, but leave it to Sir Henry Moor to Act in this matter as he should think fit." The minutes further reported that the lieutenant governor had acquiesced in the council's wishes and that he would comport himself accordingly. If those in attendance were not engaged in a round of backslapping as they left the chambers, it was only because decorum prevented it. Finally, they had found a way out.

Colden and his ministers lost no time in leaking the results of the meeting, but the response was far less than they had hoped for. On Sunday morning, Colden was roused from his bed by an officer. A sentry had found a message stuffed into an oyster shell and left outside the gate:

Sir,
As one who is an enemy to mischief of all kinds, and a Well
wisher to you and your Family, I give you this Notice that Evil
is determined against you and your Adherents and will in all
human Probability take Effect, unless Speedily prevented by
your public Declaration upon Oath, That you will never, in any
Manner, countenance, or assist, in the Execution of the Stamp
Act, or anything belonging to it; and also, that you will, to the
utmost of your Power, endeavor to get it repeal'd in England,
and meanwhile prevent its takin Effect here. Your life may
depend upon the Notice you take of this Advice.

BENVELOUS

It was also reported to Colden that a call to storm the fort and seize the stamps was circulating on the streets. Even if Colden did not sigh at such news, he well might have. Clearly, there would be no simple way out of this mess.

On Monday, Colden summoned Mayor Cruger to his offices, where he repeated his pledge that he would take no action regarding the stamps and even handed Cruger a signed declaration to that effect. As the *Gazette* reported, that gesture had little effect. Word came back to Colden that unless the stamps were delivered up to the citizenry, they would be taken away by force, "which would have been attended probably with much bloodshed."

Lieutenant Montresor's journals give a deft shorthand account of the mounting tension. "Engineers all on Duty this night to fortify the Fort," he wrote on Saturday. On the streets, he said, leaders of the protests were extracting money for their ends "from private people" under threat of death. On Sunday, the men were ordered to spike the cannon outside the walls of the fort on the Battery and in the artillery yard. The defenders now totaled "153 Rank & file and near 30 officers."

The front gates were barricaded with cordwood, and for those inside the fort duty was extended around the clock. "Even the master of the vessel who brought the Stamps," Montresor wrote, "his life being threatened, was obliged to fly."

On Monday, Captain Kennedy again refused to move the papers to any of his ships, and the sense of crisis deepened: "Advertisements throughout the Town threatening the lives of particulars. Many stragglers thronging in with arms from several parts even Connecticut, for plunder, Etc. The Fort pretty well under cover this night. The Governor's Family obliged to seek protection on board His Majesty's Ship the Coventry." Major James determined it prudent to leave the fort and observe matters from the decks of the *Garland*.

On Tuesday, November 5, Colden received a message from the city's council advising that the stamps should be delivered into its hands. The papers would be held in City Hall and guarded by their own officers. Sensing that he was at the endgame, Colden sent a message to General Gage: if townspeople were to storm the fort, he was ready to give them a "warm welcome," but he wanted the general's advice.

Gage was not disposed to be cowed by thugs, but he was also an experienced military tactician. Firing upon the mob might indeed keep it out of the fort for a time, but it would not put an end to the matter. "The consequence," said Gage, "would in all appearance be an Insurrection . . . the Commencement of a Civil War, at a time when there's nothing prepared or can timely be so, to make opposition to it."

Gage's conclusion was succinct: "The Fort tho' it can defend itself, can only protect the Spot it stands on."

With the wave seemingly about to crash, Colden called his own council together that afternoon. He shared Gage's thoughts and the demands of the town council and passed along intelligence suggesting that demonstrators had gathered a hundred barrels of powder in preparation for an assault on the fort.

Colden warned that even if they were to yield up the stamps, it might not satisfy the people. It would quite likely be seen as a sign of weakness on the government's part, not to mention a breach of his own oath of office. It was Colden's belief that this was the first step toward a civil war.

Whether his councilmen shared this dire (if prophetic) assessment, they saw no further equivocation possible. Yield up the stamps, they counseled Colden. And so, explaining to Major James that "I could not stand single," he did. "I deliver'd the Packages."

As Montresor described it, "Seven Boxes of Stamps were delivered and proceeded to the city Hall in Carts and deposited there attended by 5,000 people. I was on duty at Fort George this night. . . . The Governour ordered double Guards. . . . Major James embarked for England, where he was obliged to remain, being in danger, otherwise of his life. Two Guns fired at 4 o'clock pm for the men of War to their stations."

There was little need for double guards, as it turned out. In fact, Major James might even have returned to the city without fear of being buried, for the time being, at least. The effects of Colden's actions were instantaneous. "After which," as he wrote to London, "the Mob entirely dispersed, and the City remained in perfect tranquility, till I delivered up the Administration to Sir Henry Moore."

Hindsight would suggest that the actions of the mob were controlled largely by city officials and their influential friends, but the fact that nearly one-third of the city's population turned out to escort the convoy of stamps to their own hall also suggests that there was great accord across all social lines. Certainly, the outcry surrounding the event would be greatly influential in determining the fate of the Stamp Act.

HORNETS AND FIREBRANDS

Montresor summed up the immediate aftermath in New York using few words: "6th. Perfect tranquility (as to appearances) this day: advertisements put up about *Peace proclaimed*. The Governor's family returned from on board the Man of war. The Lawyers leveled at, by the people, to be at the bottom of this disloyal Insurection and seconded by many people of property of the place and its neighborhood."

With lawyers properly excoriated—"Hornets and Firebrands of the Constitution, The Planners and Incendiaries of the present Rupture"— Lieutenant Montresor termed the matter essentially at an end: "8th. Sailed the Edward—Cap' Davith with major James of the Royal Artillery on board for England, with dispatches to the Secretary of State from the Lieutenant Governor and General."

Colden remained to await the new governor, though his attempts to pass the buck to Governor Moore did not go unnoticed in London. Secretary Conway sent back a scathing condemnation of Colden's pusillanimous statement that he would take "no Step 'till Sir Henry Moore should arrive. It is not comprehended upon what Principle you could take upon You thus to suspend the Power of Government, 'till the arrival of the Governor."

Colden did his best to explain the realities of his situation. "At the time the Mob Demanded the Declaration from me that I should not distribute the Stamp'd Papers, they knew that no Man would distribute them and that no Man dared to Receive a Stamp'd Paper," he told Conway, arguing that he had only been following the advice of his advisers.

"The Council thought I should be under no difficulty in saying I would not do, what it was not in my power to do."

As for the matter of deferring action until the new governor arrived, it was only a matter of protocol, Colden suggested. "My promise was founded on the supposition of the arrival of Sir Henry Moore in a very short time: If any accident had happened to prevent his arrival . . . that Promise ceased; and I believe no Man would have thought me perpetually bound by it." In fact, he told Conway, he had stood up against the mob until the last possible moment, causing the council to call him an "obstinate old man."

His property and bodily safety and that of his family were at risk, and, furthermore, it would have probably meant a slaughter and the beginning of a civil war had he tried to keep the papers in the fort, he went on. He was a long and faithful servant to the Crown; instead of criticism, he said, he hoped for understanding and approval.

Of course, if hopes were horses, beggars would ride, and if Colden truly expected a pat on the back, he would forever go wanting. Still, he was spared outright punishment for his actions (there was a call by some colonists that his salary be diverted to pay for the repairs to the home that Major James had leased, but it came to nothing), and Colden would remain in office until the final days of British rule.

Colden's capitulation and Governor Moore's arrival on November 13 did not put an end to tensions in New York. Even though Montresor was ordered by the new governor to raze the defenses at Fort George and Moore issued no public statement regarding the stamps, the legislation remained in effect and milder protests continued in the town of New York and elsewhere.

News of demonstrations in New Hampshire, North Carolina, Philadelphia (where Franklin's home was threatened), and Charleston also reached London. Twelve of the colonies' stamp collectors relinquished their duties by mid-November, and though the stamp master for Georgia did not arrive until early in January 1766, his first official action was to resign.

In late November a group of three hundred men ferried themselves to Long Island in pursuit of Stamp Master Zachariah Hood, who had been spotted at a home in Flushing. On December 1, Montresor reported that a member of the Royal Artillery had stabbed a protester with a bayonet, but nothing came of it. A ship from Quebec arrived in New York with its captain holding a stamped clearance he had obtained there, and word came from Philadelphia that a ship had arrived from Barbados, also bearing a stamped permit. Protesters in Philadelphia seized the captain's papers and took them to the common, where they were burned.

On December 13, a British man-of-war intercepted one ship attempting to leave the harbor without stamped papers, forcing it to return to dock. On December 16, Governor Moore called a meeting of the New York merchants to advise them that he had ordered the navy to seize any ships attempting to leave without stamped papers. The announcement occasioned a march culminating in the burning of Lord Grenville's effigy on the common, but no rioting accompanied the demonstration. Broadsides and advertisements were posted everywhere, Montresor observed, "seditious and infamous as ever."

A week before Christmas, the first snowfall of the year blanketed the city with a six-inch carpet as a forty-person contingent of militiamen maintained its watch over the stamps in the town hall. Undeterred by the weather, a mob gathered on Christmas Eve outside Captain Kennedy's house, calling out threats that they would burn it, but they dispersed when Mayor Cruger appeared. Meanwhile, Lieutenant Montresor was deputed to draw up a proper survey of the town and its harbor; though he accepted the commission, he did so without calling attention to his charge, for reasons made obvious by such actions.

At about the same time, the town council suggested to Governor Moore that he advertise for someone to fill the vacant post of stamp master and that if no one could be found, he should issue free passes to ships so that trade could resume. It might have been deemed a clever ploy on the part of the opposition, but the governor took no notice of it.

On New Year's Eve, notices went up at the Merchants Coffee House warning that the homes—and the lives—of the captains of the men-of-war were at risk should they try to stop ships leaving New York harbor without stamped paper, but though the customs house was reopened, no stamps were issued and no ships attempted to leave. Business was essentially at a standstill in the town, and Montresor continued to work on his maps, "*Sub Rosa*, as observations might endanger ones house and effects if not ones life."

Most significantly, the threat and lingering tension in the town of New York had taken on a quasi-legitimate identity. At first, the discord was centered in the essays and broadsides attributed to individuals such as John "Freeman" Scott, or in such papers as John Holt's *Gazette*. Then the faceless "mob" had joined the fray, and whether its members were the pawns of the intellectuals or the "attorneys" or constituted the spontaneous uprising of the common people, they were similarly disaffiliated and disorganized, appearing one night to loot and burn, then vanishing. But by the end of 1765—and not only in New York—the disparate forces had begun to coalesce. What had begun as a generic epithet tossed off on the floor of Parliament had metamorphosed into a distinct reality.

On December 8, John Montresor wrote in his journal, "The Sons of Liberty they term themselves, openly defying powers, office and all authority." *They* had acquired an identity—and at last vague discontent and patriotic philosophy were joined to action and a political agenda.

11

FROM AIRY NOTHING

As the aggrieved Henry Van Schaack would attest, the men who called him to account in Albany on the evening of January 4 were just a group of Dutchmen, most of whom he was familiar with—he easily rattled off the names of thirty-six who had been present the night he was first accosted at Williams's Inn.

But two nights later, those men had become something else. In a handbill nailed to the Dutch church door, Van Schaack saw that he was now up against an *organization*: "Whereas Mr. Henry Van Schaack has by great impudence and unequal'd obstinacy drawn upon himself the resentment of his Fellow Citizens already, There are, Therefore, to advise him To meet the Sons of Liberty at Mr. Thomas Williams's, Vintner, to Morrow at 10 o'clock . . . to prevent worse consequences."

Of course, there was correspondence between men of influence and similar political leaning in New York and Albany. And Albany sent its own set of delegates to the Stamp Act Congress in October. Montresor noted in one of his journal entries early in December that the new governor, Henry Moore, was eager to make arrangement for the quartering of a garrison of troops in Albany, "great disputes having cropped up there on that score."

There is no evidence that the Dutch fire masters of Albany were operating under any brief but the common resolve now uniting the colonies. But in only two days, they left off existence as a group of concerned citizens and were now issuing public statements as the Sons of Liberty, just as their counterparts in New York, Boston, and elsewhere were. And if it was a frustration for Van Schaack to find himself forced to address an organization, as opposed to John Lansing and friends, it would have been an equally invigorating transformation for the fire masters.

In short order, the group would draft a document titled "The Constitution of the Sons of Liberty of Albany," which began, "As in our present distressed condition, while under the greatest apprehensions of yet threatening Slavery, our surest refuges seem the mercies of God, and our own fixed and unanimous resolution to persevere to the last in the vindication of our dear bought Rights and Privileges."

There were eight articles of this constitution, including: (1) the stipulation of a thirteen-man elected committee, (2) that this committee was to be formed for the purpose of considering grievances pertinent to the Stamp Act, (3) that the group would "countenance no step whatsoever to the disturbance of the public tranquility, nor private peace of any man," (4) that the group would oppose, and help bring to punishment, anyone who would injure any person or property, (5) "that we will discourage, discountenance and oppose the mean practice of dropping Letters on the Streets, setting up scandalous Libels, Verse, etc.," (6) that anyone who opposed the articles would be considered as "cold Friends to Liberty, and treated accordingly," (7) that the group held the "highest esteem of his most sacred Majesty, King George," and (8) that should any person "subscribing or publicly assenting and behaving agreeable to these Articles" be arrested or prosecuted for that behavior, then "we will do the uttermost for their relief." The document was signed by ninety-four citizens of Albany, including most of the men whom Van Schaack had identified.

On January 7, 1766, a meeting was reported at which the New York Sons of Liberty also voted to formally organize themselves, and in his diary entry of January 11, Lieutenant Montresor noted that the New York town Sons had received "advice of the Riots at Albany by the Sons of Liberty there." When Governor Moore announced that he was still in possession of the stamps originally intended for Connecticut and would be willing to issue them to anyone who applied, the local Sons issued threats against his life.

"Children nightly trampouze the Streets with lanthorns upon Poles

& hallowing," Montresor lamented. "The Magistracy either approve of it or do not dare to suppress the children." He reported that "insolent advertisements" had been placed at the coffeehouse warning against anyone daring to aid in the enforcement of the Stamp Act and passed along rumors that a group of colonists in Hartford—a "large body"— had assembled there to discuss forming "a new system of government." Some called for an intercessor such as Oliver Cromwell to seize control of the royal government while others argued for something altogether new. Only one thing was certain, Montresor said: "they were very much divided & the consequences amongst themselves were dreaded."

On January 19, word reached Montresor that a desecration almost impossible to imagine had taken place in Philadelphia: "To such a pass are matters come to . . . in a Stationers Shop was found wrote in a Blank Book, 'George by the Curse of God, usurper of Great Britain and Destroyer of the Faith.'" As Montresor—stunned that anyone would blaspheme his king—reported, "Great Enquiries were made but unfortunately to no purpose."

By February 1, the Sons in New York went so far as to form a plan to storm Fort George to seize and destroy the stamped papers belonging to Connecticut. The group formed an official committee of correspondence for "the Liberty Boys," as Montresor and others also called them, in the neighboring colonies.

When Governor Moore called his council together, seeking its opinion as to how the Stamp Act might possibly be implemented, its response was the same as it was to Colden before: the measure simply could not be enforced. Colonists continued to parade nightly through the streets of New York town, and vendors hawked papers by crying out, "The downfall of the stamp act." Similar unrest was reported in Boston, and the Sons of Liberty in Philadelphia sent word to their counterparts that they had discovered stamped permits authorizing ships' passage to the Mediterranean. The permits, which had been signed by the customs director in New York, were incinerated in front of the Philadelphia Coffee House to the approval of many.

When that news reached New York, it occasioned a rally led by two men who had assumed prominent roles in the nascent organization: John Lamb, a trader, and Isaac Sears, a thirty-five-year-old former privateer. The mob marched upon the home of Charles Williams, the naval officer for New York province, who had issued the pass, and that of Lewis Pintard, the merchant who had applied for it, intending to send a ship out of Baltimore. The two were dragged to the common, where they would have been pilloried if not for the intercession of clergymen; when both agreed to apologize, they were set free.

Meantime, colonial papers carried news from London that the matter of "what should be done with the rebellious colonies" was now being debated in the House of Commons. Grenville, who had been replaced as prime minister during the summer, remained a member of Parliament and was said to be "exceptionally warm" on the matter. He requested that a sizable force be sent to "destroy" the rabble, and a fair number of his colleagues were in support of such sentiments. Still, there were a number, including Pitt, who were equally fervent in their opposition. A letter from one British friend of the colonies published in the *New-York Gazette* predicted that all would end well: "Things will be settled to your satisfaction soon."

Though it was not reported widely, the New York Sons had taken matters to a level previously unknown in the colonies. Just before Christmas, a secret delegation, headed by Gershom Mott and Hugh Hughes, was sent to New London, Connecticut, bearing a letter from Isaac Sears. Sears, a Boston native, had earned a reputation as a daring captain during the French and Indian War, wreaking havoc on French shipping until he lost his ship in 1761. He had moved to New York at that point and turned to trading, investing principally in ships that sailed between the colonies and the West Indies.

What Sears was asking of his counterparts in Connecticut was a pledge that the people there would come to the aid of New York in the event that Grenville followed through on his threat to send troops to enforce the Stamp Act. In return, Sears promised the same. Mott and Hughes held discussions with committees in New London and Norwich, and on Christmas Day 1765, they returned with a successfully negotiated mutual defense pact. The Sons of Liberty of both New York and Connecticut agreed to march at a moment's notice, at their own expense, should proper notice be received from the other, "to the relief of those that shall, are, or may be in danger from the stamp act, or its promoters and abettors."

In addition, the two groups agreed to keep a close eye on local persons who might take actions favoring the implementation of the Stamp Act and share intelligence as need be. The groups further pledged to defend freedom of the press and to uphold the interests of all those who wished to carry on business in defiance of the odious threats of the British.

Copies of the agreement were sent to other groups of Sons in Connecticut and New York, including Albany, as well as Massachusetts, New Hampshire, New Jersey, and Rhode Island. On January 7, 1766, the full membership of the Sons of New York passed a set of resolutions that would effectively transform them from a randomly motivated association into a formally constituted organization. They pledged: (1) to go to the "last Extremity, and venture our lives and fortunes, effectually to prevent the Stamp-Act from ever taking place in this city and Province," (2) that anyone who issued or received a stamped instrument "shall incur the highest resentment of this society, and be branded with everlasting infamy," (3) that anyone carrying on business as usual without stamped papers would be protected "to the utmost power of this society," (4) that they would cast no aspersions on the character of any man, except of course, "than as he was a promoter or abettor of the stamp act," and (5) that they would maintain peace and order, "so far as it can be done consistently with the preservation and security of our rights and privileges."

On February 24, the resolves were published in the pages of the *New York Mercury*, along with a sixth article agreed to the week before during a meeting at the home of William Howard. In that addendum, the Sons of New York affirmed their belief that the general safety of the colonies and the British constitution depended upon a "firm union of the whole," and that the Sons would stand firm against any attempt to rob them of their rights and privileges. Furthermore, they pledged their willingness "to assist our fellow subjects in the neighbouring provinces, to subvert or endanger the liberties of America."

All this was reprinted without comment by the *Mercury*, though the paper did add punctuation with a bulletin recently arrived from Elizabeth-Town. There, it was said, "A large Gallows was erected . . . last Week with a Rope ready fixed thereto, and the Inhabitants there vow and declare, that the first Person that either distributes [or] takes out a Stamped Paper, shall be hung thereon without Judge or Jury."

The Sons of Liberty of Oyster Bay wrote to cheer "the measure which you have taken . . . we do heartily approve of, and that with our lives and fortunes we stand ready to assist you in the same." Sons chapters in Wallingford, Connecticut, issued a similar proclamation of willingness to go "to the last extremity, even to take the field." Chapters at Preston, Canterbury, and Stratford chimed in. At a summit meeting in Hartford, Sons delegates from across the state dedicated themselves to the perpetuation of "the union and harmony established among the Sons of Liberty" in all the colonies and created a Committee of Correspondence to further that end.

A Sons chapter in New Brunswick, New Jersey, wrote New York on February 25 that it would be ready to lend "hearts and hands" to oppose the common enemy. The Sons of Woodbridge called for a general convention to join "all the provinces on the Continent." In April, the militiamen of Springfield followed up their annual military exercises with a proclamation that they would be ready at a moment's notice to come to the aid of the Sons of Liberty of any neighboring province, and as the *New York Mercury* reported, they then drank a toast to an ample supply of arms and ammunition for the Sons of Liberty everywhere.

Sons in Providence and Newport met in support on the plan of union for all the colonies, stating it was their "indispensable Duty" to unite with Sons of Liberty "through out America in every reasonable Measure, to prevent the Execution of the Stamp Act." The Boston Sons, of course, pledged their unity with New York and sent letters out to every town in the colony urging the same. In Portsmouth, New Hampshire, and the surrounding towns, the results were similar, and in Baltimore as elsewhere in Maryland groups responded enthusiastically to a union of the colonies. Only in Philadelphia were Sons unable to secure a pledge of support, owing, says historian Edmund Morgan, to public apathy there.

Inside two years, then, vague discontent, polite protest, and petition by lawfully appointed colonial assemblies and trade agents to Parliament transformed into the formation of paramilitary guerrilla organizations, ready to do battle with the British. Poor Montresor seemed beside himself. "The Sons of Liberty arrived to that pass . . . that in case orders should arrive for Enforcing the Stamp act to seize all the Officers of the Crown and embark them for England," he reported on February 26. With the officers gone, the Sons hoped to bribe the rank and file "over to their disloyal opinions."

Still, Montresor found reason to hope. He pointed out that Governor Moore had "bought and wears two Homespun Coats made in the Colonies for the Encouragement of arts in the Colonies and as an Example for others." Meanwhile, he busied himself with finishing up the map work that Moore had commissioned. On March 3, he reported that finally the unspiking of all the field artillery had been completed, nearly four months after the mob had threatened to storm Fort George.

On March 9, the first sloop of spring sailed upriver for Albany, though the following day a storm dumped a foot of snow on the city. The Sons held a parade on the eleventh, featuring an effigy of Lieutenant Governor Colden spiking a cannon. The procession made one stop before General Gage's headquarters, and when Gage and his men refused to join in their huzzahs, the men shouted that they would have their hats off yet before the Sons were done with them.

The bad weather continued, with tides threatening to force the evacuation of Fort Edward. "A very hard Gale of wind at East with rain," as Montresor described it. "A perfect storm." One sea captain, a veteran of twenty-two Atlantic crossings, claimed that he had never seen such weather. He reported having hacked more than twenty tons of ice off his masts and rigging. Aboard that frozen ship, as it turned out, was one Captain Conner, sent by His Majesty to relieve Captain Kennedy for refusing to take the stamps aboard a man-of-war when Colden begged him. The act would have been some solace to the sulking Colden, surely.

On March 18 word came of a proposal from the New York Sons to erect a statue on Bowling Green where Governor Colden's coach had been burned. It would be the likeness of that friend of the colonies William Pitt standing in prominence there, and the place would be re-named Liberty Green.

While that prospect loomed, a more pressing matter took over the concerns of the Sons. On the nineteenth, Isaac Sears and one of his as-sociates went aboard the warship *Garland*, demanding that the ship's lieutenant, a man named Hallam, be turned over to them. According to Sears, Hallam had publicly proclaimed that were John Holt, the pub-lisher of the *Gazette*, to set foot in England, he'd be hanged for the things he'd dared to publish.

As Sears made this case, a mob gathered on the docks and began to chant, "Bring the lieutenant ashore, with a halter about his neck."

There would be no need for halters, Sears explained, if the lieutenant would deliver a written denial of the statement. What Sears received was a quick escort back to the docks, but it was not the end of things. The following day, the mob was back and a message was relayed to the ship: if Hallam did not deliver himself up to answer these charges, he would be killed, sooner or later.

When General Gage heard of all this, he must have been at his wit's end. He sent word to the captains of the warships in the harbor that he was sending additional powder and cartridges. Meantime, they should stand fast against such threats.

Continuing foul weather hampered efforts to bolster the ships' sup-plies, but at the same time it kept the protesters inside as well. On the twenty-first, the Sons assembled on the docks again, but word reached them that the ships were stocked and fortified and that any attempts on them would mean a substantial firefight. Discretion, it was determined, was the better part of valor.

There was resultant grumbling among the protesters that Gage had intervened in the matter. But that point also caused Lieutenant Mon-tresor to grouse, saying that since his arrival, Governor Moore had not once interfered with the activities of the Sons. Until Gage had stood up, the Sons never "had the shadow of Opposition to present itself against them."

The morning of March 23 dawned with a hard wind still blowing out of the northwest. Word circulated on the street that the Sons were threatening to pull down the house of the officer who had carried the messages from General Gage to Captain Conner authorizing him to fire in case of an assault on the warships.

The New York Sons were also heartened by a message sent by Colonel Israel Putnam, a legendary Indian fighter from Connecticut and one of the leaders of that colony's Sons. Putnam had established an armory with powder, guns, and ammunition, he said, and there were 10,000 men arrayed and ready to march as soon as they were summoned.

Then, while the stalemate simmered, some astonishing news arrived. On the afternoon of March 25 an express rider galloped in after a twenty-two-hour ride from Philadelphia, carrying word from that city's Sons: a ship from Ireland was just docked at Baltimore, carrying copies of a letter from a member of Parliament to a correspondent in Dublin. On January 29, it was said, the Stamp Act had been repealed.

12

FIRST TO BLINK

Though that news from Parliament would turn out to have been premature—what was meant was that repeal seemed *imminent*—it was nonetheless a great boost to the hopes of the colonists to learn that Parliament might yet come to its senses. It was well known that Lord Rockingham, Grenville's replacement as prime minister, was disposed to the repeal of the Stamp Act.

In fact, debate on the matter continued with some urgency once Parliament convened in December 1765. The news of the violence in the colonies struck conservatives such as Grenville as intolerable, with Whigs such as Pitt calling such events inevitable. While the theoretical debate raged, British merchants, stung by a drop in trade revenues, began to press for repeal of the measure based on practical considerations. Rockingham, with the aid of his close friend Edmund Burke, went to some lengths to organize the nation's merchants in lobbying their individual representatives for repeal of the act.

When Parliament reconvened in January following the holidays, King George appeared before Parliament and requested that the Houses formulate resolutions, "as may tend at once to preserve those Constitutional Rights over the Colonies, and to restore to them that Harmony and tranquility, which have lately been interrupted by Riots and Disorders of the most dangerous Nature." Rockingham followed by introducing a formal proposal for repeal of the Stamp Act.

Grenville responded that "Great Britain protects America; America is bound to yield obedience. If, not, tell me when the Americans were emancipated?" The colonists were quite happy to have British troops defend them against the depredations of French-incited savages on the western frontiers, the former prime minister argued. As a result, he said, "the nation has run itself into an immense debt to give them their protection; and now they are called upon to contribute a small share toward the public expence, an expence arising from themselves, they renounce your officers, and break out . . . into open rebellion."

William Pitt's position was that Grenville had been wrong from the beginning. Whatever the reasons, he said, "It is my opinion that this Kingdom has no right to lay a tax upon the colonies." Though he reaffirmed the authority of Great Britain over the colonies, he maintained that levying taxes was not a part of governing (a position that even modern-day Tea Party members might find startling). With regard to the acts of violence that Grenville and others found so repugnant, he said, "I rejoice that America has resisted." Had the three million in the colonies been content "to submit to be slaves," they would have provided the precedent to make slaves of every British subject.

Back and forth the debate raged, with petitions arriving daily from the members' constituencies, such as the one sent from the merchants of Bristol, "in favour of the Bill to repeal the American Stamp Act." The document lamented the sorry state of current trade with the colonies and predicted that "thousands of our Industrious Poor will soon want employ" unless the act was repealed.

Benjamin Franklin was called before the House of Commons to testify on the matter, and although the veteran statesman had been restrained when the act was being proposed, the fact that his own Philadelphia home had nearly gone up in smoke at the hands of his constituents seems to have given him a new perspective on the matter. His testimony lasted for four hours, during which the members of Parliament grilled him with 174 questions. A sampling of the exchange presents both the positions of the combatants and the practical terms of engagement:

Q. What is your name, and place of abode?
A. Franklin, of Philadelphia.
Q. Do the Americans pay any considerable taxes among themselves?

A. Certainly many, and very heavy taxes.

Q. What are the present taxes in Pennsylvania, laid by the laws of the colony?

A. There are taxes on all estates, real and personal; a poll tax; a tax on all offices, professions, trades, and businesses, according to their profits; an excise on all wine, rum, and other spirit; and a duty of ten pounds per head on all Negroes imported, with some other duties.

Q. For what purposes are those taxes laid?

A. For the support of the civil and military establishments of the country, and to discharge the heavy debt contracted in the last [Seven Years'] war. . . .

Q. Are not all the people very able to pay those taxes?

A. No. The frontier counties, all along the continent, have been frequently ravaged by the enemy and greatly impoverished, are able to pay very little tax. . . .

Q. Are not the colonies, from their circumstances, very able to pay the stamp duty?

A. In my opinion there is not gold and silver enough in the colonies to pay the stamp duty for one year.

Q. Don't you know that the money arising from the stamps was all to be laid out in America?

A. I know it is appropriated by the act to the American service; but it will be spent in the conquered colonies, where the soldiers are, not in the colonies that pay it. . . .

Q. Do you think it right that America should be protected by this country and pay no part of the expense?

A. That is not the case. The colonies raised, clothed, and paid, during the last war, near 25,000 men, and spent many millions.

Q. Were you not reimbursed by Parliament?

A. We were only reimbursed what, in your opinion, we had advanced beyond our proportion, or beyond what might reasonably be expected from us; and it was a very small part of what we spent. Pennsylvania, in particular, disbursed about 500,000 pounds, and the reimbursements, in the whole, did not exceed 60,000 pounds. . . .

Q. Do you think the people of America would submit to pay the stamp duty, if it was moderated?

A. No, never, unless compelled by force of arms. . . .

Q. What was the temper of America towards Great Britain before the year 1763?

A. The best in the world. They submitted willingly to the government of the Crown, and paid, in all their courts, obedience to acts of Parliament. . . .

Q. What is your opinion of a future tax, imposed on the same principle with that of the Stamp Act? How would the Americans receive it?

A. Just as they do this. They would not pay it.

Q. Have not you heard of the resolutions of this House, and of the House of Lords, asserting the right of Parliament relating to America, including a power to tax the people there?

A. Yes, I have heard of such resolutions.

Q. What will be the opinion of the Americans on those resolutions?

A. They will think them unconstitutional and unjust.

Q. Was it an opinion in America before 1763 that the Parliament had no right to lay taxes and duties there?

A. I never heard any objection to the right of laying duties to regulate commerce; but a right to lay internal taxes was never supposed to be in Parliament, as we are not represented there. . . .

Q. Did the Americans ever dispute the controlling power of Parliament to regulate the commerce?

A. No.

Q. Can anything less than a military force carry the Stamp Act into execution?

A. I do not see how a military force can be applied to that purpose.

Q. Why may it not?

A. Suppose a military force sent into America; they will find nobody in arms; what are they then to do? They cannot force a man to take stamps who chooses to do without them. They will not find a rebellion; they may indeed make one.

Q. If the act is not repealed, what do you think will be the consequences?

A. A total loss of the respect and affection the people of America bear to this country, and of all the commerce that depends on that respect and affection.

Q. How can the commerce be affected?

A. You will find that, if the act is not repealed, they will take very little of your manufactures in a short time.

Q. Is it in their power to do without them?

A. I think they may very well do without them.

Q. Is it their interest not to take them?

A. The goods they take from Britain are either necessaries, mere conveniences, or superfluities. The first, as cloth, etc., with a little industry they can make at home; the second they can do without till they are able to provide them among themselves; and the last, which are mere articles of fashion, purchased and consumed because the fashion in a respected country; but will now be detested and rejected. The people have already struck off, by general agreement, the use of all goods fashionable in mourning. . . .

Q. If the Stamp Act should be repealed, would it induce the assemblies of America to acknowledge the right of Parliament to tax them, and would they erase their resolutions [against the Stamp Act]?

A. No, never.

Q. Is there no means of obliging them to erase those resolutions?

A. None that I know of; they will never do it, unless compelled by force of arms.

Q. Is there a power on earth that can force them to erase them?

A. No power, how great so ever, can force men to change their opinions. . . .

Q. What used to be the pride of the Americans?

A. To indulge in the fashions and manufactures of Great Britain.

Q. What is now their pride?

A. To wear their old clothes over again, till they can make new ones.

Though Franklin's testimony would not have moved a man of Grenville's ilk, it is difficult to imagine any fence-riding member of Parliament listening to such back-and-forth without seeing the unmistakable course to take. An army might counter acts of insurrection, but how could it force a man to buy a stamp or a shirt he did not want?

At the same time, there was some sentiment in Parliament for a compromise position. When Benjamin Franklin was asked what he thought the opinion of the American public might be about a measure repealing the Stamp Act but reaffirming the sovereignty of Parliament over the colonies, he opined that nothing short of repeal of the Stamp Act itself would be acceptable. When he was asked if Americans would think that it was their violent actions that had forced Parliament into submission, Franklin said no. Reason alone was what dictated the need for repeal.

With such testimony fresh in members' minds, George Grenville introduced "An Act for the better securing the dependency of His Majesty's dominions in America upon the Crown and Parliament of Great Britain." Referred to as the Declaratory Act, the measure was presented as companion legislation to a bill repealing the Stamp Act. The Declaratory Act was a close copy of the Irish Dependency Act of 1719, stipulating that Ireland was subordinate to and dependent upon the British Crown and that the king, with the advice and consent of Parliament, had full power "to make laws and statutes of sufficient validity to bind the Kingdom and people of Ireland." However, Grenville appended four words to that wording that would in time prove incendiary: "*in all cases whatsoever*" [italics added].

With the understanding that the two measures would go forward together, an accord was finally reached. By a vote of roughly two to one, the Stamp Act was repealed, the Declaratory Act passed, and the legislation ratified by King George on March 18.

❖ ❖ ❖

Two hundred and fifty years later, such news would have been beamed around the world in moments, but as it was, the American colonists remained on tenterhooks, with tension and uncertainty to prevail for two months. In New York, General Gage tried to move the powder and guns stored on shore to the warships in the harbor, where they would be less likely to fall into the hands of the Sons. It might have been a wise idea, but not a single local craft could be hired for the purpose, and marines were forced to use their dinghies for the laborious process.

Meanwhile, discord arose within the ranks of the British. When Governor Moore asked Lieutenant Governor Colden for copies of the letters he had received from London during his term as acting chief, Colden refused. Lieutenant Montresor petitioned Governor Moore for a plot of some 10,000 acres on the Connecticut River, but the governor refused, telling Montresor that he intended the land for his own wife and children.

Nor were the Sons quietly waiting for further word from London. As Montresor described it, "Five Ruffians or Sons of Liberty fell on an Officer of the Royal Americans on the Common about Dusk, behind his Back, and beat him unmercifully and broke his sword, which he had drawn in his Defence." Word came from Connecticut that a group of forty men identifying themselves as Sons had "pillaged and ransacked" a gentleman's house there for the offense of "being a neutral person and not declaring his sentiments."

By that time, Montresor had begun to display signs of the budding satirist in his clipped notes. Though the early April weather at last turned mild and the gale winds relented, "The sons or Spawns of Liberty and Inquisition," he said, were "still venting threats and Insulting the Crown and Officers under it."

He seemed to find it presumptuous that these "Heroes of Liberty" now maintained an office, kept careful minutes of their various meetings, and sent news and records of their accords "to their licentious fraternity throughout the different Provinces." At the same time, more ships were arriving up and down the coast of the colonies, bearing word that Parliament had indeed repealed the Stamp Act early in February. Still, there was no official confirmation, and there were signs that even if the act had been repealed it would not matter.

The Sons were determined to have every restriction on trade removed from the colonies, and they also wanted an end to the jurisdiction of the royal courts of admiralty. A colonist accused of a crime should be entitled to a trial with a jury composed of his peers, and there should be no appeal of the verdict in any British venue.

A contingent of Sons was at work drilling out the spikes that had been driven into the cannon on the Battery, an endeavor that Montresor found vaguely pointless. The guns were old and their carriages rotted, he said, no longer able to support the weight of the metal. The rusted weapons would be of little use in any battle—"Let them try," the lieutenant seemed to say.

A rumor came that "2,000 men from Westchester" were on the march to New York, and all troops and officers were ordered inside the fort. On the following day, two ships attempted to slip into the harbor past the sentinels. The *Garland* fired warning shots, bringing one of the ships to, while the other fled.

The next day, Isaac Sears led a party of men on board the merchant ship that had been prevented from unloading its goods. The group seized several crates of beer and ale, along with a quantity of good English cheese. As a spirited rally ensued on the common, another rumor came in from Boston that the Stamp Act had indeed been repealed.

A man named Swinney, described as "an inflammatory news-carrier and monger" who'd enjoyed a fair share of the purloined cheese and ale, jumped on a horse and began to gallop through the city streets, crying huzzahs "To Pitt!" and "No more king!" His ride might have occasioned more of a flurry, but before he traveled far, a butcher with a fierce loyalty to His Majesty stepped from his shop and, with a deft swing, clubbed Swinney unconscious from his horse.

Though the rumor of the act's repeal once again proved premature, copies of William Pitt's stirring defense of the colonies did in fact arrive and were widely circulated, and the Sons were confident that the end was near. A few days later, on May 5, the *New York Mercury* advertised that a play would be performed that evening at the Chapel Street Theatre. The piece, *The Twin Rivals*, was described as a comedy and would include a "Song in Praise of Liberty." Appended to the advertisement was a note adding, "As the Packet is arrived, and has been the Messenger of good News relative to the Repeal, It is hoped the Public has no objection to the above Performance."

The producers' hopes were to be dashed, however. Scarcely did the nearby church bells toll six and the play begin when sympathizers of the Sons, heedless of the promised song to liberty and indignant "that such Entertainments should be exhibited at this Time of public distress," burst into the theater "with noise and tumult." As the lights went out and the fracas escalated, patrons battled toward jammed exits and dived out windows to escape.

"Thus ended the comedy," the *Newport Mercury* drily reported, "in which a boy unhappily had his skull fractured, his recovery doubtful." Others lost wigs, watches, purses, and caps, and the poor actor who was to have played the part of Mrs. Mandrake was carried outside still wearing his dress and "whipped for a considerable distance."

May 7 brought the first day of summer weather to New York, and Montresor reported, "The Sons of Liberty, otherwise the Sons of Tyranny, who now call themselves the Redressors of Grievances held a council whether they should not secretly Barbacue an officer of the 27th [Regiment] for speaking disrespectfully of them."

Meanwhile, little business was being conducted. Five ships full of goods languished at the New York docks, Montresor reported, and word circulated that as a result of the Stamp Act boycott, the merchants had no funds to pay their bills due in London. It was all a pretense, however, he said, for the markets were high and workmanship, materials, and goods very costly, "which plainly demonstrates that the country cannot complain of poverty." As further proof, he cited the high prices and brisk trading of "Beaver skins, the price of which, greater or less, is the standard by which one may judge of the riches of this country."

In Connecticut, the situation was dire, the lieutenant reported. Colonists there had recalled their governor and a number of elected assemblymen, and established a Committee of 500 who had renounced "all future connections with Great Britain," though they maintained their "allegiance to King George III." Reports came in that in rural areas, squatters had taken possession of deeded lands and had no intention of giving them up. "No law prevails," Montresor lamented. Indeed, it seemed that civilization in the colonies, as the British conceived of it, was nearly at an end.

Then, on May 20, more than two months after the fact, word finally came that the king had given his assent to the repeal of the Stamp Act. Montresor reported the ensuing "hideous Din" of church bells and hundreds of boys running through the streets with "poles upon which were hoisted Handkerchiefs, papers, etc., in imitation of the late Mob, attended with repeated Huzzahs."

"Friday night to the inexpressible Joy of all," reported the *Boston Post-Boy*, "we received . . . the important News, at the Repeal of the Stamp Act, which was signed by His Majesty the 18th of March last." The news set the bells in the town ringing, "the Ships in the Harbour display'd their Colours, Guns were discharged in different Parts of the Town, and in the Evening were several Bonfires." Debtors were released from jail, a holiday was proclaimed for the following Monday, and that evening the Sons of Liberty "erected a magnificent pyramid, illuminated with 280 lamps."

Similar rejoicing was reported in Connecticut, in New York, and across the colonies. Whereas public gatherings of the past six months had been occasions primarily of strife, suddenly "All was Loyalty to the King, Blessings on the Parliament of Great-Britain, Honour and Gratitude to the Present Ministry, and Love and Affection to the Mother Country."

At midnight on the evening of the holiday celebration in Boston, the *Post-Boy* reported, "upon a Signal given in the Common, and the Beat of a Drum, the Populace retired to their respective Dwellings, the

Lights were put out, and the Town was hushed in an unusual silence."
Virtually overnight, it seemed, order and harmony were restored, yet,
even for the most optimistic souls in the colonies, it must have seemed
too good to be true.

Montresor's observations suggest that not everything was magically
erased by the decree of His Majesty. The Sons of Liberty, he said, fell
into a vehement argument as to who should lead their celebratory procession in the streets of New York. When the resident clergy of the
Church of England presented an address to Governor Moore from the
assembly, Moore refused to attend the ceremony or accept the document. And trouble remained in Connecticut, where the members of the
colonial assembly refused to recognize the state's newly appointed governor or swear their oath of allegiance to the king.

While business resumed in New York and Governor Moore held a
public meeting at the Merchants Coffee House to assure constituents
that there would be no appeals in the British courts of any jury verdict
in the colonies, a true test of the Sons' willingness to forgive and forget
came when the warship *Hind* sailed into New York on May 25, carrying with her Major James, the despised artillery officer who had threatened to jam stamp papers down their throats.

Immediately, threats began to circulate that the house in which
James had resided would be pulled down if he attempted to move back
in. When it was suggested that James might seek to be indemnified for
the losses he had suffered in November, letters arrived at the homes
of assemblymen, warning of dire consequences should they authorize
a penny. Though nothing came of such threats, Montresor wrote of
nightly marches and demonstrations by the Sons of Liberty. Though
the Stamp Act was repealed and duties on sugar and molasses were
reduced, resentment lingered.

For one thing, some of the more astute of the Sons of Liberty pointed
to the Declaratory Act that had come hand in hand with the legislation
of repeal. At a meeting at the liberty tree, a notably handsome live oak
that graced the pasture of a Mr. Mazyck in Charleston, Christopher

Gadsden warned the assembled mechanics and artisans against "the folly of rejoicing at a law that still asserted and maintained the absolute dominion of Great Britain over them." The somewhat chastened group agreed with Gadsden that they should never relax their vigilance or indulge "the fallacious hope that Great Britain would relinquish her designs and pretensions." The meeting concluded with the assembly joining hands and swearing their everlasting intention to defend against the encroachment of tyranny, but for most in Charleston, as elsewhere, with the immediate source of irritation gone, the prospects for future strife seemed remote.

13

BETTER DAYS

One of the issues that did not disappear along with the Stamp Act was the problem of money in the colonies. With the economy already depressed, trade down, and receipts as well as expenditures curtailed by local governments, the simple withdrawal of a plan to impose additional taxes did little to put more money into circulation.

Along with the veiled implications of the Declaratory Act, the Currency Act passed by Parliament in 1764 put an end to the practice of the issuance of paper money by the colonies, notes that were based primarily on the value of mortgaged land. The act was passed in large part because of pressures by British merchants, who complained about the wild fluctuations in the value of the currency they were asked to accept as payment for their goods. Henceforth, trade would have to be carried out in pounds sterling, gold, or silver. Since there was relatively little British currency circulating in the colonies and the colonies had no gold or silver mines, this meant that the colonists were going to have a difficult time buying anything from Great Britain.

Having no paper money of their own affected the local economies as well. In South Carolina, historian Walsh points out the particular impact of the law on the planters. When the value of crops in a given year was not sufficient to pay for the goods bought from merchants or the services rendered by mechanics and artisans, any further purchases were simply impossible. Money could not be borrowed because there literally was no money.

Nor were the mechanics or merchants spared. Without money coming in, goods necessary for manufacture or resale could not be purchased.

And how could a shipfitter expand his business if there was no money to pay the help? Bartering allowed for some commerce to continue, but it was scarcely the way to break an economy out of the doldrums, Stamp Act or no.

One trader interviewed in the *South-Carolina Gazette* complained that even in the rare instances where a hardworking master carpenter, bricklayer, or painter earned 30 to 40 shillings per day, he could not "possibly pay House-Rent, Cloath and feed his family, and pay Five Pounds out of his poor Pittance to purchase a Cord of Firewood."

Trade out of Charleston was down significantly as well. South Carolina tanneries had exported 20,000 hides to New England manufacturers in the first half of the decade; following the repeal of the Stamp Act, they shipped half of that. Barrel makers' business was down by a quarter and shipwrights' by half. At the same time, prices for food rose by as much as 60 percent.

Another bit of legislation passed by Parliament in March 1765 went relatively unnoticed in the wave of resentment against the Stamp Act. The Quartering Act of 1765 required the colonies to house and feed British soldiers in barracks constructed at their expense. If the barracks were not provided or were not of sufficient size, communities were obliged to house the soldiers in local inns, stables, and public houses. And if there were still redcoats left in the streets, the communities were to make available any uninhabited houses, sheds, barns, or other buildings "as shall be necessary" for the purpose.

In addition, the act declared, "That in case any innholder, or other person, on whom any noncommission officers or private men shall be quartered by virtue of this act . . . shall be desirous to furnish such noncommission officers or soldiers with candles, vinegar, and salt, and with small beer or cyder, not exceeding five pints, or half a pint of rum mixed with a quart of water, for each man *per diem, gratis*, and allow to such noncommission officers or soldiers the use of fire, and the necessary utensils for dressing and eating their meat."

Though the colonists had for the most part been willing to quarter British troops on the march during the French and Indian War, the notion of doing so in peacetime seemed an unnecessary burden, just one more hardship foisted upon them by Parliament. A proposal by General Gage to send six hundred troops to be quartered in Albany had already occasioned protests there, and in 1766, when Gage proposed that a contingent of nearly three times that many should be housed in New York, residents were inflamed. It amounted to the same thing as the Stamp Act: taxation without representation.

In June, the troops arrived in New York and were housed, for the most part, in barracks situated on the north side of the common. From the moment of their arrival, there was hostility between troops and townspeople.

The townspeople resented the fact that they were paying for what amounted to an occupying force, and the troops found the demonstrations regularly held on the south side of the common insulting. Particularly annoying to the troops was the sight of the "liberty pole" that the Sons erected on June 4, as part of the celebration of the birthday of King George. That event, described in detail in the *Gazette*, the *Mercury*, and elsewhere, featured considerable drinking and feasting, including the roasting of "two fat oxen."

The principal spectacle of the evening was the torching of a ship's mast that had been planted in the common with a dozen tar barrels lashed to its top and two dozen cords of wood stacked at its base. Following a twenty-five-gun salute, the bonfire was lit and the whole went up in a blaze that prompted great cheering. The Sons of Liberty also erected a second pole on the same day with a sign affixed—"George, Pitt, and Liberty"—identifying it as the symbol of the successful rebellion of the citizenry against the Stamp Act. Boston had its liberty tree, Charleston its liberty oak, and now New York had its liberty pole.

Theories abound as to the source of a tree or pole as an axis around which such passions came to revolve, though the pagan-oriented maypole and its associated celebration seem a sensible explanation. In some European communities the maypole was a permanent fixture on the town common dating from medieval times, though it was the center of celebration only once a year, usually marking the onset of spring or

summer and often carrying the banners or symbols of the local craftsmen and artisans.

Though the practice of an annual maypole celebration was discour-
aged in England because of the bacchanalian associations attached,
those would have only helped endear the notion to the rebellious Sons
who flooded New York Common in 1766 to celebrate. The men might
still be British subjects, but they had been reborn as a decidedly independent species, and the liberty pole was a permanent, priapic statement of that fact.

The British soldiers who marched daily past that pole were well
aware of what it stood for, of course, and on the close and sultry afternoon of August 10, a group of men from the 28th Regiment decided
that enough was enough. Armed redcoats stood watch while a pair of
their fellows put their axes to work, and within a few minutes, the first
liberty pole was felled.

The following day, a scorching one according to observers, found a
crowd of three thousand assembled on the common to hear Isaac Sears
demanding an explanation from the officers of the regiment as to why
the "Tree of Liberty" had been cut down. According to Montresor, and
despite the hurling of significant insults and threats by the mob, no response was forthcoming from the assembled troops until some of the
mob began to toss stones and bricks at the redcoats.

At that point, the troops broke ranks and charged the mob with fixed
bayonets. Though no serious injuries resulted, some have called the
skirmish the site of the first blood spilled in the Revolution.

Before the confrontation got completely out of hand, British officers
rushed to intervene. One protester swung a club at a British captain,
who drew his sword in response. At that, several in the mob produced
pistols and a stalemate ensued. When the commanding officer of the
28th appeared, he listened to the complaints of Sears and promised an
investigation. If any of his men were at fault in the incident, he said,
they would be punished. Meantime, in the interest of the public safety,
the common would be cleared.

The following day found a series of handbills posted by the Sons about New York promising that they would have their revenge upon the troops and that any attempt to carry on their daily parades through the streets would result in disaster. Nonetheless, the troops paraded, though the guard was doubled. A number of townsmen were hauled to the city court, charged with making threats of death against troops and officers, and one British officer was charged for making a similar threat against a man who had called him a "rascal."

While all this was going on, the Sons marched upon the common with an even taller mast, this one emblazoned "George, Pitt, and Liberty" and bearing an ensign fluttering at its top. Though the pole was permitted to stand, the men of the 28th ringed the common with their bayonets fixed, denying anyone entrance to the grounds. Though crowds shouted and surged, no violence ensued.

Handbills were posted calling for citizens to forgo any interaction with the troops, and a petition was circulated asking that all troops and fortifications be withdrawn from the city. On the wretchedly hot evening of August 15, a group of men armed with clubs and sticks stopped a coach bearing a British officer who resembled the hated Major James. They demanded that the officer step down so they could carry out their intention of burying him alive upon the spot. When the shaken officer emerged from the coach and identified himself as one Captain Heathcote, a disappointed murmur swept through the crowd. Heathcote was free to leave, a spokesman explained, but he should carry a warning to his compatriot James.

As the heat wave continued unabated, tensions rose. The Sons advised market vendors that they were not to sell goods to soldiers or officers and drew up complaints against the mayor when he proved unwilling to press charges against any of the officers or men. A proposal went to General Gage requesting that soldiers not on duty be prohibited to carry their sidearms. A broadside declared that if the Sons were not rendered justice for their tree being cut down, then "they will revenge themselves on the Soldiers as God and Nature has enabled them."

Major Brown, the commander of the 28th Regiment, was served with two writs seeking damages of £5,000, but they were ignored. One afternoon, as the military parade was making its rounds through the streets, a merchant ran from his shop to demand a sword from one of the guards. The soldier gave the man "his advice with the butt end of his musket, which settled him," according to Montresor, "and so marched on."

An artillery detachment was deployed at the barracks, and light cannon were placed at the end entrance, along with an additional pair at the fort, which had been unarmed since Moore's arrival. Thunderstorms swept across the city but did little to lessen the heat, with readings hovering in the 90s even at night. Eighty members of the 28th Artillery Detachment were ordered to the city on August 26, a day on which the temperature soared to 103 degrees.

The writs that had been served on Major Brown were thrown out in court. In answer, persons unknown heaved rocks—along with a volley of insults and threats—through the major's windows. Montresor was dispatched to make a proper survey of the islands in New York harbor and its approach, with an eye toward their eventual fortification.

When Montresor returned from his fieldwork to begin work on the charts and plans, Governor Moore again summoned him to his offices. He was to complete his map work quickly, the governor explained, and then he was to go on to a matter of the utmost secrecy: the outline of a military plan for moving a "considerable body of troops" through an "inhabited country in North America." Just what country that might be, Moore was not prepared to divulge, but, given the events of the past several months, Montresor could guess.

The *New York Post-Boy* complained of the uneasiness among the population, given "that such a number arm'd men, without any visible occasion for them are station'd among us, and suffer'd so to patrol the Streets, as in a Military or conquer'd Town." On September 23, a contingent of troops marched from the barracks across the common to the site of the liberty pole that had been standing since mid-August. Orders were barked, axes were unsheathed, and in moments the second pole had fallen. It might have been the spark that set off the powder keg, but miraculously the day and evening passed without incident.

Early in the morning of September 25, a sentry rounding the barracks at the north side of the common stopped short. The sun was not yet risen and mist still drifted across the fields, but there was no mistaking what was silhouetted in the distance against the southern sky: somehow, during the night, a third liberty pole had materialized where the previous two had stood.

14

TOWNSHEND FANS THE FLAMES

M ost scholars theorize that it was Governor Moore who authorized the cutting down of the first two liberty poles on New York Common, and it is also probably Moore who advised against cutting down the third, for a time at least. After all, the city had managed to get through a period of torrid weather and inflamed passions without any serious outbreak of violence. If the Sons of Liberty could not rest without a ship's mast planted in the middle of New York Common, perhaps it was best to let it stand.

Certainly, the leadership of the Sons of Liberty in the various colonies seemed to feel that a certain stability was restored, even if some nonetheless warned of the need for vigilance. Reverend Mayhew wrote to his Boston counterpart, James Otis, that a valuable lesson had been learned in the sharing of information between the colonies. It was the understanding that groups in every province were united by a common cause that had led to the defeat of the Stamp Act, Mayhew said, and he urged that the Massachusetts Assembly take the lead in maintaining communication even in the wake of victory. It should seek to "perpetuate union among ourselves, by all laudable methods," he told Otis.

In December 1766, Samuel Adams wrote to Christopher Gadsden of Charleston in support of the notion that the Stamp Act had been successfully rebuffed chiefly through solidarity. Though Adams was confident that the common resolve expressed and the friendships formed would deter the "most virulent Enemy from making another open attempt upon their rights as Men & Subjects," he seemed to have given up on the possibility of maintaining any serious correspondence among the chapters. Still, it was a pity, he told Gadsden in closing, that a union and correspondence of the merchants in all the colonies could not continue.

In that same letter, Adams, who was clerk of the Massachusetts Assembly by that time, repeated his often cited opposition to the provisions of the Quartering Act. Not only did the requirement that colonists pay to keep His Majesty's troops constitute "a tax" but it also established the unfortunate precedent of the maintenance of a standing army even in peacetime. In Adams's opinion, standing armies were by their very nature a constant threat to liberty.

Still, things were not looking so bad for liberty in Boston. Adams and the other liberal members maintained control of the Massachusetts Assembly and effectively warded off the efforts of Governor Bernard to pack his council with conservatives and cronies such as Hutchinson. On March 18, Adams, Otis, and other influential Sons of Liberty organized a celebration to commemorate the one-year anniversary of the repeal of the Stamp Act. Food and drink were served to a cheering public at the gaily decorated Faneuil Hall, which housed the Boston Town Assembly, and the liberty tree on nearby Boston Common was lit by candles and torches.

Such celebrations were calculated moves by Adams and other leaders, of course, attempts to remind citizens of the value of their previous efforts and the need to remain vigilant. And if a contemporary Fourth of July celebration contains only a vague reminder of the events that brought it into being, such was not the case in Boston in 1767. As one participant wrote in his diary entry for the date, "I never saw more Joy than on this occasion."

Joy, unfortunately, would be relatively short-lived in the colonies. In the early summer, Charles Townshend, the British chancellor of the Exchequer, introduced into Parliament a series of measures designed to sidestep the opposition that had arisen to the Stamp Act and raise some badly needed revenue. Interest on the £137 million national debt had risen to nearly £5 million, and total revenues were projected at scarcely £8 million for the year. What Townshend cobbled together was a plan that would not only raise money but also create a system under which the colonies would ultimately pay for their own upkeep.

The first of the five measures that are commonly referred to collectively as the Townshend Acts was the Revenue Act, which would, in Townshend's view, reestablish the right of Parliament to raise revenue from the colonists, even if the word "tax" was studiously avoided in the wording. To opponents in Parliament, Townshend pointed to the ultimate clause of the Declaratory Act, which affirmed the right of that body to pass legislation binding upon the colonies "in all cases whatsoever."

Furthermore, he argued, stalwart supporters of the colonies, including Benjamin Franklin himself, insisted that the colonists had been opposed to the Stamp Act principally because it was a levy on the "internal" business of each province. Thus the brilliance of his Revenue Act, Townshend maintained. Because it would place new duties on items not manufactured in the colonies and imported solely from England—paper, glass, lead, paint, and tea—it was an "external" levy on trade, and therefore the colonists could make no protest.

It might have sounded good in theory, but in practice, Townshend's sophistry would be taken for just that in the colonies. In fact the distinction between "internal" and "external" taxes floated by Franklin and others at the time of debate regarding the Stamp Act was a sophistic maneuver, one of the attempts to bring reason to bear on a volatile situation. When men were taking to the streets of Boston, Providence, Charleston, Albany, Philadelphia, and New York and pulling down the homes of customs officials, they were far beyond considerations of the niceties of "internal" versus "external"; they were simply taxed out.

Along with the Revenue Act, a companion piece of legislation was passed: the Indemnity Act, which repealed duties on tea imported into England. The measure was intended to help prop up the British East India Company, which was losing a good deal of its domestic market share to less expensive Dutch tea routinely smuggled past British customs. While it meant a loss in revenue, on the one hand, Townshend pointed out that the Crown would make a portion of it up on the new duties paid on tea imported by the colonies (3 pence per pound). British tea merchants would prosper, the national treasury would be protected, and the colonists would have no grounds upon which to complain.

Commentators have differed as to their estimation of Townshend's motives. Some say that the legislation was vindictive and political rather than practical, given that there would be something of a net loss to the national treasury; others maintain that there was nothing cynical about the treasurer's moves. The country needed money, Townshend believed that the colonists endorsed the principle of trade duties, and this was a way to proceed, establishing the precedent of the power of Parliament over the colonies into the bargain.

The third prong of Townshend's program was a piece of legislation that created a new agency to be called the American Board of Customs Commissioners, which would be charged with enforcement of all trade regulations pertaining to the colonies and headquartered in Boston, well known as a center of smuggling operations. Some commentators cite the establishment of this board as the true tipping point of the buildup to the American Revolution, given that it created a policing agency specifically designed to regulate the raising of revenue in the colonies.

It is doubtful that Townshend would have seen it that way. As the historian Robert Chaffin explains in his careful analysis of the Townshend programs, the establishment of the board was the only way to ensure that the new duties would in fact be collected. Over time, the existing customs officials had grown estranged from any sense of loyalty to the Crown, becoming little more than lackeys to the smugglers and making more by accepting bribes than they did in salary. Honest officers feared for their physical safety and were often the target of damage suits brought in courts stacked against them. Basing oversight of the system in the colonies, Townshend argued, would not only allow for easier enforcement but be more economical as well.

A corollary measure, the Vice Admiralty Court Act of 1768, would establish district offices of the admiralty court system (headquartered in

Halifax, Nova Scotia) in Boston, Philadelphia, and Charleston. Those courts, much despised in the colonies because they did not have juries attached, were far more likely to support the efforts of the new customs officials in prosecuting accused smugglers.

There was at least one bit of undeniable chicanery included in Townshend's plan: though the preamble to the Revenue Act stated that its purpose was "for making a more certain and adequate provision for defraying the charge of the administration of justice, and the support of civil government, in such provinces where it shall be found necessary; and towards further defraying the expenses of defending, protecting, and securing, the said dominions," Townshend let it be known that he intended to set aside a portion of the funds generated to pay the salaries of the colonial governors. Traditionally, those salaries had been paid by the colonial assemblies, but that arrangement was prone to the sorts of problems recently exacerbated in Massachusetts, where the assembly could withhold payment to a governor who was too conscientious in his allegiance to Parliament.

Along those lines, Townshend also took action to bring the recalcitrant New York Assembly into line for its failure to comply with the terms of the Quartering Act, requiring support of General Gage's troops in that colony. The New York Restraining Act was passed along with the Revenue Act on July 2 and officially suspended the authority of the colony's assembly until it was willing to come up with the funds. Ultimately, the New York Assembly would comply, though, in its resolution approving the delivery of the funds, the representatives made no mention of either the Quartering Act or the Restraining Act, insisting that they were making a free and voluntary gift toward the expense of keeping the troops.

However onerous all this might seem, the fact is that Townshend's proposals were mild compared with those of others in Parliament. Lord Shelburne, for instance, pushed his own agenda for the upstart colonies, which included a requirement that troops be billeted in private homes and criminal punishment be applied for untoward criticism of king and Parliament.

Townshend's plan won the day, however, aided by a speech that has been called one of the most compelling ever presented in the House of Commons. He had actually spoken on behalf of his proposals earlier in the day on May 8 and then, assuming his work was done, had gone to dinner with colleagues. Townshend, who suffered from epilepsy, had appeared in Parliament with an eye bandaged from a fall during a seizure the previous day and was already a bit worn down.

After dinner, he and his companions ordered a bottle of champagne to toast what all hoped would be a successful outcome for the measures still being debated. They'd barely drained their glasses when a messenger arrived at the table. Members still had their doubts, and Townshend's presence was required on the floor. Though one member of Parliament wrote that Townshend appeared "half drunk" when he returned to speak and another described him as "in liquor," the Treasury minister's passion carried the day. As MP Horace Walpole wrote, "Half a bottle of champagne, poured on genuine genius, had kindled this wonderful blaze."

The performance essentially put an end to debate and earned Townshend the nickname "Champagne Charlie" among popular scribes. Whatever a colonial audience might have thought of it, the speech, which lasted about an hour, was for Walpole "the most singular" of its kind and was filled with "torrents of wit, ridicule, vanity, lies, and beautiful language." Townshend would have his way.

Though one might have expected all this to provoke an uproar in the colonies far beyond what the Stamp Act had elicited, the immediate reaction was mild. One of the most significant responses came in the form of a series of letters penned by thirty-five-year-old John Dickinson, a Philadelphia attorney and descendant of a wealthy landowning family of Quakers. Though raised on a plantation in Delaware, Dickinson had studied law in both Philadelphia and London and was a sophisticated observer of the developing political situation.

In his twelve-part series, *Letters from a Farmer in Pennsylvania*, which began circulating in December 1767, Dickinson dismissed the notion that there was any meaningful distinction between "internal" and "external" taxes. The Townshend duties were bald-faced attempts to raise revenue from the colonies, he said, and had nothing to do with the "regulation of trade." Parliament did indeed have sovereignty in matters that affected the whole of the British Empire, but when it came to the matter of raising revenues and deciding what monies were to be allocated to the mother country for assistance in anything affecting their internal operations, the colonial assemblies were the sole deliberators.

Generally regarded as constituting "the literary event" of the prerevolutionary period in the colonies, Dickinson's letters begin in a simple, engaging fashion:

> *My dear Countrymen,*
> *I am a* Farmer, *settled, after a variety of fortunes, near the*
> *banks of the river* Delaware, *in the province* of Pennsylvania. *I*
> *received a liberal education, and have been engaged in the busy*
> *scenes of life; but am now convinced, that a man may be as*
> *happy without bustle, as with it. My farm is small; my servants*
> *are few, and good; I have a little money at interest; I wish for*
> *no more; my employment in my own affairs is easy; and with a*
> *contented grateful mind, undisturbed by worldly hopes or fears,*
> *relating to myself, I am completing the number of days allotted*
> *to me by divine goodness.*

But in short order Dickinson moved to share his fears that too little attention had been given to an act of Parliament "as injurious in its principle to the liberties of these colonies, as the *Stamp Act* was." Specifically, he explained, he was referring to the act suspending the powers of the New York Assembly:

> *If the* British *parliament has legal authority to issue an order,*
> *that we shall furnish a single article for the troops here, and*
> *to compel obedience to* that *order, they have the same right to*
> *issue an order for us to supply those troops with arms, clothes,*
> *and every necessary; and to compel obedience to* that *order*

also; in short, to lay any burthens *they please upon us. What is*
this but taxing us at a certain sum, *and leaving to us only the*
manner *of raising it?*

It was a direct rebuttal of Townshend's claim, pointing out that there
was no difference in principle between a tax of a penny and one of a
pound, and a stance that found great favor among the colonists, who
had come to an awareness of their power through the struggle against
the Stamp Act. In his third letter, Dickinson addressed the issue of just
how far it might be necessary to go in defense of freedom from such oppression:

The English history affords frequent examples of resistance by
force. What particular circumstances will in any future case jus-
tify such resistance can never be ascertained till they happen.
Perhaps it may be allowable to say generally, that it never can
be justifiable until the people are fully convinced that any fur-
ther submission will be destructive to their happiness.

The series of essays was published and widely circulated about the
colonies in serial form from December 1767 through February 1768, yet,
as popular as they became, Dickinson knew that the relatively conservative Pennsylvania Assembly was unlikely to mount any official
challenge to the Townshend measures. Accordingly, he wrote to James
Otis in Boston, expressing his hope that the assembly there would take
action. "The Liberties of our Common Country appear to me to be at
this moment exposed to the most imminent Danger," he said, explaining
why he had begun to publish his letters and enclosing a copy of the first.

Dickinson gave Massachusetts much of the credit for forcing the repeal of the Stamp Act and suggested that if Otis agreed with the sentiments expressed in the attachment—that the threat implied in the
Townshend measures was even more dire than that of the Stamp Act—
then possibly he might want to share the "Farmer's" letter with the Sons

in Massachusetts and others who would be sympathetic. Their common cause was nothing less "than to maintain the Liberty with which Heav'n itself 'hath made us free,'" Dickinson said, insisting to Otis that "the most destructive Consequences must follow, if these Colonies do not instantly, vigorously, and unanimously unite themselves, in the same manner they did against the Stamp Act."

Still, Dickinson called for moderation. Despite the importance of the cause, he said, "I hope it will not be disgrac'd in any Colony, by a single rash Step. We have constitutional methods of seeking Redress; and they are the best Methods." He closed with a similar rejoinder, telling Otis, "The Moderation of your Conduct in composing the Minds of your Fellow-Citizens, has done you the highest Credit with us."

Otis's reply, along with most others, was positive, but meantime, the Sons of Liberty in Boston were not sitting idle. Samuel Adams was instrumental in leading the Boston Town Assembly to issue a ban on the importation of some fifty items, including those named in the Revenue Act, which would no longer be imported after December 30, 1767. The Committee of Correspondence sent copies of the resolution to all towns in Massachusetts as well as to every major city throughout the colonies, asking that they join the embargo. By early spring, a number of cities, including New York, signed on, but Philadelphia held out. Though Benjamin Franklin wrote home that news of the boycott alarmed British merchants, Philadelphia's absence from the coalition was a serious blow to the endeavor.

In January 1768, Adams convinced his fellow liberals in the Massachusetts Assembly to draft a petition directly to King George, asking that the revenue acts be rescinded. The colony had been developed principally by investments made by the colonists themselves, not by the Crown, the document began, yet Britain gained significant profit by trading with the province, supplying most of its manufactured goods. The petition went on to reiterate what were now familiar precepts, most of them contained in Dickinson's letters: that residents of the colony could be taxed only by their own elected representatives, that it was not practicable for the colony to have a representative in the distant Parliament, and that residents of the colony were not truly free so long as the revenue acts oppressed them. The petition closed with a plea to the king to grant relief to his loyal subjects.

Though Adams initially found it difficult to convince his colleagues to send out a call to the other colonial legislatures, asking them to send their own similar petitions, he finally won out, composing a circular that would accompany a copy of the Massachusetts petition. In his letter, he spent considerable time arguing the unconstitutional nature of taxation without representation, but he attacked the specifics of the Townshend Acts as well. One of the most troubling aspects was the notion that the Crown would henceforth be paying the salaries of the colonial governors and judges, thereby removing them from any influence of their own constituencies.

Most important, Adams was quick to assure the Massachusetts agent who would bear the petition to London, it should be understood that no colonist harbored any desire for independence. In a letter of January 22, 1768, drafted on behalf of the assembly to Lord Rockingham, Adams insisted that the residents of Massachusetts were well aware of "their happiness and safety, in their union with, and dependence upon, the mother country." Even if an "independency" were offered them, Adams said, "they would by no means be inclined to accept."

In a letter penned the following week to the chief judiciary officer of Great Britain, the generally sympathetic Earl of Camden, Adams reiterated, "The subjects in this province, and undoubtedly in all the colonies, however they may have been otherwise represented to his Majesty's ministers, are loyal: they are firmly attached to the mother state: they always consider her interest and their own as inseparably interwoven, and it is their fervent wish that it may ever so remain." All they desired, he emphasized, was to have their rights respected and restored.

Such protestations of loyalty did not convince everyone, of course. General Gage wrote to London in March 1768, saying that anyone with sense could see the trend. First, the colonists had refused to be taxed on their internal affairs. Now they were denying the obligation to pay import duties. "They mean to go on step by Step," he said, " 'till they throw off all subjections to your laws."

As for protestations of loyalty to the king, Gage insisted, the colonists might acknowledge the king for a time but soon enough would "deny the prerogatives of the Crown, and acknowledge their King no longer than it shall be convenient for them to do so." The ultimate aim of the colonies was for "independency," he declared, and the sooner everyone in England understood it, the better.

When copies of the Massachusetts petition and circular letter reached London in April, Parliament was not in session, but the king's ministers immediately foresaw the possibility of a second pan-colonial congress coming into being, to develop a coordinated resistance to the Townshend Acts. Accordingly, the secretary in charge of colonial affairs wrote immediately to Governor Bernard of Massachusetts, directing him to order the assembly to retract the circular letter at once; if they did not disavow the letter, the assembly would be dissolved.

On June 30, the Massachusetts Assembly met and voted on the matter, and by a vote of 92 to 17, they refused to rescind the circular. Samuel Adams, the house clerk, was directed to write a letter to Lord Hillsborough, secretary of state in charge of the colonies, justifying the refusal, and in a letter of his own to Hillsborough, Governor Bernard shared an interesting bit of behind-the-scenes jockeying between Otis and Adams that had ensued. Since Adams had not been asked to read his letter to the assembly, no one would know its contents—theoretically, at least—until it was read by its intended recipient. Governor Bernard, however, offered the following fly-on-the-wall dialogue between Otis and Adams as an example of his adversaries' political cunning, all of it "from a gentleman of the first rank" who happened to be in the representatives' anteroom at the time:

When Otis asked Adams bluntly what he intended to do with the letter to Lord Hillsborough, Adams replied casually, "To give it to the printer to publish next Monday."

By that point, Otis understood the value of sharing the various passionate appeals with the broadest possible audience, but still he was concerned. "Do you think it proper to publish it so soon," Otis asked, "that he [Hillsborough] may receive a printed copy before the original comes to his hand?"

Why would that small point matter? Adams responded. "You know it was designed for the people, and not for the minister."

Of course Otis knew as much, but still he wondered whether Adams was being carried away by his own importance. "You are so fond of your own drafts that you can't wait for the publication of them to a proper time."

It was a moment at which the discussion might have taken a truly contentious turn, but Adams put an end to it. "I am clerk of this House," he reminded Otis, "and I will make that use of the papers which I please."

On the heels of its resolution to refuse to rescind the circular, the assembly also voted a committee headed by Samuel Adams into being, its business being to draft a petition to the king, this one calling for the removal of Bernard as governor. As Adams's biographer John Alexander points out, the assemblyman seemed uncannily prepared for the task, given that he had a fourteen-paragraph draft ready for the assembly's consideration by that same afternoon. It was a rather daunting list of complaints, one of the kindest being that Bernard possessed "an arbitrary disposition," but before the assembly got the chance to consider the document, Bernard dissolved the body.

Meantime, the situation on the streets and docks of Boston was deteriorating. The Board of Customs Commissioners had begun operations late in 1767 and proved itself to be even more vigorous in its operations than Townshend or anyone else in Parliament had probably envisioned. The commissioners did operate independently of local government, but in a particularly unfortunate manner. One of the first actions of the new commission was to deploy its own harbor patrol fleet, which soon came to operate essentially as privateers.

Since there were no funds allocated to pay the crews, it was understood that the proceeds would come from the sale of seized contraband. But in short order, the question of what was contraband and what was legitimate became murky indeed, prompting great complaint from local merchants and traders, who often found their goods seized upon dubious pretexts. Worse yet, when such cases did end up in court, they were heard by the newly expanded admiralty courts, where the verdicts regularly vindicated the actions of the customs "agents."

Still, the new commissioners were troubled by threats from their doughty constituency and were petitioning London for a show of military support from the day they landed, when they were escorted to their offices by a crowd of a thousand or more, bearing their hanging effigies and signs that proclaimed "Liberty & Property & no Commissioners." Though local merchants might have said otherwise, the commissioners in short order complained to London, "we shall find it totally impracticable to enforce the Execution of the Revenue Laws until the Hand of Government is strengthened. At present there is not a ship of war in the [Massachusetts] Province, nor a company of soldiers nearer than New York."

Finally, in mid-May, the *Romney*, a fifty-gun British warship, was dispatched from Halifax to Boston harbor, under the command of Captain Corner, who found it necessary to bolster his crew by impressing a few colonial seamen from ships he passed along the way. Impressment had been an issue of contention in the colonies for some time, but never had the issue been more inflammatory. The moment the *Romney* dropped anchor, a group of citizens confronted Corner, demanding the release of their fellow citizens. Corner denied having forced any colonist into service and dismissed the men, who promptly went to Samuel Adams for help. Adams drafted a request from the assembly to the governor, requesting his intervention in the matter, but he might have saved himself the trouble.

At that point the distressed citizens rowed out to the *Romney* under cover of darkness and managed to spirit one of the impressed seamen away. That action heightened security on the warship, however, preventing any further rescue operations. The committee of citizens then tried negotiating with Corner, offering to place a willing seaman on board in exchange for one of their friends who was desperate to return to his rightful place.

The captain's response was not calculated to win the hearts and minds of the local populace. "No man," he told them, "shall go out of this vessel. The town is a blackguard town, ruled by mobs: they have begun with me by rescuing a man whom I pressed this morning; and, by the eternal God, I will make their hearts ache before I leave it."

The incident only hardened the lines between customs officials and local traders, including John Hancock, one of the city's most prominent. From the day that word arrived of the passage of the Townshend Acts, Hancock vowed that he would never allow a British customs officer to board one of his ships, and he was steadfast in his criticism and social ostracism of the newly arrived customs officials.

As it happened, one of Hancock's ships, the *Liberty*, arrived in Boston harbor from Madeira on May 9, carrying a cargo of twenty-five casks of wine, for which the appropriate duties were paid. The vessel remained at Hancock's wharf for the next month, gradually being loaded with cargo for a return trip to London. By June 10, two hundred barrels of whale oil and twenty barrels of tar were in the *Liberty*'s hold when agents of the Board of Customs Commissioners arrived, searched the ship to discover this cargo, and ordered the ship promptly seized. The *Liberty* was towed from the docks and out into the harbor, where she was anchored alongside Captain Corner's *Romney*.

The issue was a technical one, stemming from the provisions of the 1764 Sugar Act: the ship's captain had not filed for a formal permit to transport the items *before* loading its cargo. It was a common practice for shipowners to file for such permits after the fact simply to expedite the flow of paperwork. But the letter of the law was quite clear, and John Hancock was now paying the price for his disrespect and his ties to Samuel Adams, James Otis, and the Sons of Liberty. If the seizure were upheld, one-third of the value of the ship and its goods would go to the governor, one-third would go to the informant who had alerted officials to the illegal loading (a longshoreman in the pay of the governor), and one-third would go to the Crown, through the hands of the customs commissioners.

There is speculation that the seizure of the *Liberty* was actually planned to take place upon her arrival in early May, based upon the fact that the twenty-five casks of wine for which Hancock had paid duties constituted only about one-quarter of the ship's capacity. Lacking any evidence that additional goods had been off-loaded under cover of darkness, however, Governor Bernard and the commissioners, it is theorized, waited for a chance to sting Hancock and finally hit upon the technicality to seize both his ship *and* the valuable cargo.

The response of the local citizenry to the seizure of the *Liberty* was perhaps the most significant aspect of the affair. As marines nailed up the broad arrow on the ship's mast to mark her as an impounded ship and others began to cut the lines in preparation for her towing, word spread quickly about the docks. Within minutes, a crowd of some five hundred gathered and began pelting the marines with rocks and paving stones.

When the marines pulled the *Liberty* out of range, the crowd turned its anger upon the customs agents who had led the raid. The pair were dragged through the streets, spat upon, and stoned, and the windows of their homes were smashed with rocks. Men hauled a small boat belonging to the commissioners out of the water, dragged it to the common, and set it on fire.

Well aware of what had happened in Boston and elsewhere in the lee of the Stamp Act, the customs commissioners quickly gathered up their documents and cash on hand and fled their offices, stopping only to snatch their families from their homes before making their way out to the safety of the *Romney* and, eventually, Castle William, the fortification that guarded the entrance to Boston harbor. Governor Bernard, fearful that this would be the riot that would end him, hastily sent a message to General Gage, begging for reinforcements; in response, Gage sent a pair of regiments on the march to Boston.

Adams took the opportunity to address the restless populace beneath the liberty tree on the common. "We will support our liberties, depending upon the strength of our own arms and God," he assured the crowd. Handbills went up about the town calling upon all Sons of Liberty to meet again the next day on the common, but rain sent them first to the

1,200-seat Faneuil Hall and then—when that proved too small—to the Old South Church meeting hall, where James Otis was welcomed with an ovation from some two thousand Sons and their supporters.

Otis, who could be red hot one moment and exceedingly deliberate the next, called on this occasion for moderation and order, affirming his belief that their grievances would be addressed. "If not," he said, "and we are called on to defend our liberties and privileges, I hope and believe we shall, one and all, resist even unto blood; but I pray God Almighty this may never so happen."

John Hancock, meantime, viewed the matter more from a businessman's perspective. The day following the seizure, he sent representatives to the commissioners, offering to post bond for the value of his ship and his cargo so that he could send the *Liberty* on to England while the courts deliberated the case. The commissioners, taken aback by the ferocity of the demonstrations, agreed, though as part of the deal, they wanted Hancock to make a written promise to restrain the mob from any further interference with the activities of the commissioners or their agents.

The historian O. M. Dickerson, who describes the actions of the commissioners at the time as little less than "customs racketeering," says that the arrangement fell apart because Hancock was intelligent enough to know that signing such a pledge, even if he had the power to sway the mob, would amount to an admission that he had incited them to violence in the first place and would be used against him in subsequent court proceedings. Others, such as Hancock's biographer Harlow Unger, say that Hancock would have gone along with the plan had it not been for James Otis and Samuel Adams, who rushed to his home when they got wind of the proposition. It would be seen as nothing less than treason against the Sons of Liberty were Hancock to relent on any pretext—a vindication of the governor's position, the activities of the customs commissioners, and the Townshend Acts themselves.

Whether it was pressure from the increasingly militant Adams and Otis or distrust of the commissioners' motives is uncertain, but Hancock did decline the deal, and, on August 1, the admiralty courts dosed him with his medicine: the *Liberty* and her contents were bound over and divided by the Crown.

Commissioners also sought to press smuggling charges against Hancock, but the case eventually fell apart because of lack of evidence. Meantime, the merchants of Boston retaliated by signing a nonimportation agreement, to begin on January 1, 1769, banning the importation of glass, painters' colors, tea, and paper until the new duties on those items were rescinded. In addition, the importation of all other products from Great Britain was forbidden for a year's period, except for a few things deemed impossible to live without: buckshot, duck, hemp, fishhooks and fishing lines, and salt.

Over the ensuing year, groups in New York, Connecticut, Delaware, Rhode Island, and elsewhere issued similar decrees, and in Virginia, the plantation owner George Washington wrote on April 5, 1769, to his neighbor George Mason in support of the notion. "Something should be done to avert the stroke and maintain the free that we have derived from our Ancestors," he said. "How far then their attention to our rights and priviledges is to be awakened or alarmed by Starving their Treade and manufactures remains to be tried."

However, merchants loyal to the king continued to stock their own warehouses, key cities such as Philadelphia did not exhibit their solidarity with the bans, and trade essentially continued. Even more distressing to the populace of Boston was the prospect of the arrival of troops meant to stamp out the incipient flames of treason that Governor Bernard insisted to his superiors had been lit by Adams, Otis, and others.

In September, word came from Bernard that troops were on the way to Boston. The news provoked a town meeting where Adams oversaw the issuance of a number of resolutions, including the insistence that the stationing of an army in Boston without the people's assent violated the terms of the British Constitution. Bernard's response was to point out that the colony had in effect disbanded its own assembly by defying the king's decree to retract the circular letter—thus it had no business complaining that it enjoyed no conduit into its governance.

Adams then called for a convention of representatives from all

Massachusetts towns and districts to consider the grave situation, with the results of its deliberations and decisions to be sent to every newspaper in the colonies. Though more than a hundred communities representing virtually all of Massachusetts did send representatives to the conference, the results fell short of what Adams might have wished for. As its first order of business, the body petitioned the governor to reconstitute the assembly, but Bernard refused, calling the convention "illegal" and directing the delegates to disperse. "The King is determined to maintain his entire sovereignty over this Province," Bernard said in his reply to the impromptu convention, "and whoever shall persist in usurping any of the rights of it shall repent his rashness."

It was just the sort of response that Adams and others might have hoped for. At the first town meeting called to consider the prospect of the stationing of troops, Otis and Adams spoke before a display where four hundred muskets were arrayed. The implication was obvious: colonists might well have to shoulder arms to fend off an occupying force.

But if Adams and Otis expected a call to arms from the present body, they would be disappointed. After a week of debate and discussion the convention agreed on little more than an affirmation of the now-dissolved assembly's actions and the lament that their constitutional rights had been maligned. "We hold that the sovereignty of King George the Third is entire in all parts of the British empire. God forbid that we should ever act or wish anything in repugnation of the same," the delegates resolved. It was a tame response that would have had Bernard gloating. On the same day that the convention disbanded, there arrived in Boston harbor eight warships and four armed schooners bearing two battle-hardened regiments sent down from Halifax. No musket fire opposed them.

Though Bernard boasted in letters to Hutchinson that it was he who had put the fear of God into the colonists, it is just as likely that the absence of James Otis until halfway through the proceedings accounted for that body's indecisiveness. Though Otis's absence was never explained, it points to a growing rift between the more restrained Otis and the always outspoken Adams.

It also affirms the notion that for most colonists, the prospect of an armed insurrection was simply inconceivable. They were in large part farmers, merchants, blacksmiths, and journeymen who had enough of a struggle just making ends meet in the rawboned wilderness. They wanted their concerns heard and their burdens relieved, but they were certainly not thinking of shooting someone to achieve those aims. It might be one thing for a group of their rowdy city-boy cousins to smash a few windows and scare the daylights out of some foppish, wig-wearing Tories, but—just as there would be a long wait for Huey Newton or Stokely Carmichael to gain credibility during the civil rights struggle— relatively few colonists in 1769 were ready to take marching orders from the likes of Samuel Adams.

15

THE ROAD TO MASSACRE

On the afternoon of October 1, 1769, while marines stood by their cannon, ready to provide covering fire if it should come to that, the first troops of the 14th and 29th Regiments began to leave their ships for the Boston docks. Once ashore, and seven hundred strong, they marched through the streets to Boston Common, bayonets fixed, accompanied by an artillery company towing two cannon. Boston was now officially an occupied city, and for some commentators, it marked the point at which Samuel Adams, and by extension the Sons of Liberty everywhere, abandoned forever the illusion that the colonies could exist as a dependency of Great Britain.

Though Adams issued no proclamation and penned no private wish for "an independency" on that day, a number of his close acquaintances would write that the sight of an occupying army marching through the streets of his city must have signaled that he could no longer harbor any thoughts of compromise. As resolute as Adams and others had been in defending the constitutional principles of liberty, it now seemed that the British were equally determined to demonstrate their dominion.

Benjamin Rush, who would serve with Samuel Adams in the Continental Congress, said that Adams had told him that "the first wish of his heart" was independence, "seven years before the war." And when he was asked to comment on Rush's statement, John Adams agreed that it was probably at the time of the British occupation that his cousin had reset his course. From that point on, Adams undertook a prodigious counteroffensive, not with a musket or a sword but with a pen.

Just a few weeks previously, the Sons of Liberty had held a grand outdoor dinner near the Liberty Tree Tavern in Dorchester to commemorate the repeal of the Stamp Act. First on the list of names of the 350 in attendance was "Adams, Samuel," and next was "Adams, John." Also in attendance were James Otis, a young silversmith named Paul Revere, and many others who would become well known to patriots. Cannon were fired and multiple toasts were drunk, including toasts to the cause of liberty and "the speedy removal" of oppressors.

In a subsequent diary entry, John Adams noted the value of such gatherings in cementing the resolve of those present. "They render the People fond of their Leaders in the Cause, and averse and bitter against all opposers," he said, adding that despite the multitude of toasts, he had not seen a single person intoxicated. But he might also have added the impact of such gatherings on the leaders themselves and, in particular, upon the passions of his cousin Samuel.

Samuel Adams was a true believer. But his passion for this cause was rooted in his certainty that he was simply the messenger for the will of his fellow, ordinary citizens. It would be a pity, he once wrote, for anyone "to despise their neighbor's happiness, because he wears a worsted cap or leathern apron"; and, to his latest days, his sympathies were with the craftsman, the laborer, and the poor.

The importance of the information shared by the various Committees of Correspondence in combating the Stamp Act and the Townshend Acts was not lost on Adams, nor did he mistake the impact of the various colonial newspapers in reprinting letters and proclamations issued far and wide. The writings of "Farmer" Dickinson impressed Adams, but he was also well aware that the widespread dissemination of those essays was key. In the months that followed the occupation of Boston, Adams undertook a series of essays intended for publication in newspapers and focused specifically upon the irrationality of maintaining a standing army in a peaceful town.

Put the soldiers on the unsettled frontier where they might be useful, perhaps, he said, but keeping them in Boston to enforce the unconstitutional acts of Parliament was simply a mark of that body's intention to subjugate the colonists and deprive them of their rights. And because soldiers behaved differently from ordinary citizens, he argued, especially in being willing to obey any order without reasoning whether it was lawful or otherwise, the very notion of a constitutional government was threatened. Easily enough, Boston could find itself effectually governed by a military junta.

One of the more compelling visions of the passionate Adams is passed along by his early biographer William Wells: shortly after Adams's death, his wife spoke of the many nights she had awakened to find herself alone in bed, lamplight from the adjoining study leaking through a cracked door, the incessant whisper of her husband's pen the only sound in the house. Wells also quotes Joseph Pierce, an acquaintance of Adams, as having often passed by the house well past midnight to see the study lamp burning. It meant only one thing to Pierce: "Sam Adams was [in there] hard at work, writing against the Tories."

At that time, Adams, along with Boston's town clerk, William Cooper, came up with an idea for efficiently transmitting word of what was going on in Boston to newspapers in the other colonies, a practice that transformed the very nature of the medium in the process. They would compile a weekly summary of events that took place in Boston, along with commentary, and distribute the accounts, a "Journal of the Times," to other papers, urging them to reprint the material in the interest of the general welfare.

Up until that point, newspapers were for the most part compilations of letters, essays, appeals, and harangues by publishers and their associates; advertisements; public notices; reprints of governmental reports and edicts; and the like. There were no "reporters" as such, and "news" of the day was passed along in the form of what a "gentleman of Philadelphia" or "a traveler recently arrived from Charleston" might have written in a letter or shared in conversation with "a prominent citizen of this town" at the coffeehouse or tavern.

The "Journal of the Times," or "Journal of Occurrences," as it was also known, changed all that. It might be argued that it was the first time in the history of the colonies that there was a real demand for such information on the part of a wide readership and that circumstances would have demanded the creation of such a news service sooner or later, even if Adams had not conceived of it. But the fact remains that Adams, though unnamed in the bulletins, became the veritable Walter Cronkite of his time, and his news service became an invaluable piece of the march toward revolution.

The first installment, titled "Journal of Transactions in Boston," was published in the October 13 issue of John Holt's *New-York Gazette* and contained a summary of the events attendant on the troops' arrival in Boston. Later in the afternoon of their arrival, as the story detailed, the commanding officer of the newly arrived troops "went to the Manufactory House, with an Order from the Governor," and requested that the occupants remove themselves within two hours, "that the Troops might take Possession." Instead of receiving a "compliance," the story continued, he found that "the Doors were barr'd and bolted against them."

When the no doubt flummoxed commander appealed to the town council, earnestly entreating, out of "compassion for the troops," according to the report, the selectmen granted them refuge in Faneuil Hall, in part because the next day was the Sabbath and any possibility of conflict should be avoided. "Thus the Humanity of the City Magistrate permitted them a temporary Shelter, which no Menaces could have procured," the writer says. The piece concludes with what would become Adams's standard postscript: "The above Journal you are desired to publish for the general Satisfaction, it being strictly Fact."

Contemporary readers might quibble about the purity of that final declaration, but the impact upon the readership of the day was certainly no less than that upon the late-twentieth-century television viewer when Cronkite leaned forward to declare that what had just been delivered was unequivocally the news of the day, and good night. Circulation of the "Journal of the Times," recounting various thefts, humiliations, beatings, and even rapes committed by troops stationed in Boston and New York, as well as the widespread corruption and malfeasance of customs officers, spread quickly across the colonies, and the paper became standard reading fare even in England.

All the while, Adams and his fellow writers reminded readers that all such depredation and discord stemmed from the Townshend Acts and that the practical response to be made was to join in the nonimportation agreement. Finally, in March 1769, when the reluctant merchants of Philadelphia joined with those of Boston, New York, and the other principal northern cities, it seemed as if economic pressures might yet force Great Britain to relent.

In addition, Bostonians had further reason to rejoice when rumors of Governor Bernard's imminent departure for England, where he was to join the peerage, began to circulate. And although tensions between the troops and townspeople never entirely disappeared, both sides had reason to keep the peace. If there were no eruptions of violence from the mob, Adams could more easily maintain his position that the troops were a waste. As for the troops and especially the commanders responsible for keeping their men in line, a return to the placid surroundings of the Nova Scotia wilderness was a far more pleasant prospect than the continual harassment they lived with in Boston and New York. By August 1, 1769, Bernard would sail for London and General Gage would have transferred two of his four regiments out of Boston, along with the artillery company.

Adding to the mood of euphoria on his way out of the city, the despised Bernard let it be known that he and other colonial governors had been advised by ministers in England that no plans existed to levy any further duties on the colonies. In fact, the administration was planning to propose to the next Parliament that the Townshend duties on paper, glass, and lead paints be eliminated, leaving only the "necessary" levy on tea. The mid-August celebration staged by the Sons of Liberty in Boston was an exuberant one indeed.

But for Adams and the more perspicacious of the leadership, a portion of the liquid in the glass of oppression might have been emptied, but it was nonetheless yet half full. If two regiments had been withdrawn from Boston, two still remained. And if a tax on tea remained, then in principle nothing was changed. Until all duties—including those dictated by the Sugar Act—were rescinded, Adams maintained, the fight must continue. A tax of a penny was the same as a tax of a pound.

Even in distant Charleston, the Sons were working diligently to unite with their northern cousins. In the South, however, the political forces driving the opposition to the Townshend Acts were quite different. The merchants of Charleston were little affected by the duties imposed, for, unlike their Boston and New York counterparts, they carried on almost no illegal trade; duties were simply passed on to their customers, and the more British-manufactured goods that passed through their hands, the more they profited. They were simply not interested in joining a radical movement that threatened their own livelihoods.

The planters, artisans, and mechanics, however, suffered greatly because of the prohibition of paper currency and the demand that they settle their debts with the merchants in specie. With no money to expand plantings or hire new help, prospects for those interests were gloomy indeed. In the end, it was the mechanics and the planters who constituted the radical element in South Carolina.

Though Christopher Gadsden was himself a successful merchant, he had long before cast his lot on the side of resistance. In 1769, in fact, he advertised in the *South-Carolina Gazette* that he was no longer a merchant representing British interests but a "Country Factor," brokering local produce for export at the highest possible prices. Unless the colonies were in control of their own economic policies, he understood, they would always be subject to the capriciousness of Parliament and the enactment of measures that would hamstring development. He eventually became instrumental in putting together the alliance of South Carolina's planters and mechanics, who greatly outnumbered the merchants in the province.

In an aggrieved letter to his superiors, South Carolina lieutenant governor William Bull complained that there were far too many like Gadsden among his constituencies, embracing, in his words, "the political principles now prevailing in Boston, which kindles a kind of enthusiasm very apt to predominate in popular assemblies and whose loud cries silence the weaker voices of moderation." Bull called Gadsden "a violent enthusiast to the cause" and lamented that he expressed "with great vehemence the most extravagant claims of American exemptions."

In Bull's eyes, Gadsden and the influential planter John Mackenzie (of whom Bull groused, "whose education at Cambridge ought to have inspired him with more dutiful sentiments of the Mother Country") were the most effective supporters of the drive to secure unanimity on the nonimportation agreement. "At public meetings, whether in Taverns or under the Liberty Tree, they direct the motions as they previously settle the matter," Bull grumbled.

By late June 1769, Gadsden succeeded in effecting an agreement between planters and mechanics (including a prohibition on the importation of Negro slaves from England), and within a few weeks, a goodly number of merchants agreed to sign as well. By the end of the year there would be 142 signatures on the agreement and only thirty holdouts, the so-called irreconcilables.

In his study of the Sons of Liberty in South Carolina, Richard Walsh points out that a significant number of artisans and skilled workers in the province were encouraged by the call for the development of American manufacturing to fill the void left by the nonimportation of various British goods. A society titled "Lovers and Encouragers of American Manufacturers" was established and a proposal to create a paper mill in the colony circulated.

Gadsden had his critics, of course, most of them successful merchants who feared the loss of the status quo and claimed that opposition to the Townshend Acts set the colonies irrevocably on a road to calamity. "To be independent of Great Britain, would be the greatest misfortune that could befall," wrote the irreconcilable planter William Wragg.

Gadsden's reply to such wealthy loyalists as Wragg (who was buried in Westminster Abbey following his death in a shipwreck while on his way to England in 1777) was consistent in pointing out that in the end the repercussions of the onerous duties affected those colonists little able to bear it. "In arbitrary governments," he wrote, "tyranny generally descends, as it were from rank to rank, through the people, til' almost the whole weight of it, at last, falls upon the honest laborious farmer, mechanic, and day labourer. When this happens, it must make them poor, almost *irremediably* poor indeed."

✦   ✦   ✦

As such jockeying continued in Charleston, the Sons of Liberty in New York were also becoming a significant force in the local political scene. For a number of years prior to the upheaval that began in 1765, the most powerful machine of influence was that managed by James DeLancey, a trader who initially allied himself and his party with the interests of conservative merchants and landholders.

Politics in New York, however, has always been a brawling, pragmatically directed arena, a "dirty business," in the words of the historian Roger Champagne. Votes were bought, influence was peddled, and payoffs and kickbacks were routine, and whatever it took to maintain power was far more important to the players than allegiance to ethics or morals, or steadfast adherence to a political platform. And the skilled workmen and artisans of New York composed a significant portion of the electorate. There were about four thousand white males over the age of twenty-one living in the city at the time, of whom nearly 70 percent held voting rights, either by dint of the ownership of an estate worth £40 or by paying a registration fee. Because the latter was a relatively modest 2 shillings, 3 pence for mechanics, that class came to constitute nearly half of the total electorate.

Accordingly, as the sentiments of the voting populace began to swing toward the progressive interests led by Philip Livingston in the wake of the Stamp Act Congress, DeLancey countered by forging an alliance with Isaac Sears and his fellow Liberty Boy mechanic John Lamb.

In the election of 1768, called to reconstitute the provincial assembly that Governor Moore had dissolved in February for its failure to comply fully with the terms of the Quartering Act, the DeLancey candidates took back control of the assembly and rewarded Sears by naming him the city's first potash inspector, considered a plum appointment. Suddenly, the conservative DeLancey machine was the party of the public interest, at the forefront of opposition to the Quartering Act and mobilization of merchants in support of the nonimportation agreement.

Nor did the liberty pole lose the attention of the city's patriots. Following the 1767 celebration held on the common to commemorate the repeal of the Stamp Act, the *New York Journal* reported that on the night of March 18, following the conclusion of the festivities, "a few very mischievous Spirits among the Soldiery" left the barracks late in the night and cut down the third liberty pole, which had stood since the previous fall.

The following day, according to the *Journal*, "the Inhabitants" erected yet another pole, larger yet and banded with iron "to a considerable height above ground." That same night, the British soldiers returned and attempted to cut the fortified pole down, then tried to dig it up when those efforts failed. Time or exhaustion stymied the troops, however, and on the night of March 21 they returned to try to blow the pole up with gunpowder. "But this also fail'd," according to the *Journal*.

On Sunday night a contingent of citizens installed a surveillance party in a home overlooking the common. In the wee hours, a small party of soldiers armed with clubs and bayonets was observed moving toward the common, but when members of the watch went to confront them, the soldiers withdrew. On Tuesday afternoon, the resolute band of redcoats was observed making its way toward the common, carrying a ladder commandeered from a nearby construction project. Apparently it was the soldiers' intention to climb past the iron bands that had foiled their earlier attempts to cut the new pole down.

This time, the *Journal* reported, the men were spotted by an officer who ordered them back to their barracks. When word of the incident was passed up the chain of command, orders from Governor Moore and General Gage put an end to the siege once and for all. "Since, all has been quiet," the *Journal* said, "and we hope this Matter, in itself trivial . . . will occasion no farther Difference."

In fact, "the Post," as the *Journal* called it, did occasion no further difference for almost three years, during which a relative calm prevailed in the city, though the governor did once again suspend the assembly in 1769 for failing to meet its obligations in support of the troops. At the same time, the DeLancey faction betrayed a promise to Isaac Sears that it would vigorously oppose the Quartering Act and instead brokered an agreement with Governor Moore that would allow the colony to once again print its own currency, if only half would go toward the provisioning of the troops. In short order, Sears and Lamb, along with their more moderate fellow Son Alexander McDougall, switched their allegiance back to the Livingston faction. Such was politics in New York.

In September 1769, Governor Moore suddenly fell ill and died, thrusting Cadwallader Colden back into the post of acting governor. Though eighty-one by then, Colden was determined to show that he still had the moxie for the permanent position he had long coveted. He followed through on the agreement on currency with the DeLancey faction, and in late November, the assembly authorized the payment of £2,000 for support of the troops.

Predictably, demonstrations flared up on the common, and on December 16, an anonymous writer circulated a broadside addressed to "the betrayed inhabitants of the city and colony of New York," complaining that the DeLancey forces had abandoned their constituents in allocating funds for the support of troops sent, "not to protect but enslave us." The broadside was signed, "A Son of Liberty," and the DeLancey-led legislature struck back with the offer of a reward of £100 for the name of the author.

Protests continued into the new year, and on Saturday night, January 13, a group of British soldiers again made their way to the common, where they managed to bore a hole into the liberty pole and pack it with gunpowder. They were about to detonate the charge when patrons from the nearby Montagne's Tavern spotted them and called a general alarm. The charge misfired, sparing the pole, but the soldiers rushed into the tavern "with drawn Swords and Bayonets," according to a report in the *New-York Gazette*, breaking crockery, lamps, and windowpanes, "insulting the company and beating the Waiter."

This insult provoked the publication of a harangue against the troops and the Quartering Act and a call for a meeting at the liberty pole at noon the following Wednesday, when "the whole matter shall be communicated." What the Sons of Liberty discovered when they made their way to the common on the seventeenth was dismaying, to say the least.

In "the dead hour" of the previous night, said the *Post-Boy*, British soldiers quartered in a house near the common had made their way back to the liberty pole and once again packed a cavity they had chiseled out with gunpowder. That time the charge was detonated, and the pole was shattered. The soldiers gathered the fragments and carried them to the doorstep of the shuttered Montagne's Tavern, depositing them in a pile.

Outraged citizens milled about the shattered stump of the liberty pole, muttering at the audacity of the troops. Someone pointed to the nearby house where a few troops were billeted and called out the suggestion that they pull it down. The "Aye!"s were thunderous, and the group began a march toward the house.

The soldiers billeted there, almost certainly the same ones who had destroyed the pole, arrayed themselves before the house, their bayonets and cutlasses drawn, jeering and daring the citizens to try their damnedest. It might have been the occasion for a bloodbath, but a contingent of British officers arrived, accompanied by a squad of local magistrates, and the confrontation was squelched.

By Friday, the troops took the rather surprising measure of printing a broadside of their own and were bustling about the city, handing out copies and nailing others to posts and door frames. The piece began with a ditty:

> *God and a Soldier all Men doth adore*
> *In Time of War, and not before;*
> *When the War is over, and all Things righted,*
> *God is forgotten and the Soldier slighted.*

And it continued by making sport of the Sons of Liberty, "as these great heroes thought their freedom depended upon a piece of wood." These Sons of Liberty ought to be more properly called "the real enemies to Society," the broadside continued, calling upon the populace to throw their support to the troops, who suffered through the blaze of summer and the freezing nights of winter on their behalf.

As one soldier nailed a copy onto a posting board at an outdoor market near the wharves, Isaac Sears, who'd gotten wind of what was going on, approached and snatched the man by his collar, demanding that he explain his actions. Posting libelous claims against the citizenry was a serious offense, Sears said. He would drag the man to the mayor and see what happened then.

A second soldier, who'd been carrying the stack of handbills while his partner did the nailing, started toward Sears, but a fellow Son intervened, grabbing him by the arm and spinning him about. A third soldier pulled his saber and started toward the melee, but Sears snatched up an ox-horn snuffbox and flung it at the swordsman, striking him solidly between the eyes. It was enough to send the soldier fleeing for reinforcements, while Sears and his companion dragged their two captives to the mayor's house.

As a crowd gathered and Sears began his explanation of the incident, a party of some twenty soldiers from the barracks advanced, swords and bayonets drawn. At the mayor's house, the soldiers called out for the release of the two men inside, and the leaders of the company—clearly intoxicated, according to the account of the matter in the *Gazette*—began pounding on the door.

A magistrate ordered the soldiers to desist and return to their barracks, and the mayor came to the door to repeat the edict. The two captives, meanwhile, took one look at the volatile scene developing outside and decided they'd take their chances with Sears and the mayor. With that rebuff from their own comrades, the redcoats began a retreat, followed by the crowd of citizens who'd gathered to watch the spectacle.

The procession made its way—with insults flying back and forth—to the summit of Golden Hill, a field near the intersection of modern-day Fulton and Cliff Streets and just a few blocks southeast of the common, where a second party of soldiers happened upon their beleaguered comrades. Emboldened by the reinforcements, the soldiers who'd been driven from the mayor's house turned to face the crowd members who were pressing in on them, brandishing clubs and hurling catcalls.

There was a moment when the matter might have passed, the British retreated back to their barracks, the crowd returned to the wharves and the market—but then one of the British party, noticeable for the expensive silk stockings and buckskin breeches he wore, called out an order. "Soldiers, draw your bayonets," he barked, "and cut your way through them!"

The crowd members, none of whom was armed with more than a cudgel or a barrel stave, surged backward, pushing through a narrow passage between buildings for escape. "Where are your Sons of Liberty now?" one of the soldiers cried, lunging toward a townsman with his bayonet. A nearby townsman swung at the soldier, who parried the blow with his rifle. The townsman's club flew from his hands, and the next moment, the pair were fleeing down the alleyway, pursued by enraged soldiers.

As the two rounded a corner and sped toward the safety of the nearby wharves, Francis Field, an unsuspecting resident identified by the *Gazette* as "one of the people called Quakers," stepped from the doorway of his home to see what the commotion was about. At that same moment, one of the soldiers rounded the corner to see Field emerging from the doorway. Assuming that he was under attack, the soldier swung his cutlass at the astonished Field. The hilt of the blade caught Field across the cheek, spraying blood over them both. The blow would probably have killed Field, but as he staggered back, the tip of the blade struck the door frame and lodged there, saving him from its full force. With Field down and clutching his bleeding cheek, the soldier ran on with his mates after the fleeing crowd.

Residents carrying out their normal business gaped as citizens galloped through their ranks, screaming, "Murder!" and pursued by red-faced troops fueled by months of pent-up fury. A tea cart vendor who stepped unknowingly into the path of a frenzied soldier took a blade across the shoulder, and a fisherman on his way to the docks nearly lost a finger when he held up a hand to stop an onrushing redcoat.

Back on the hill, where a few stalwart citizens stood their ground, the fighting was intense. One man took a thrust with a bayonet that threatened his life. The magistrate who had ordered the troops from the mayor's home found himself with only a long stick in his hands, up against two soldiers armed with swords. They backed him into a corner and were advancing with murderous expressions when a neighbor rushed out with a halberd in hand and tossed it to the cornered magistrate. Suddenly the confrontation took on a new character.

Two men with cutlasses now found themselves facing a desperate law officer brandishing a six-foot steel-tipped pike, a glistening ax blade affixed near its head for good measure. It was the same weapon, wielded by a Swiss infantryman, that is said to have split the skull of Charles the Bold, Duke of Burgundy, thus ending the Burgundian Wars. The soldiers had probably not read of such events, but they did not need to; their quarrel with the magistrate was over.

As word of the riot spread, officers from the barracks arrived to call the soldiers off. The injured—none of whom would die—were carried off and tended to, but the deeper wounds would remain unhealed. Some commentators have called the blood spilled on Golden Hill the first to be shed in the Revolution, but there were far worse actions to come.

16

AFFRAY IN KING STREET

Surprisingly enough, the Battle of Golden Hill did not escalate into a full-scale uprising. That evening there were minor incidents—one lamplighter was assaulted by soldiers; another had his ladder pulled out from under him while carrying out his duties—and the following day there was a scuffle on Nassau Street that ended with one soldier slashed across the shoulder and a citizen losing two teeth to the butt of a bayonet, but the city somehow receded into calm.

When the city government itself declared that under no conditions would a replacement liberty pole be allowed to rise on the common, Isaac Sears did not quarrel. Instead, he purchased a lot nearby and arranged for the city's fifth liberty pole to be erected there. It was the largest, most elaborate yet, a forty-six-foot ship's mast topped by a twenty-two-foot metal flagstaff and a gilded weather vane spelling out "Liberty." The pole was hauled from the wharves through the streets by six garland-draped horses and accompanied by a crowd of thousands. As a brass band played, the pole, its base protected by iron strips and bands, was planted in a twelve-foot-deep hole reinforced with timbers and boulders. If Sears had learned anything in his years of struggle, it was the enduring strength that this symbol lent to his cause. It was "just a piece of wood," but that was like calling a nation's flag "just a piece of cloth." Sears was certain of one thing: so long as there was a fight, there would be a liberty pole for his side to rally by.

In occupied Boston, meantime, tensions persisted as well, and Samuel Adams was forced to carry on the struggle to keep the merchants united behind the nonimportation agreement without the aid of his compatriot

James Otis. Though Adams's stridency could alarm the more conservative of their constituency, Otis could be counted on as the calming influence: "Don't worry, now, that's just Sam."

But Otis was not immune to the occasional fit of temper, and for some time in 1769, he was chafing at the rumor that the customs commissioners had written home calling Otis an enemy of the king. There were in fact attempts by some in Parliament to have the leaders of the Sons of Liberty arrested and brought to England to be tried as traitors, but nothing came of them. Still, the possibility of being shanghaied and tried on capital charges was not a trifle. When a friend produced copies of some of the damning private correspondence sent by Governor Bernard and the commissioners during the summer, Otis blew up.

In the September 4 issue of the *Boston Gazette*, he placed a public notice stating that he possessed "full evidence" that the four customs commissioners, including one John Robinson, had defamed him "in a manner that is not to be endured" as a traitor and part of "a general combination to revolt from Great Britain." Nothing could be further from the truth, Otis declared. He was a faithful subject of the king, and, furthermore, he was demanding personal satisfaction from those named. In other words, Otis was challenging the four commissioners to a duel. He had not yet received an answer, he said in his notice, but meantime he begged that no one in England give any credence to the abusive representations made by the commissioners, for their word was of no more merit than that of Francis Bernard, the governor.

It was quite a proclamation, particularly since Otis printed the notice under his own name. One could only imagine the gossip that flew about the city that day, as well as the collective intake of breath that must have silenced the British Coffee House when Otis walked in at seven the following night. At one table in the establishment sat Commissioner John Robinson, along with a number of his customs agents and some officers of the British army and navy.

Words, as the saying goes, were exchanged. Robinson swung his cane, striking Otis, and Otis returned the favor. As one of Otis's early biographers stated, "Great confusion then ensued."

The lights went out, and Otis, who had imprudently gone to the coffeehouse alone, found himself surrounded. A young man named Gridley who was passing by in the streets heard Otis's cries and rushed in to help, but he was quickly beaten and tossed out. When the lights came back on, Robinson was gone, out a back door, and Otis was on the floor, bleeding from a head wound. Several billy clubs and an empty sword scabbard lay nearby.

Otis was taken home and treated for his wounds, while Samuel Adams took to the press, decrying the incident as a cabal arranged by Robinson to assassinate Otis. Though it was something of an overstatement on Adams's part (Robinson would ultimately agree to pay Otis £2,000 in settlement of a resulting civil suit), the affair did have something of a terminal influence. Otis would eventually recover from the physical effects of the beating, but the psychological impact proved more significant. Though he had always been mercurial, his periods of highs and lows intensified, and he gradually withdrew from public life; he would never again regain his place as the placating complement to Adams.

Adams, however, continued his efforts to keep the town's merchants solidly behind the nonimportation movement. In October, he was successful in convincing the merchants' committee and the town council to agree to continue the nonimportation agreement past the scheduled expiration date of December 31 to such time as Parliament agreed to rescind *all* duties in effect upon the colonies.

It is safe to assume that the incident of Otis's beating aided Adams in his efforts, but townspeople were still disturbed by the daily sight of redcoats patrolling their city and irked by the constant presence of customs men lurking in the harbor and at the docks. On the evening of October 28, a man named George Gailer, suspected to be a customs informant, encountered a group determined to instruct him concerning the error of his ways. The men snatched up the quarrelsome Gailer, tarred and feathered him, then paraded him through the city streets. When a soldier tried to put a stop to the spectacle, the men offered to decorate him similarly and put him into the cart with Gailer.

Gailer the informant would survive his treatment, but it is worth noting that although the practice of tarring and feathering may sound quaint to the modern ear and although it was based in the intent to ridicule, it was no laughing matter to the recipient. In a study of this practice, which enjoyed a resurgence during colonial times, the scholar Benjamin Irvin notes that the concept derived from the medieval period, dating back at least as far as an 1189 proclamation by King Richard I of England, in which he decreed that any of his crusaders who stooped to thievery during their noble missions "were to have their heads shaved, to have boiling Pitch dropped upon their Crowns; and after having Cushion-Feathers stuck upon the Pitch, they were to be set on shore, in that figure, at the first place they came to."

Certainly, the image of a hapless crusader wandering about a forlorn promontory with eyes peering out of a blanket of black tar and bristling feathers (one observer said victims looked as if they'd been stuck by thousands of darts) might be construed as demeaning, even ludicrous, but there would be little funny about it for the victim. Though the practice was sometimes modified to a simple dipping of a victim in a barrel of molasses followed by a tumble in a pile of goose fathers, victims in the colonies did not always get off so easily.

The most common "tar" used in the practice was gum taken from pine trees. Sometimes it was heated, causing serious blistering of the skin; sometimes it was applied straight out of the barrel with a trowel. Sometimes the recipient was allowed to remain clothed, but it was not always so. And depending on how much time elapsed in the usual parading of the offender about the community, the tar could easily harden, making its removal exceedingly difficult.

Try to imagine removing hardened tar from hair, face, ears, nose, eyes, and genitals. Most victims of the practice lost a good deal of body hair; those lucky enough not to have strips of skin peeled away with the tar suffered severe rashes. Surely, to be tarred and feathered was a humiliating experience, but it was a painful one as well.

In any case, Adams responded to criticism of such incidents by pointing out that had there been no unconstitutional levies and no unnecessary occupation of troops, such things would never take place. In a letter to London, Thomas Hutchinson complained that Adams was pressing for the removal of the remaining troops to Castle William. Meanwhile, with the coming of the new year, Adams found the tide turning against him on the nonimportation issue.

Largely because associations in the other colonies were unwilling to extend the terms of nonimportation to the Sugar Act and other duties, Adams was forced to be content with Boston's decision to do the same; nonimportation would cease once the Townshend duties were abolished. Though this flew in the face of his fears that the tea tax would constitute a fearsome precedent if it remained, the clamor for an increase in business and the enjoyment of goods too long forgone was simply too strong. Still, he kept up his effort to brand several prominent irreconcilables as traitors to the cause of liberty and to urge a public boycott of their businesses.

A group of more than 1,300 jammed Faneuil Hall in late January to hear the names of several merchants castigated as "importers" and ignored Hutchinson's orders to disperse. At the same meeting, a resolution calling for abstinence from drinking tea was passed, and shortly thereafter, several groups of Boston women joined in by forming their own agreements "against drinking foreign TEA."

Still, irreconcilable merchants continued to import the product, and tensions remained high. On February 22, 1770, protesters picketed outside the shop (on present-day Hanover Street) of Theophilus Lillie, a dry-goods retailer and one of the merchants identified by the town meeting as an "obstinate and inveterate enemy." Though Lillie was but one of four merchants singled out by the council as an "importer," he went to the trouble of publishing an indignant reply in the *Boston Chronicle*, a conservative paper supporting the interests of the Crown. In the piece, Lillie complained that although he was no politician it did strike him as strange that "people who contend so much for civil and religious liberty" should be so ready to deprive others of theirs.

In Lillie's view, he was just an ordinary merchant trying to make a living who had made the mistake of ordering some goods from England before nonimportation was agreed upon. By the time the goods arrived, the agreement had gone into effect and he had been forced to store the goods, a state of affairs that he described "as punishment for an offence before the law for punishing was made." What most annoyed Lillie was the principle of the thing: "If one set of private subjects may at any time take upon themselves to punish another set of private subjects just when they please, it's such a sort of government as I never heard of before."

Such niceties of logic served only to call particular attention to Lillie, however, and on the Thursday in question, a day when town schools released their restless pupils early, a demonstration formed outside Lillie's shop. One of the boys (he would have been the son of a working-man) carried a sign in the shape of a hand with a pointing finger aimed at Lillie's shop and bearing the legend "importer." A second of the boys planted a pole topped with a likeness of Lillie's head in the ground nearby, and catcalls and hurrahing began.

Soon after, Ebenezer Richardson, a known informant employed by the despised customs commissioners, happened by and took offense at the demonstration. He first tried to wrest the sign away from the youth carrying it, and when that failed, he made a rush at the pole bearing the effigy of Lillie, but that went no better. Richardson, who was something of a buffoon according to contemporary press accounts, then retired to his home, which was not far from the site of the demonstration.

Some of the boys trailed Richardson to his home, exchanging insults with him all the way. When Richardson reached his house, he turned upon his tormentors, and, as it is reported in the *Boston Gazette* of February 26, "swore by GOD that he would make the Place too hot for some of them before Night." If they did not go away, he added, he would "make a Lane through them."

At this point, garbage began to pelt the Richardson home, and Richardson's wife ran out to gather up the slops and hurl them back at the crowd. In short order, rocks and paving stones began to rattle the boards of the house. One window was shattered and then another.

Richardson, who had fled inside the house with his wife as the bricks began to fly, appeared at one of the gutted windows with a musket raised. It was the sort of bravado that only inflamed the crowd to new heights. A hail of bricks and curses flew at Richardson, who raised his musket to his shoulder . . .

. . . and fired.

Sammy Gore, a boy at the front of the crowd, took several buckshot pellets to his hands and thighs. Eleven-year-old Christopher Seider, later identified as an uninvolved passerby drawn by the commotion, took the brunt of the charge in his chest and died a few hours later.

By that point, the crowd of unruly boys had been supplanted by a mob of adults, who stormed the house and dragged Richardson into the street. He was carried to Faneuil Hall, where witnesses confirmed the events surrounding the shooting and a panel of magistrates ordered him held in the county jail for trial.

"This innocent Lad is the first whose Life has been a Victim to the Cruelty and Rage of the *Oppressors*," said the *Gazette*, and even if the language was overblown, the account had the statistics correct. Young Seider was the first clear casualty of the nascent war.

In a postscript either penned or approved by Samuel Adams, the account used the unfortunate outcome as the basis for a swipe at the occupying troops. "It is hoped the unexpected and melancholy Death of young Seider will be a Means for the future of preventing any, but more especially the Soldiery, from being too free in the Use of their Instruments of Death," the piece opined, closing with an announcement of the funeral that would take place on the afternoon of February 26: "It is hoped none will be in the Procession but the Friends of Liberty, and then undoubtedly *all* will be hearty Mourners."

The event was indeed a celebration of unity. The procession began with an invocation beneath the liberty tree and wound through the streets with a parade of 500 boys marching in front of the casket and 1,500 or so townspeople following. John Adams remarked that he had never seen a funeral of such size. "This Shows there are many more Lives to spend if wanted in the Service of their Country," he wrote in his diary entry for the day. "It Shows too that the . . . Ardor of the People is not to be quelled by the Slaughter of one Child and the Wounding of another."

The *Gazette* reminded its readers that indeed the boy had died "in his Country's Cause," and Phillis Wheatley, a slave educated by her Boston family, wrote a poem memorializing young Seider's death (she misspelled his name) that began:

> *In heaven's eternal court it was decreed*
> *How the first martyr for the cause should bleed*
> *To clear the country of the hated brood*
> *He whet his courage for the common good.*
>
> —"On the Death of Mr. Snider, Murder'd by Richardson," 1770

There is little doubt that whatever was to account for the incident, it would surely serve to solidify the position of the radicals and Adams's appeal for unity of the colonists in opposition to the British. It might have even become the event that Bostonians would remember as the beginning of the Revolution in their town had it not been for the events that ensued just four days later.

On March 2, Patrick Walker, an off-duty British soldier looking for part-time work to supplement his salary, approached the rope-making factory of John Gray. It was an example of one more activity that hardened the common public against the soldiers' presence in their midst, for not only did the redcoats insult and threaten the citizens (and sometimes woo away their sweethearts and bed their daughters); they were often willing to take temporary work at lower wages than the locals.

"So you want a job, do you?" one of Gray's workmen is said to have asked Walker.

Indeed he did want a job, the eager Walker responded.

"Then go and clean my shithouse," the workman responded, a witticism that provoked gales of laughter from his nearby cohorts and no end of retellings by historians (the richest account is probably that of Hiller Zobel).

Walker might not have been bright, but he was no coward. He fell upon the workman and a brief tussle ensued, one in which the soldier fared little better. In short order, then, two day laborers pummeled Walker into submission. Understandably, the hapless soldier ran off with the jeers of the workmen trailing him.

Shortly, however, Walker reappeared with at least eight of his comrades, spoiling for a rematch. The rope makers were more than happy to give it to them, and once again they came out on top. By this time the factory was giddy with triumph.

The self-congratulation was soon interrupted, though, for inside fifteen minutes yet one more contingent of troops returned, this time at least forty strong. This time the two sides went at each other with clubs and rope maker's tools, but the outcome was no different. The soldiers were chased from the rope yards and hounded all the way back to their barracks.

Similar skirmishes took place on the streets over the next three days with civilians proclaiming their superiority and soldiers threatening revenge. During one fight, a soldier suffered a broken arm and fractured skull. As General Gage would admit, the stationing of troops proved to be an exercise in futility. "The people were as Lawless and Licentious after the Troops arrived as they were before," he lamented.

Then, on the night of March 5, matters came to a head. There were rumors afloat that a brawl was planned between the sides, but whether that is true or not, there was no shortage of hotheads on the streets looking for trouble. It was a chill night lit by a quarter moon, the streets frozen, the remains of a light snow still on the ground. As one early account penned by Richard Frothingham had it, "as though something uncommon was expected, parties of boys, apprentices, and soldiers strolled through the streets; and neither side was sparing of insult."

A group of soldiers left Murray's Barracks on Brattle Street, "armed with clubs and cutlasses, bent on a stroll." At Brattle Street Church they encountered a crowd that was collected there, most of its members carrying canes and clubs. "Wretched abuse" was exchanged, and fighting ensued yet again. As that was going on, Captain John Goldfinch, who was making his way back to the barracks, passed by a sentinel's station on King Street near the Boston customs house. Loitering nearby was a young barber's apprentice, Edward Garrick, who shouted an insult. According to the apprentice, the captain was a scoundrel who had not paid him for dressing his hair.

What Captain Goldfinch thought of this is not recorded, but it is known that the sentinel stepped from his guard box and clubbed the apprentice to the ground with a blow from the butt of his musket. After a moment, the boy made his way dazedly to his feet and ran off crying.

Goldfinch hurried on toward the barracks only to find his way blocked by the scuffle that had erupted outside Brattle Street Church, where townsmen were now pelting the troops with snowballs and chunks of ice and church bells tolled an alarm in the background. Goldfinch shouted orders for his men to repair to the barracks, and calm seemed restored, at least for the moment.

"For a little time," says Frothingham, "there was nothing to attract to a centre the people who were drawn by the alarm bell out of their homes on this frosty moonlit memorable evening; and in various places people were asking where the fire was." Possibly fifteen minutes of peace constituted the fulcrum upon which history was balanced. And then things changed.

At a quarter past nine a group of agitated townsmen rushed down King Street toward the customs house, led by the bruised barber's apprentice. As they approached the sentry box, the apprentice stopped and pointed. "That's him!" he cried. "That's the soldier who hit me!"

The crowd surged forward at that. "Knock him down!" someone shouted.

"Kill him!" a second called.

By now the young soldier, John White, had deserted his sentry box and was backing carefully up the icy steps of the customs house, loading his musket as he went. It might have seemed the right thing to do at the time, clobbering the insolent barber's apprentice while his commanding officer watched, but now, as an angry mob closed in upon him and his numb fingers fumbled with his weapon, he must have entertained regrets.

A snowball, more ice than snow, burst against his chest, and a jagged chunk of ice, enough to have felled him, flew past his head. The soldier raised his musket. "Stay back, damn you!" he called. A hail of snowballs and chunks of ice came in answer.

"Fire if you will!" came a cry.

"Damned coward!" another called.

One bystander burst into the nearby barracks to say that the life of the customs house sentry was in danger, and Captain Thomas Preston, the officer of the day, rushed to the headquarters of the main guard, several hundred feet from the confrontation. In moments, a detail of seven, led by a green sergeant, set out at a trot toward the customs house, bayonets fixed.

The troops elbowed their way through the menacing crowd, using their bayonets to prod anyone slow to get out of the way. They arrayed themselves before the crowd at the base of the steps, and the sentry hurried down from the shelter he'd taken from the ice and stones the crowd was hurling at him.

Captain Preston came through the crowd then. "Make way!" he shouted, shouldering aside townsmen until he joined his troops. There were nine of them facing off the mob of fifty or so: Preston, the shaken sentry, and the seven men Preston had sent.

Preston might have been about to shout an insult at the crowd, or perhaps an order to disperse, but that is when a heavy ball of ice and snow burst upon his forehead. Perhaps Preston thought it was the prelude to a charge, or perhaps he was simply outraged by the insult.

"Fire!" he cried to his men as a hail of ice and snowballs rained upon them all. "Damn you, fire! Be the consequence what it will!"

One soldier did fire, just as a townsman strode forward and brought his cudgel down across the soldier's hands. The soldier stumbled back with a cry, his weapon tumbling to the frozen pavement. The townsman barely paused, lunging toward Preston with a mighty roundhouse of a swing.

The club was aimed at Preston's skull, but the officer ducked, and the blow glanced off his shoulder, sending his hat sailing. The rest of the troops were firing now. Seven shots were fired, or eight. Some swore they had heard eleven.

Five men lay on the pavement, three of them killed instantly. Two others would die by morning.

Samuel Gray, of the rope-making clan, was killed on the spot, "the ball entering his head and bearing off a large portion of his skull." He'd just called out to his fellow protesters not to worry: "My lads, they will not fire."

Crispus Attucks, a hulking "mulatto man," and one of those who'd been involved in the original fighting by the Brattle Street Church, was also killed at once. He was leaning casually on a cordwood stick he carried for a club when he took two balls, one of which went through a lung and traveled on to pierce his liver.

Also dead was the seventeen-year-old James Caldwell, who lived nearby. He'd come out into the street and turned to ask someone in the crowd what was going on when two balls took him in the back.

A ball went through the stomach of Samuel Maverick, also seventeen, "son of the widow Maverick" and apprentice to an ivory carver. He would bleed until morning and finally die.

And there was Patrick Carr, said to be "a seasoned Irish rioter," who worked with a leather breeches maker in Queen Street. He took a shot in the hip that exited out his side. He too would linger and bleed, and finally die.

Six more were seriously wounded, and as the stunned and shaken townsmen tended to the victims, the soldiers were reloading. They might have fired again if Captain Preston had not ordered a withdrawal to the main guard headquarters. Meantime, several companies of the 29th Regiment were drawn up there, a third of their number deployed in the kneeling position, ready to fire.

While Dr. Joseph Warren, a close associate of Samuel Adams, hurried to tend to the wounded and dying, a deputation of citizens made their way to Lieutenant Governor Hutchinson's home to alert him of what had happened. The entire town was on its way to King Street, they told him, and full-scale warfare was about to erupt.

Hutchinson, never popular in the city, made his way to the gory scene with caution. When he arrived at King Street, he went to the office of the main guard and called for Captain Preston.

It was a simple question he had for Preston: "Do you know, sir, you have no power to fire on any body of the people collected together, except you have a civil magistrate with you to give orders?"

Preston's reply was even more simply couched. "I was obliged to," he said, "to save the sentry."

This exchange, overheard by some in the crowd, resulted in a cry that became a chant: "To the town house, to the town house."

The townspeople were demanding an immediate response to the matter by Hutchinson, and he was wise enough to grant it. "The law," Hutchinson assured them at a gathering inside the town council chambers, "should have its course; he would live and die by the law." Hutchinson ordered the troops arrayed outside the main guard to repair immediately to the barracks and ordered Captain Preston and the eight soldiers who had fired upon the crowd jailed, pending a proper inquiry. It was 3 a.m. by the time Preston was remanded behind bars and the populace largely dispersed, but Hutchinson managed to avert a total disaster.

The following morning presented a stunning scene to the citizens of Boston. As the *Gazette* reported, any passerby could view "the Blood of our Fellow Citizens running like Water through King Street and the Merchants Exchange, the principal Spot of the Military Parade for about 18 months past."

Modern-day readers seeking a way in which to comprehend the power of the incident (and the attendant press accounts) upon the citizenry might look to the images published in the press following the shootings at Kent State University on May 4, 1970. On that day, Ohio National Guardsmen called to control an antiwar rally on the campus fired sixty-seven rounds in thirteen seconds, killing four students and wounding nine others. Though some supporters of the guardsmen argued that the troops had feared for their lives and that some of the young people were of questionable background, such considerations mattered little to most of the nation. The "Kent State Massacre," as it became known, is generally conceded to be the event that swung the last of the undecided populace toward a call for the end of the Vietnam War.

At 11 a.m. on March 6, 1770, citizens of Boston met in Faneuil Hall and formed a committee headed by Samuel Adams, Dr. Warren, John Hancock, and others to present a petition to Hutchinson demanding the immediate withdrawal of all troops to Castle William in the harbor. Hutchinson wasted little time in responding.

His answer was sent to the committee at the meeting hall at Old South Church, where an ever-burgeoning mass of citizens had gathered to share their outrage and determine their future course of action. Hutchinson began with an apology for the events of the previous evening and a promise that the law would indeed take its course in the matter. Furthermore, he said, the troops of the 29th Regiment would be removed immediately to Castle William. Until word was received from General Gage, however, the troops of the 14th Regiment, who had taken no part in the evening's conflict, would be kept in the town barracks and would be "laid under such restraint that all occasion of future disturbances may be prevented."

It would have been a bit like promising the outraged students at Kent State that the only guardsmen who would be left to patrol the campus were those who promised to be good, and the meeting of Bostonians (now swollen to roughly four thousand) was quick to respond. Adams and the others were soon back in Hutchinson's office bearing a second resolution. "Nothing less will satisfy than a total and immediate removal of *all* the troops," Adams informed the governor, reminding him that if he had the power to remove one regiment, he surely had the power to remove two.

Adams's logic had little effect upon Hutchinson, who felt he had done more than enough to mollify the citizens. He sent word to his council that he would have no further use for them on that day and prepared to leave his offices. At that point, Colonel William Dalrymple, the commander of the troops, intervened. Perhaps the lieutenant governor should consult with his council as to these demands, he said. In fact, if the council felt that all the troops should be removed, Dalrymple would not object.

Hutchinson was surprised but gave in to Dalrymple's urging and convened the council once more following dinner. At that meeting, the governor sat in disbelief as the council members one by one suggested compliance with the townspeople's demands. There were said to be 10,000 citizens in Boston and towns nearby who were ready to take up arms. If it should come to that, there was no hope that their forces could prevail.

Hutchinson wrangled with the council well into the night, warning of the precedent such an action would set, but it was to no avail. In the end, the council affirmed its unanimous opinion and the disgruntled Hutchinson passed the word along to Colonel Dalrymple, appending the notation that nonetheless, as governor, he held no personal authority to order the removal of the troops. Dalrymple felt that appendix to be an unnecessary equivocation, but Hutchinson was resolute: if the council and the local commander wished to take responsibility for the matter, he would not oppose it, but he was certainly not going to back down to Adams and his cohorts.

Soon enough, word that the troops would be removed was passed to a cheering crowd at Old South Church. Colonel Dalrymple would begin his preparations in the morning, Adams advised. "There would be no unnecessary delay until the whole of the two Regiments were removed to the Castle." According to town records, Adams, John Hancock, and other leaders of the Boston Sons formed a committee to supervise a night watch patrol to keep order on the streets until the troops were actually redeployed.

On the afternoon of Thursday, March 8, the third day following the shootings, more than 10,000 citizens took part in the funeral procession for the victims. The bodies of Samuel Gray, Samuel Maverick, James Caldwell, and Crispus Attucks were interred in a single vault in the city's cemetery. As the *Boston Gazette* put it, "The aggravated Circumstances of their Death, the Distress and Sorrow visible in every

Countenance, together with the peculiar Solemnity with which the whole Funeral was conducted, surpass description."

Patrick Carr, the fifth to die, would linger for a week before expiring of his wounds late on March 13: eventually he would join the others in their common grave. Though press accounts speculated that more among the wounded would soon follow, all recovered, though some historians would later point to young Christopher Monk, a shipbuilder's apprentice, as the sixth victim of the shootings. Monk, seventeen at the time, was shot near the spine, and though newspaper accounts described his condition as grave, he pulled through. Monk never completely recovered, however, and lived out his remaining ten years in a compromised state, supported by the charity of others.

One might suppose that the Boston Massacre, as it became known, would have occasioned a mammoth upheaval among the populace. But Samuel Adams and other leaders went to considerable lengths to maintain calm. For one thing, the hated troops were on their way to Castle William. For a second, Adams had long contended that stationing an army in the midst of a peaceful town was an invitation to disaster, and it seemed that he had been proved right. He had no desire to see further violence erupt, for it would only support the claims of loyalists that Boston was an ungovernable nest of radicals and firebrands.

Considerable friction remained between Hutchinson and Adams, of course, but neither wanted further bloodshed. Adams concentrated his efforts on revitalizing the nonimportation movement in the town, convincing 212 of the city's 225 merchants to agree to halt all sales of tea until Parliament agreed to repeal all the revenue acts. In what he considered the ultimate act of humiliation, Adams saw to it that the names of the thirteen recalcitrants were entered into the town records for posterity.

At the same time, responding to the charges of critics that the nonimportation agreement only perpetuated the sour economy, the town assembly set about a public works project that would provide employment for out-of-work tradesmen and "the poor." Soon the committee announced what might be termed the first American public welfare project, the building of three new ships that would put the citizenry back to work.

Sniping continued between Hutchinson and Adams, of course. Hutchinson enraged Boston leaders when he passed along a decree from the colonial minister in London that future meetings of the colony's assembly were to be relocated to Cambridge. That was a violation of the colony's charter, Bostonians complained, arguing quite correctly that it would lead to a diminution of their influence. Hutchinson stood firm, however, pointing out that he was only following the orders of the king.

Meanwhile, word reached Boston that Parliament had in April removed all duties save for that on tea. It was a serious blow to the non-importation agreement, and though Adams's vociferous protests kept Boston merchants mindful that even one tax was the crack through which a multitude of future incursions might intrude, the accord that he had in large part been responsible for began to fall apart in New York and elsewhere in the colonies. Once New York and Philadelphia merchants fell, Boston would not be far behind, and on October 12, those merchants declared that the only British import no longer to be sold would be tea.

As 1770 drew to a close in Boston, Samuel Adams must have seen it as a doleful time. A year before, as redcoats marched through the streets of his city, he would have sensed that the time for an ultimate confrontation with the abusive mother country was at hand. The confrontation between citizens and troops in April could have only convinced him further. Now, with his colony's legislature banished to the hinterlands and the support of the city's merchants evaporated, it would have seemed that the moment was lost.

17

TRIAL OF THE CENTURY

Until the case of Captain Preston and his men went to trial in Boston in late 1770, the successful defense of the New York publisher John Peter Zenger on charges of libel had stood as the most significant legal triumph of the colonies over the Crown. But the precedent to be set in this case involved more than principles. Blood and bodies had been strewn about the streets of Boston by the hands of British troops, and the decision of the courts in this case would have a huge impact in the land.

From the outset, Samuel Adams pressed for a speedy trial, in part to ensure that the frustrated public did not erupt in violence while waiting for justice to be done. Of course, he was also motivated by his own desire to see the villainy of the troops exposed for the wider world. In turn, though Hutchinson cited a number of "unavoidable circumstances" as reasons for delay, the governor would surely have understood the wisdom of putting off the trial for as long as possible, until the public pulse calmed.

In any case, the first trial did not begin until October 24, with a Whig attorney, Robert Treat Paine, appointed as prosecutor in the case of Captain Preston. Acting in Preston's defense were Josiah Quincy and John Adams, who, though no zealot, was by then well known as a sympathizer of the Sons of Liberty.

Years later, Adams would write in his *Autobiography* in explanation of his decision to aid in the defense of the soldiers, "Endeavours had been systematically pursued for many Months, by certain busy Characters, to excite Quarrells, Rencounters and Combats single or compound in the night between the Inhabitants of the lower Class and the Soldiers, and at all risks to enkindle an immortal hatred between them."

Of the events of the night of March 5, he continued, "I suspected that this was the Explosion, which had been intentionally wrought up by designing Men, who knew what they were aiming at better than the Instrument employed." Adams left it open to interpretation who these "designing men" who had manipulated the masses and the soldiers were, but whether he meant Hutchinson and his supporters or Samuel Adams and his men, it was the principle of law that dictated the right of the latter to a fair trial.

Adams wrote that he had been at the home of a friend the night of the shootings. When he and his friends heard the ringing of the bells, they ran into the street, thinking at first that there was a fire. When passersby recounted the events, Adams hurried to King Street to find the rioters dispersed and the troops arrayed near the barracks and the church on Brattle Square. "I had no other way to proceed," he said, "but along the whole front in a very narrow Space which they had left for foot passengers. Pursuing my Way, without taking the least notice of them or they of me, any more than if they had been marble Statues, I went directly home to Cold Lane."

After that harrowing experience, Adams said, he spent the night tossing and turning, consumed by the implications of the situation. "If these Poor Tools should be prosecuted for any of their illegal Conduct they must be punished," he said. But, he continued, "if the Soldiers in self-defense should kill any of them they must be tried, and, if Truth was respected and the Law prevailed, [they] must be acquitted. To depend upon the perversion of Law and the Corruption or partiality of juries would insensibly disgrace the jurisprudence of the Country and corrupt the Morals of the People."

The next day, James Forrest, a loyalist merchant, appeared in Adams's office to beg him to take on the defense of Preston, as it seemed unlikely that anyone else among the largely liberal corps of Boston attorneys would take on the job. Forrest had just been to see the young

Josiah Quincy, and Quincy had said he'd defend Preston only if John Adams would join his team.

Adams deliberated, telling Forrest that of course he believed that any defendant whose life was at stake ought to have the counsel he preferred. But he also warned his petitioner that the case "would be as important a Cause as ever was tried in any Court or Country of the World." And if Forrest and Preston expected any shenanigans from him as a defense attorney, they should look elsewhere.

"He must therefore expect from me no Art or Address, No Sophistry or Prevarication in such a Cause; nor any thing more than Fact, Evidence and Law would justify," he emphasized. Forrest assured Adams that Preston was well versed as to Adams's rectitude and was willing to entrust his life to Adams's hands.

Adams nodded. "If he thinks he cannot have a fair trial of that issue without my assistance," he said finally, "then without hesitation he shall have it." With that Forrest pressed a guinea into Adams's hand, and the deal was sealed.

John Adams may not have resorted to chicanery, but he certainly availed himself of every ethical tool at his disposal. During the impaneling of the jury, he exercised every one of his twenty-two available challenges to ensure that not a single Whig or Son of Liberty was chosen. Among those seated were the baker who held the contract to supply Preston's regiment with bread and a man whom Samuel Adams complained was a known friend of Preston, a person who'd been overheard saying he would "sit 'til Doomsday" before joining in a verdict against the captain.

Given Adams's insistence that he had taken on the task of defending the soldiers because of his awareness that they had been manipulated into their plight by men desirous of causing a cataclysm, his refusal to put the Boston mob on trial for having provoked the attack perplexed his cocounsel, Quincy. Why not paint Preston as a man terrified by a crowd well known to have been spoiling for a fight for weeks? The mob had already started one riot that had resulted in the death of a young man and had also, just days before the shootings, shattered the arm and skull of another soldier.

Furthermore, Quincy pointed out, the prosecution had introduced similar inflammatory testimony against the troops, including that of a friend of Matthew Killroy, one of the accused soldiers.

"Did you ever hear Killroy make use of any threatening expressions against the inhabitants of this town?" the prosecutor asked his witness.

"Yes," the witness replied, "one evening I heard him say, he never would miss an opportunity, when he had one, to fire on the inhabitants, and that he had wanted to have an opportunity ever since he landed."

But Adams was resolute in his refusal, leading to speculation by General Gage and Lieutenant Governor Hutchinson that John Adams was more concerned about protecting the reputation of the Sons of Liberty than the welfare of his clients. "Such a disposition appeared in Adams to favor the Town," Hutchinson wrote to Gage, that various loyalists "spoke to me & told me they expected the cause was lost."

That was not the case, however. For one thing, Adams was probably confident that he would prevail without such testimony, and furthermore, as he would later say, such testimony would have actually "hazarded his clients' lives." Though Adams never explained just what he had meant, some historians have theorized that the words suggest that he feared a great uprising of the people, perhaps even a lynching of his client, were he to parade a series of witnesses damning the populace and their cause.

However, the legal scholar John Phillip Reid proposes a far more practical explanation for why Adams was reluctant to paint the Boston mob as a bloodthirsty band prowling the streets on a nightly basis and panting for a chance at mayhem. Had he done so, Reid theorizes, Captain Preston would have necessarily been viewed as having been reckless in leading his troops out from the barracks that fateful night, into an arena where he should have known calamity might well result. In that lawyer's view, the shootings would then have been Preston's fault.

As it was, Adams rested his defense of Preston on the answer to one question: did the captain order his men to fire or not? Eyewitnesses testified that indeed Preston had given that order. Preston said that he had not. In fact, the captain said in his deposition, as he had been explaining to one person in the crowd why it was that he would not have his men fire, someone had stepped forward and struck one of the soldiers with a club. The soldier, "having received a severe blow with a stick, stepped a little on one side and instantly fired."

As Preston turned in surprise, someone delivered a blow to his arm, "which for some time deprived me of the use of it." Had he taken the blow to the head, it would have surely killed him, he added. Townsmen were charging the troops with clubs and hurling ice, shouting, "Damn your bloods, why don't you fire?"

Instantly—fearing for their lives—three or four of the soldiers had fired, Preston testified, and soon after, "three more in the same confusion and hurry." In the next seconds, the mob had fled, according to Preston's account, leaving behind the three who had died at once. "The whole of this melancholy affair," said Preston, "was transacted in almost twenty minutes."

Though no transcript of the trial remains, the result is well known: Preston was acquitted, and if John Adams had done nothing else in the years to come, his place in history was secured. As he would later write, it was the most exhausting case he would ever try, all the more for the popular sentiments that assailed him. The resultant suspicion of his motives "never will be forgotten as long as History of this period is read," he said. "The Memory of Malice is faithfull, and more, it continually adds to its Stock; while that of Kindness and Friendship is not only frail but treacherous."

Subsequent events cast some doubt on Adams's assertions, however. The trial of the soldiers was continued to the next term of the court, and meantime there was an election called to fill the seat of Otis, forced to resign as the city's representative to the colony's assembly, owing to his declining health. At the meeting called to fill the vacancy, Adams—who had never so much as attended a Boston Town Meeting—was nominated to run against a shipwright named Ruddock, said to be very popular among the mechanics and merchants. Nonetheless—and all memory of malice aside—Adams won the election in a landslide, taking 418 of the 536 votes cast.

Though Adams was dubious as to the wisdom of placing himself squarely in the public eye, his sense of duty and the encouragement of his wife, Abigail, that he had done as he ought, led him to accept the place that would launch a fabled political career. He would come to take more than a little satisfaction in his decision, of course, and enjoyed telling the story of a former governor's response when told who now made up the Boston delegation to the Massachusetts Assembly: Mr. Cushing (the loyalist merchant Thomas Cushing), Mr. Hancock, Mr. Samuel Adams, and Mr. John Adams, the former governor was told.

"Well," the aging minister replied, "Mr. Cushing I know and Mr. Hancock I know, but where the Devil this brace of Adamses came from I know not."

Meanwhile, the trial of the soldiers was fast approaching. Though buoyed by Preston's acquittal, Adams still had the lives of eight men in his hands. His approach in this instance was to argue that the soldiers had fired in defense of their lives. And because he could argue that the men had simply followed their commander's orders in marching to the scene of the disturbance, he could more freely characterize the situation and the composition of the mob in a fearsome aspect.

The soldiers had actually petitioned to be tried along with Preston, arguing that "we did our Captain's orders, and if we do not obey his command should have been confined and shot for not doing it." That petition for a common trial had been denied by the court, however, and the subsequent exoneration of Preston had put Adams into something of a bind. Preston might have ordered the men to the scene, but Adams certainly could not argue that the captain had commanded them to fire.

The prosecution called witnesses characterizing the soldiers as provocateurs in the days leading up to the shootings and introduced the testimony that Private Killroy had been overheard stating his fervent wish for a chance "to fire on the inhabitants"; Adams countered with those describing the mob as a bloodthirsty gang of thugs. James Bailey testified that he had seen Crispus Attucks bludgeon Private Hugh

Montgomery with the cordwood staff he had been leaning on when shot and vividly described the hail of ice and stones hurled at the troops. Perhaps most powerful was the hearsay testimony introduced by the surgeon of Patrick Carr, one of those who had lingered before dying. Carr told him that as a native of Ireland, he was no stranger to confrontations between troops and citizens, the surgeon said. But Carr "had never seen [troops] bear half so much before they fired."

As to his own feelings about the soldier who had shot him, Carr harbored no ill will, even as he lay dying. "He forgave the man, whoever he was, that shot him. He was satisfied he had no malice, but fired to defend himself."

Adams's summation to the jury was masterful and unapologetic as to the makeup of the crowd. They were, Adams said, "most probably a motley rabble of saucy boys, negroes and molattoes, Irish teagues and out landish jack tarrs. And why we should scruple to call such a set of people a mob, I can't conceive, unless the name is too respectable for them: The sun is not about to stand still or go out, nor the rivers to dry up because there was a mob in *Boston* on the 5th of *March*."

What he wished was for the members of the jury to put themselves in the places of the soldiers on that night. The crowd, Adams said, "were huzzaing and whistling, crying damn you, fire! why don't you fire? So that they were actually assisting these twelve sailors that made the attack . . . ice and snow-balls were thrown . . . there were some clubs thrown from a considerable distance across the street," and oyster shells as well. "Would it have been a prudent resolution in them, or in any body in their situation, to have stood still," he asked, "to see if the sailors would knock their brains out, or not?"

In his instructions to the jury, Judge Peter Oliver created a precedent for what would become known as the "dying declaration" or "deathbed" exemption to the inadmissibility of hearsay evidence, saying, "This Carr was not upon oath, it is true, but you will determine whether a man just stepping into eternity is not to be believed, especially in favor of a set of men by whom he lost his life."

In less than three hours, the jury was back with a verdict of not guilty for six of the soldiers. There were two—Hugh Montgomery and Matthew Killroy—who were proved to have fired, however, both of whom were found guilty of manslaughter, a charge that normally carried a sentence of death. Those two, however, invoked a plea of "benefit of clergy," which permitted the commutation of their sentences. Instead of being executed, they would have a brand placed upon their thumbs.

Looking back at the incident near the end of his long career, John Adams proclaimed it one of his most satisfying accomplishments. "Judgment of Death against those Soldiers would have been as foul a stain upon this Country as the Executions of the Quakers or Witches," he said. "Although the Clamour was very loud, among some Sorts of People, it has been a great Consolation to me through Life, that I acted in this Business with steady impartiality, and conducted it to so happy an issue."

His cousin Samuel was not as happy with the verdicts, though he was not so much aggrieved that Preston and the soldiers had escaped mortal punishment. To understand, the modern reader might again use the example of the Kent State Massacre as a guide. Though that incident turned the tide of public opinion against the war, there were relatively few who wanted the blood of National Guardsmen in return for the tragic deaths of the young victims. Nearly everyone, however, saw the folly in the thinking that had sent troops into such a situation in the first place.

Similarly, Samuel Adams hoped that the trials of Preston and his men would establish the folly of maintaining a standing army in a community during peacetime. He lamented that although a great deal of testimony had been introduced attesting to the hostile atmosphere of Boston, including the brawl at the rope works and the specter of citizens walking the streets armed with clubs, "nothing appeared there, to show the Cause and even the necessity of it."

In Samuel Adams's view the people had a right to organize and arm themselves with clubs because they were in danger from the troops. There was no reason for the troops' presence in the city, he contended, and furthermore, if they had not been there, no one would have died.

It is an issue that he and his cousin differed upon profoundly. As John Adams would write to a friend a few years after the Revolution, "I begin to suspect that some Gentlemen who had more Zeal than Knowledge in the year 1770 will soon discover that I had good Policy, as well as sound Law on my side, when I ventured to lay open before our People the Laws against Riots, Routs, and unlawful assemblies. Mobs will never do—to govern States or command armies. I was as sensible of it in '70 as I am in '87. To talk of Liberty in such a state of things—!"

18

CHARRED TO THE WATERLINE

By the end of 1770, it might have seemed that serious conflict between the colonies and England could be averted after all. John Adams, one of the "brace of Adamses" and member of the Boston Sons of Liberty, had successfully defended British soldiers who'd shot colonists dead in public and not a soul had taken to the streets in protest, though not for want of Samuel Adams's trying. That half of the brace of Adamses published a series of articles in the *Boston Gazette* that were reprinted widely, signing himself as "Vindex," poring over the testimony presented at the trial, reinterpreting facts, questioning the veracity of witnesses for the defense, and generally portraying the events of March 5 as the slaughter of innocents by depraved agents of an evil empire. "This Kilroi's bayonet was prov'd to be the next morning bloody five inches from the point," he wrote in a letter of December 17. "It was said to be possible that this might be occassion'd by the bayonet's falling into the human blood, which ran plentifully in the street, for one of their bayonets was seen to fall. It is possible, I own; but much more likely that this very bayonet was stab'd into the head of poor Gray after he was shot, and that this may account for its being bloody five inches from the point—Such an instance of Savage barbarity there undoubtedly was."

An incendiary pamphlet, "A Short Narrative of the Horrid Massacre in Boston," was hurried into print in London by the house of Edes and Gill, containing only the depositions of townspeople that were unfavorable to the soldiers. And though a more balanced follow-up edition, "A Fair Account of the Late Unhappy Disturbance in Boston," would be published shortly thereafter, containing some two dozen affidavits that supported the soldiers' actions, the concept of the events as a "massacre" was already alive. Still, no immediate repercussions ensued.

Historians debate whether the events of March 5, 1770, were the most consequential of those leading up to the Revolution, and controversy regarding the culpability for the deaths and the motives of the prosecution and defense teams fills the pages of journals to this day. If indeed there was a river of discontent flowing in the colonies at the time, however, it seemed to have dived underground.

In an entertaining summary of the shifting tides of opinion regarding the massacre, the historian Randolph Adams noted that in fact it might be true that John Adams had taken on the case of Preston out of principle and for the retainer of a single pound sterling—but, he also notes, the records of General Gage, not unearthed until the 1930s, indicate that John Adams, Josiah Quincy, and the others who assisted with the defense of Preston and the soldiers were actually paid a fee of £105 for their work, and, furthermore, Captain Preston considered sacking Adams halfway through the trial and replacing him with a more conservative associate.

As Randolph Adams said of the endless refortification and debunking of the details of such a momentous event, "Verily, we have a 'new school of history' about every twenty years." But, in the end, and whether it will ever be proved if it was the Americans or the British in the wrong on the night of March 5, Adams wrote, "there can be no doubt that the bloodshed was never forgotten."

That said, the aftermath of the saga's conclusion was apparently placid. Merchants were relieved of the burden of nonimportation, and business on land and by sea was returned nearly to normal. The law had had its say on the matter of the shootings, and no one wanted more bloodshed on the streets. Some historians have referred to the months that followed as the "quiet period," a time during which Governor Hutchinson could report to Hillsborough that his colony reflected a more "general appearance of contentment" than it had since the Stamp Act had first soured relations.

In New York, things had been similarly quiet since early in 1770, with memories of the confrontations surrounding Golden Hill having faded, but the flags still fluttered from the liberty pole near the common to remind the people from whence they had come. Shortly after the planting of that splendid pole, however, it was revealed that the author of the acrimonious broadside attacking the DeLancey faction's accommodation with the British was the well-known Sons of Liberty leader Alexander McDougall. Like his friend and associate Isaac Sears, McDougall had done well as a privateer plundering French ships during the Seven Years' War and was now a prosperous trader with sizable landholdings near Albany and also the owner of a tavern near the city docks.

Affluence would not save him in this instance, however. When testimony from the printer of the broadside revealed the identity of its author, McDougall was charged with libel against the government and jailed. Though he could have made bail on the charges, he instead chose to remain in jail while Sears and other Sons trumpeted the outrage of his imprisonment through press accounts in New York and across the colonies.

McDougall languished martyrlike in jail for three months before prosecutors brought him to trial. Had he been convicted, it might have provided a spark for further protest in New York, but when the printer who identified McDougall died suddenly, the prosecution's case collapsed, and McDougall went free.

It would prove to be the last event of incendiary potential for some time in the previously contentious city. As in Boston, with business on the upswing and employment and wages increasing, discontent suddenly seemed an antique premise. The first statue in the city's history was dedicated in August 1770 on Bowling Green, where not long before the governor's coach had been burned, along with effigies of hated oppressors. Instead of martyrs or champions of liberty depicted there, the monument featured a most regal George III triumphantly placed astride his horse.

In fact, the most victimized person in the city—at least in his own eyes—would have been the unfortunate Cadwallader Colden. Since

Henry Moore's departure in 1769, the long-suffering Colden had hoped that his steadfast loyalty would be rewarded with the promotion to governor, but it was not to be. Instead, John Murray, a Scottish nobleman, was appointed to the post. Murray, the Earl of Dunmore, and something of an opportunist, turned out not to be popular with anyone in New York, including Colden.

Although Murray was appointed in January, he did not make his way to New York until October, whereupon he demanded 50 percent of the pay that Colden had been collecting as acting governor. Colden, not surprisingly, declined to comply, and William Smith, Jr., trying to curry favor, suggested that Murray, now in office, rule in his own favor. That was too much even for Murray, however; the new governor settled by submitting a petition to London that would eventually be declined.

Worse yet, just days after he officially assumed his post, Murray received word from London that he was being transferred to Virginia, where the previous governor, Lord Botetourt, had died. Murray, who had taken the posting in New York as a move to advance his fortune, was outraged at being sent off to the hinterlands. According to Smith, who quickly saw the futility of trying to ally himself with such a venal hothead, Murray gave himself a farewell dinner, where he "took too Chearful a glass." After drinking himself into incoherence, Murray brawled with his councilors, called his successor, William Tryon, a coward, and delivered a solid blow to the chest of the new governor's secretary. Following that display, he staggered out into the New York streets in a rage, followed at a respectful distance by his worried servants.

"Damn Virginia!" he is said to have shouted beneath the window of the prominent Tory surgeon Jonathan Mallet. "I asked for New York. New York I took, and they have robbed me of it."

His superiors might well have been worried that Murray, left in the post at New York, could provoke another uprising by the force of his personality alone. "Was there ever such a blockhead?" Smith wrote in his diary. Soon enough, the earl was on his way to Virginia.

With yet one more governor gone, Colden's hopes were once more buoyed, but just as quickly they were dashed, for the king had already decided to promote Tryon, the governor of North Carolina, to the New York post. Tryon would remain New York's governor into the Revolution, and faithful Colden, ever the bridesmaid, would die in 1776, in Flushing, at the age of eighty-eight.

Meanwhile, in Charleston, and despite Christopher Gadsden's exhortations, agreement on nonimportation also teetered in the wake of Parliament's reduction of the Townshend duties. At a meeting of townsmen in December 1770, Gadsden and other leaders of the city's Sons spoke spiritedly on behalf of "the expiring liberties" of the country, which it seemed "the merchants would sell like any other merchandise." Gadsden argued that whatever the colonists might need from Britain they could easily get from Holland, but it was for naught. In South Carolina the die had long been cast; the vote to continue nonimportation failed. The meeting ended with a halfhearted gesture in Gadsden's direction: a committee was appointed to "encourage" American manufactures, and the merchants did agree to abstain from importing tea, but it was clear that the steam was out of the radical movement in Charleston too, at least for the time being.

As for the pledge to encourage local artisans, no grants were allocated by the assembly to any South Carolina craftsman or mechanic. In fact, imports into South Carolina from England quadrupled in 1771. At the same time, activity in the slave trade, which had briefly been blocked by the nonimportation agreements, quickly resumed. Though fewer than 2,000 slaves per year on average had been brought to South Carolina prior to nonimportation, the number increased to 5,000 in 1772 and 8,000 in 1773. The slave population, which had stood at 80,000 in 1769, grew by 1773 to 110,000, nearly half again as large. Modern sensitivities to the practice aside, the burgeoning population of slaves meant a corresponding drag on opportunity for craftsmen and laborers of the time. How could a free man earn a decent living, they lamented, when there were so many around him who were forced to work for nothing?

Certainly, Sons of Liberty leaders such as Samuel Adams, Isaac Sears, and Christopher Gadsden remained unrelenting in their efforts to remind their fellow citizens of the dangers of collaborating with a designing enemy, but they were cast into much the same position as Ulysses trying to exhort his sailors to leave the land of the Lotus-eaters.

It should be remembered that nearly 90 percent of the entire population of the colonies at the time was farmers, men far removed from the centers of population, whose struggle was an unrelenting one, with the land and the seasons and an array of natural plagues, far more so than with any aspect of politics. There had in fact been minor uprisings in the hustings over the issue of land rights, and there had been indignation over the arbitrary granting of vast tracts to cronies of the British ministry, but those had been of minor concern to the merchants, traders, and political activists, in whom wealth and influence were concentrated.

If the British had been content with the benefits that began to accrue to them from the moment the Townshend duties were repealed, perhaps the present-day boundaries of Canada would have extended south to Key West and westward to San Diego. But of course they were not.

Enforcement of the duties on tea, molasses, and other products still on the books remained spirited through the early 1770s, with despised customs agents active in Boston, New York, Charleston, and elsewhere. In Providence, long a smugglers' stronghold, passions were inflamed by the appearance, in March 1772, of an armed British schooner, the *Gaspée*, on the waters of Narragansett Bay. As Deputy Governor Darius Sessions, a resident of Providence, wrote to Governor Joseph Wanton in Newport, residents of Providence had been "much disquieted" by the arrival of the *Gaspée*, which, according to Sessions, "much disturbed our Navigation. She suffers no vessel to pass, not even packet boats, or others of an inferior kind, without a strict examination, and where any sort of unwillingness is discovered, they are compelled to submit, by an armed force."

What principally troubled Sessions and others among the population was that Lieutenant William Dudingston, the commander of the *Gaspée*, would present no formal authority to conduct such business, and Sessions urged the governor to inquire into the matter, as Dudingston seemed to be comporting himself essentially as a privateer. Governor

Wanton wasted no time in sending a letter to Dudingston demanding that he produce evidence of his authority to the high sheriff or face the consequences.

Dudingston's reply to the governor was fashioned of the same stuff that would one day prompt a fabled film line: "Badges? . . . I don't have to show you any stinking badges."

Dudingston informed Wanton that he was the commander of one of His Majesty's warships and that was all anyone needed to know. As for the rest, the rum-running miscreants of Rhode Island could mind their own business and keep an eye out for him into the bargain.

It was not the answer the governor was looking for, a fact of which he quickly informed Dudingston. He demanded that the lieutenant produce written authority for his actions, and furthermore, he said, "I expect that you do without delay, comply with my request of yesterday, and you may be assured that my utmost exertions shall not be wanting to protect your person from any insult or outrage on coming ashore."

As Judge William Staples, the first chronicler of the *Gaspée* affair, put it, "Here ended the correspondence between the Governor and the Lieutenant."

Instead of answering the governor's demands, Dudingston passed copies of the correspondence to Admiral John Montagu, the commander in chief of the British fleet in the colonies. On April 6, Montagu wrote back to Wanton in a manner that made it clear that the British forces considered themselves to be the final arbiters of what constituted their authority.

As to the letters of Wanton's that he viewed, Montagu termed them "of such a nature I am at a loss what answer to give them, and ashamed to find they come from one of his Majesty's Governors." Dudingston had been assigned to the Narragansett waters for the good of the citizens, Montagu reminded Wanton, "to protect your province from pirates and to give the trade all the assistance he can, and to endeavor, as much as lays in his power, to protect the revenue officer, and to prevent (if possible) the illicit trade that is carrying on at Rhode Island."

In short, Dudingston was only doing his duty, and furthermore,

Montagu scolded, "it is your duty as a governor, to give him your assistance, and not endeavor to distress the King's officers for strictly com-
plying with my orders." Nor should any of the more scurrilous of the
province's citizens undertake to interfere with the *Gaspée* and her men.
He had already informed Dudingston, the admiral said, "that, in case
they receive any molestation in the execution of their duty, they shall
send every man so taken in molesting them, to me."

Rumors reached Montagu that there was talk in Providence of sending out an armed vessel to "rescue any vessel the King's schooner may
take carrying on an illicit trade," but he minced no words about such an
idea: "Let them be cautious what they do; for as sure as they attempt it,
and any of them are taken, I will hang them as pirates."

Furthermore, Montagu said, he would forward copies of Wanton's
unfortunate letters to the home secretary, who just might have words of
his own for an impertinent colonial governor. "I would advise you not to
send your Sheriff on board the King's ship again, on such ridiculous er-
rands," he concluded. "The Captain and Lieutenants have all my orders
to give you assistance whenever you demand it, but further you have no
business with them, and, be assured, it is not their duty to show you any
part of my orders or instructions to them."

This, of course, prompted a barely contained response from Governor Wanton informing Montagu that he, too, would be sending copies of
their correspondence to London, and suggesting that Montagu be careful about hanging any colonists. Such posturing continued back and
forth for several days and might have gone on even longer had it not
been for the events of June 9, a day upon which the watch aboard the
Gaspée, which continued resolutely in the course of her duties, called
out an alarm. The packet boat *Hannah* had been spotted moving fur-
tively along the shallow waters on the northwestern side of the bay, near
Pawtuxet, about five miles south of Providence.

Dudingston gave orders, and soon the *Gaspée* was in full sail, closing
in upon the *Hannah*. The adventure might have ended with a heave-to
and a boarding, inspection, and seizure of the sort that had ignited the
recent passions of the citizens, had it not been for the fact of its being

low tide and Dudingston's overeagerness to show who was in charge. In any case, there was a sudden lurching of the *Gaspée*, then a decisive jolt, and in the next moment the crew of the warship was watching the *Hannah* shrink rapidly in the distance from the decks of their own vessel, now run hard aground.

The captain of the *Hannah*, Benjamin Lindsey, who had left Newport earlier in the day, continued his way north to Providence, where he arrived near sunset and quickly spread the word as to what had taken place. The tides would not rise sufficiently to free the *Gaspée* until at least midnight, he reckoned, and in short order, the merchants of Providence hit upon a way to solve the difficulties that Dudingston and his ship had created for them.

John Brown, a prominent merchant and leader of the local chapter of Sons of Liberty, sent men to gather eight longboats from about the harbor and to muffle their oars and oarlocks. Shortly after sunset, a man was sent along Main Street, beating a drum and passing the word to curious townsmen: the *Gaspée* had run aground not far south in Narragansett Bay, and any true Son of Liberty who wished to join the party should hurry to the docks. The troubles of the recent weeks would soon be corrected.

Ephraim Bowen, twenty-seven at the time, was one of the first townsmen to heed the call. "About 9 o'clock," Bowen said, he lit out for the meeting place, a well-known lodging house and tavern at the docks. "I took my father's gun and my powder horn and bullets and went to Mr. Sabin's, and found the southeast room full of people, where I loaded my gun, and all remained there till about 10 o'clock, some casting bullets in the kitchen, and others making arrangements for departure."

Finally word came, said Bowen. "Orders were given to cross the street to Fenner's wharf and embark; which soon took place, and a sea captain acted as steersman of each boat."

If he harbored apprehensions as to what the adventure might bring, he did not record them. He noted only that the flotilla proceeded in tight, silent formation through the darkened waters until the shadow of the *Gaspée* loomed almost atop it, some fifty yards away.

Despite the muffling of the oars, there was no masking the approach of eight longboats at such a distance. Abruptly, the sentinel on board the motionless *Gaspée* called into the night, "Who comes there?"

But there was no answer. The sentry called again, but still no response came. There were the sounds of scurrying about the decks of the *Gaspée*, and moments later Lieutenant Dudingston, coatless, his shirt a pale glow in the darkness, appeared atop the starboard railing to hail the approaching party with a pistol in one hand and a cutlass in the other.

"Who comes there?" the lieutenant's voice rolled across the quiet waters this time. Still there was no answer.

John Mawney, another Liberty Boy from Providence who had volunteered to join the assault as the party's surgeon, listened intently. The men in his boat had filled it full of staves and paving stones, though no barrel making or street paving was intended on this voyage. Mawney was in the last boat, but he was close enough to hear when Captain Abraham Whipple, the assault party's leader, finally broke the silence.

"Who comes there?" came the cry again from the motionless *Gaspée*, and this time, with his party fully assembled, Captain Whipple answered. "I want to come on board."

"Stand off," was Captain Dudingston's response. "You can't come on board."

At that, Whipple blew up. "I am the sheriff of the county of Kent, God damn you. I have got a warrant to apprehend you, so surrender."

When Dudingston did not answer, Whipple made his fateful declaration: "I am come for the commander of this vessel, and have him I will, dead or alive." At that he turned to the boats lined up beside him. "Men, spring to your oars."

At that moment, Joseph Bucklin, a man standing on the main thwart of one longboat, turned to Ephraim Bowen. "Ephe," Bucklin said, "reach me your gun and I can kill that fellow."

Without hesitation, Bowen handed over his musket. Bucklin steadied himself, aimed at the white-shirted figure at the gunwale of the *Gaspée*, and fired. There was a groan, and Dudingston's figure disappeared from atop the railing.

Bucklin turned back to Bowen with satisfaction as the longboats surged forward. "I have killed the rascal," he said, handing over the musket.

In seconds, the longboats were alongside the *Gaspée*. If Bowen and the others in the assault party expected resistance, they did not encounter it. The terrified crew of the *Gaspée* were scattering like mice, fighting one another to make it through the entrance to the hold.

As his longboat approached the *Gaspée*, surgeon Mawney spotted a rope hanging from the warship's bow. He snatched hold and heaved himself off the deck, intending to pull himself aboard the *Gaspée*, but his hands slipped on the wet rope. Mawney felt himself hurtling down toward the waters beside the grounded ship.

It was a short fall. Instead of a plunge into the depths, Mawney splashed to a jolting halt on the same sandbar that had seized the *Gaspée*, his knees scarcely touching the waterline. Mawney stared for a moment in surprise, then seized the rope more tightly and scrambled up over the gunwale and on board.

A companion from the longboat tossed him a barrel stave, and Mawney, thinking himself to be the first of the assault party on board, turned to a sailor fumbling at the anchor windlass nearby. Mawney raised his stave and was about to bring it down on the skull of the sailor at the windlass when the man cried out, "John, don't strike."

Mawney, recognizing it as the voice of Samuel Dunn, the captain of one of the other longboats in the party, froze in midswing. He and Dunn stood alone, watching the last of the *Gaspée*'s crew crowding down the hatchway toward the hold.

Mawney strode quickly to the hatchway, calling after the frightened sailors. They had no reason to fear, he said. He ordered them to return on deck and bring some cord so that their hands could be tied. They'd be escorted to the nearby shore, he told them, but they would not be harmed.

"They brought some tarred strings," said Mawney, who then busied himself in the hatchway, tying up a pair of frightened British sailors. And that is when John Brown, the Providence merchant who had put the foray together, approached him somberly. The surgeon was needed up on deck immediately, Brown said, concern evident in his voice.

When Mawney asked Brown what was wrong, the merchant glanced about before answering. "Don't call names," Brown said, "but go immediately into the cabin. There is one wounded, and will bleed to death."

Mawney made his way quickly to the ship's cabin, where he found Lieutenant Dudingston reclining on the deck, a pool of blood spreading about the boards beneath him. Someone had covered him with a thin white woolen blanket, which Mawney quickly pulled aside.

Someone handed Mawney a lantern, and the surgeon bent to examine the wounded officer. Dudingston had taken Joseph Bucklin's shot in the left groin, Mawney saw, and the blood was pouring out freely. Thinking that Dudingston's femoral artery was severed, Mawney pulled off his vest and tore his shirt from its collar to his waistband, intending to use it to stanch the bleeding.

At that Dudingston raised a hand to stop him. "Pray, sir, don't tear your clothes, there is linen in that trunk."

Following Dudingston's gesture, Mawney turned to find none other than Joseph Bucklin standing beside the officer's trunk. Mawney told him to break the trunk open and shred some of the linen there to make a compress. Bucklin managed to get the trunk open and find the linen, but as it was new, he could not manage to "lint" the fabric.

Mawney held the heel of his hand pressed tightly to Dudingston's wound while Bucklin fumbled at his task, and after a moment the surgeon called for his townsman to replace him at Dudingston's side. The two quickly exchanged places, and while Bucklin did his best to stanch the bleeding of the man he had shot only minutes before, Mawney tore the linen into strips. If indeed Dudingston's femoral artery was severed, a bandage would be of little help, but Mawney's instincts as a doctor led him nonetheless.

When he was ready, Mawney gave Bucklin the signal to lift his hand from Dudingston's wound and the surgeon quickly applied the makeshift compress, then wrapped it tightly with strips of cloth. The three men stared down at Mawney's handiwork, where an ooze of blood was already welling up. All that might have been done was done, each knew; from here it was up to the fates—and then the bleeding stopped.

Fists were pounding on the cabin door now—they had been throughout the entire operation, in fact—and Mawney finally went to open it. There was a crowd of townsmen there, all of them clamoring for a chance at the officers' liquor stores, some of which had been lifted from a Providence-bound sloop. "Many rushed in and attacked the bottles," the disapproving Mawney reported. "I having boots on, stamped on them, and requested others to assist, which was readily done. During this, Mr. Dudingston was carried out of the room, and I never saw him after."

In the aftermath, the sailors aboard the *Gaspée* were given the opportunity to gather up their clothes and belongings, then were put ashore, along with the wounded Dudingston, at nearby Pawtuxet. Mawney, Bucklin, Bowen, and most of the others in the party were sent ahead toward home, while one boat remained behind for the leaders, including John Brown.

They had not rowed far toward Providence, Mawney recalls, when a glow began to light the sky behind them. He turned to witness what they already guessed was happening: it was the *Gaspée*, timbers, masts, and sails ablaze, burning to the waterline.

The following day, Lieutenant Governor Sessions sent an urgent message to Governor Wanton, informing him of what had taken place. "A very disagreeable thing has lately happened," he began before providing a brief description of the events and explaining that he had already gone to see the unfortunate Lieutenant Dudingston at Pawtuxet.

Sessions assured Dudingston that he would happily afford him money, surgeons, or removal to a more convenient place—anything that he might need—but the lieutenant declined, asking only that Sessions see that his sailors made their way safely to Boston or to the royal ship *Beaver*, stationed at Newport. When Sessions asked Dudingston if he would be willing to give a statement as to the true nature of the events, the lieutenant again declined. He would first have to make a report to his commanding officer, he explained, adding that "if he died, he desired it might all die with him."

Sessions added in his letter to Governor Wanton the depositions of two sailors who had been aboard the *Gaspée* at the time of the attack, their descriptions differing only slightly. The lieutenant governor closed by suggesting that the governor might wish to issue a proclamation quickly, offering a sizable reward for the apprehension of the persons responsible.

Wanton took Sessions's advice, "strictly charging and commanding all his majesty's officers within the said colony, both civil and military, to exert themselves with the utmost vigilance to discover and apprehend the persons guilty of the aforesaid atrocious crime," and offering a reward of £100. There soon came aggrieved letters from Admiral Montagu to Governor Wanton, urging him to expend every effort to find the culprits. The invading party, given the crew's description of their dress, speech, and actions, were almost certainly all "gentlemen" from Providence, he added.

Wanton assured both Montagu and his superiors in the Home Office that he would spare no effort in running the perpetrators to ground, though in his letter to the Earl of Hillsborough, the governor was quick to remind the secretary of state for the colonies that the actions of Dudingston and others had produced a most lamentable effect upon trade as well as the spirits of his constituents, thereby contributing to the affray.

A month or so after the incident, with Dudingston on the mend, Admiral Montagu sent Wanton an affidavit from a sixteen-year-old slave who claimed to have been with the raiding party, identifying John Brown and several other members of the Sons of Liberty in Providence as the ringleaders. "I received the enclosed account," Montagu told Wanton, "and, although it comes from a negro man, it carries with it the appearance of truth, as it agrees in many circumstances with Lieutenant Dudingston's letter."

In turn, Wanton produced affidavits from the slave's family members and his owner stating that the young man in question had not been off the plantation where he had been kept for more than a month bracketing the date of the incident, and that the affidavit produced by Montagu must necessarily be a forgery. Furthermore, Wanton told the admiral, his wish that the matter be adjudicated by the admiralty court had been rejected by the provincial court. The *Gaspée*, even if she had in fact been operating as a ship of His Majesty, had been thirty miles inside the entrance to Narragansett Bay when she ran aground, far from the "high seas." The incident thus lay within the purview of the local authorities.

The exchange marked the end of correspondence between the admiral and the governor, and though the Home Office would issue a proclamation offering a reward of as much as £1,000 for apprehension of the ringleaders or perpetrators, no one stepped forward to claim the prize. The frustrated and indignant Home Office finally appointed a rarely convened Royal Commission of Inquiry to meet at Newport and call all witnesses forward who might have knowledge of the matter. The five-person commission included Governor Wanton, along with the chiefs of the supreme courts of Massachusetts, New York, and New Jersey and the judge of the vice admiralty of Boston, though it was the last four (all staunch loyalists) who conducted most of the commission's business.

The group began its hearings early in January 1773 and continued work until late in June, and although it was successful in obtaining several accounts of the events that agreed substantially in the main, the members were, rather remarkably, unable to identify a single colonist who might have taken part in the melee. "After exerting ourselves to the utmost of our abilities," the justices agreed, they were forced to admit failure.

There was one witness, a sailor attached to the *Gaspée*, who had identified one participant by name, the justices allowed, but even that was not of much help: "Peter May, in his deposition, mentions one person only, by the name of Greene, whom he says he saw before on board the *Gaspée*; but the family of Greene being very numerous in this colony, and the said Peter not giving the Christian name or describing him in such a manner as he could be found out [May described "Greene" as a tall, slender man with brown hair], it is impossible for us to know at present the person referred to."

As to the contentions of Aaron Briggs, the young slave who claimed to have assisted in the assault on the *Gaspée* and who identified several Providence Liberty Boys by name, the commissioners were equally dubious. For one thing, whatever Briggs had told the British commander who had taken him into custody had probably been elicited by the commander's threat to hang him from a yardarm if he didn't tell everything he knew about the burning of the *Gaspée*. As they put it:

> Touching the depositions of Aaron, the negro, we humbly conceive it our duty to declare to your Majesty, that the conduct of Capt. Linzee tended too strongly to extort from a weak or wicked mind declarations not strictly true; that some parts of said depositions falsify others; that allowing the account he gave of the time he left the Island called Prudence, the place of his residence, on the night the *Gaspée* was burnt, and his return thither, to be true, or even near the truth, must render his being at the taking and destroying her, totally impossible, the distance being so great between Namquit Point and said Island. In addition to all which, there is full and satisfactory evidence to prove him, the whole of that night, to have been at home, and the request which he deposed was made him, to carry a person off said Island that night, and which he declared was the occasion of his going from home, proved on the examination of the very person, to be an absolute falsehood; and therefore we are most humbly of opinion, no credit is due to said Aaron's testimony.

Despite the Crown's outrage and the lure of a veritable king's ransom in reward, the Sons of Providence kept their counsel. Bowen and Mawney would live fifty years more before sharing their accounts, and in the meantime, the *Gaspée*'s demise would ignite another fire.

19

PRELUDE TO A PARTY

Despite the ultimate failure of the Royal Commission of Inquiry to identify a single culprit responsible for burning the HMS *Gaspée*, colonists in Rhode Island were more than a bit apprehensive about the outcome when the hearings were first announced. Had any colonists been identified by the commission as having taken part in the affair, they would have been transported to England and tried on charges of treason, by decree of the king himself. "The civil magistrates and officers within our said Colony of Rhode Island, are entrusted with the power and authority to arrest and commit to custody such of the persons concerned in the plundering and destroying the Gaspee schooner," read the king's proclamation, "and in the inhuman treatment of our officer who commanded her, against whom any information shall lay, taken in order to the said offenders being sent to England to be tried for that offence." The receipt of a death sentence under such circumstances was a very real possibility.

When originally faced with the prospect, Lieutenant Governor Sessions wrote to Samuel Adams in late December 1772, asking his advice on how best to proceed. On January 2, 1773, Adams answered, telling Sessions that he suspected that the Home Office was intent on revoking the rather liberal charter under which Rhode Island had operated from its inception. The convening of such an extraordinary court of inquiry with the power to send a colonist to Great Britain for trial was yet one more violation of the Constitution guaranteeing British subjects a right to trial by jury of their peers, he opined. "I have long feard that this unhappy Contest between Britain & America will end in Rivers of Blood," he said, suggesting that indeed times were dire. Still, in Adams's mind there was little Sessions could do. Perhaps Governor Wanton could attempt a postponement of the commission's proceedings until he could confer directly with London. At the very least, Adams suggested, the Rhode Island Assembly ought to consider sending a circular letter to the other colonies detailing the threat in the matter, one that would "represent the Severity of your Case in the strongest terms."

Adams considered the maintenance of Committees of Correspondence, first employed during the Stamp Act crisis, as the most effective tool at the colonists' disposal during this otherwise "quiet" period, and he quickly convinced the Boston Town Assembly to resurrect a twenty-one-person committee in November 1772. Governor Hutchinson at first pooh-poohed the enterprise. Sending letters of complaint back and forth, opined Hutchinson, "is such a foolish scheme that they must necessarily make themselves ridiculous."

However, when Hutchinson realized that Adams was being successful in encouraging the formation of such committees in most towns of consequence in the province, his tone changed from dismissal to complaint and finally to condemnation of a troubling theme that began to develop in the missives flying back and forth. Colonists were beginning to question the supreme authority of Parliament, he railed, and in an appearance before the assembly in early January 1773, he asserted that there could be no gray area in this matter. "I know of no line that can be drawn between the supreme authority of Parliament and the total independence of the colonies," he said.

Stirring as it may have seemed to the governor, it turned out to be an unfortunate declaration, for Adams and the members of the assembly wasted no time in using the governor's own words against him; if it were true, said Adams, that the citizens of the province were either the mere servants of Parliament *or* totally independent, and if it could be equally safely assumed that the men who had negotiated the colony's charter in 1691 would never have given away their freedom, then logically there could be little doubt that Hutchinson himself regarded his constituents as independent of Parliament.

Adams pointed out that most colonial charters granted the power of governance to the colonies themselves and promised only that the laws enacted therein would be "not repugnant to the laws of England." A long response to the governor drafted in large part by Adams on behalf of the assembly on January 26, 1773, painstakingly detailed a number of instances in which various British monarchs had acted to affirm the independence of the colonies from Parliament. From the beginning, Adams argued, the colonies had not been considered "within the realm of England," and therefore they could not be considered subject to the laws governing that realm. Certainly, the inhabitants of the colonies had never given their assent to governance by Parliament, Adams said, and they were not about to give it now.

In his speech to the assembly, Hutchinson drew a dire picture for any colonists who might be desirous of an independency. The colonies would be gobbled up in a trice by the Spanish, the French, or the Dutch, he warned, and *then* they would find out what misery truly was. To that Adams responded by wondering whether it truly would be a "misfortune," for the oppressive measures the colonies were now laboring under seemed misfortune aplenty.

In the end, Adams said, it appeared as if the governor were suggesting that indeed there was a need to choose between subservience and independence, and furthermore, if the governor expected "to have the line of distinction between the supreme authority of Parliament, and the total independence of the colonies drawn by us, we would say it would be an arduous undertaking, and of very great importance to all the other colonies; and therefore, could we conceive of such a line, we should be unwilling to propose it, without their consent in Congress." What Adams was suggesting in those fateful lines was the formation of a Continental Congress in which the prospect of independence would be formally considered.

Still, despite that not-so-veiled threat, Adams said, things did not have to come to such a pass. The people of Massachusetts, he insisted, had not in the least "abated that just sense of allegiance which we owe to the King of Great Britain, our rightful Sovereign; and should the people of this province be left to the free and full exercise of all the liberties and immunities granted to them by charter, there would be no danger of an independence on the Crown."

Adams's protestations meant little to Hutchinson, who saw it all as hairsplitting by an opponent who was already determined to lead the colony toward independence. Hutchinson drafted a scathing response that reaffirmed his own legal reasoning, which occasioned an equally indignant reply from the assembly, and back and forth it went, well into 1773, though the implications of a desire for independence that had provoked their debate had already reached a much wider audience.

In Boston, a little-known visiting minister from England, John Allen, delivered a sermon at the Second Baptist Church that utilized the *Gaspée* affair to warn listeners about greedy monarchs, corrupt judges, and conspiracies at high levels in the London government. Allen then expanded his spoken sermon into a letter to Lord Dartmouth titled "Oration of the Beauties of Liberty": "Suppose your Lordship had broke the Laws of his king, and Country; would not your Lordship be willing to be tried by a Jury of your peers, according to the Laws of the land? How would your Lordship like to be fetter'd with irons, and drag'd three thousand miles, in a hell upon earth?" The resulting document was distributed widely about the colonies, becoming one of the more popular political pamphlets of the run-up to the Revolution.

Meanwhile, in Virginia, word reached the House of Burgesses of the discord in Massachusetts and of the *Gaspée* inquiry in Rhode Island. On March 12, the burgesses voted to follow the lead of the local committees in Massachusetts and formed the first colony-level Committee of Correspondence, "to consist of fifteen members, any eight of whom to be a quorum; whose business it shall be to obtain the most early and authentic intelligence of all such Acts and resolutions of the British Parliament, or proceedings of administration as may relate to, or affect the British colonies in America, and to keep up and maintain a correspondence and communication with our sister colonies." One of the original members of Virginia's committee was Patrick Henry; another was the young burgess Thomas Jefferson.

"This House is fully sensible of the necessity and importance of a union of the several colonies in America, at a time when it clearly appears that the rights and liberties of all are systematically invaded," the Virginia resolution stated. Thus, "in order that the joint wisdom of the whole may be employed in consulting their common safety," the burgesses also resolved to try to convince all other colonies to join. The first order of the committee's business would be to draft "a circular letter to the several other houses of assembly on this continent, enclosing the aforesaid resolves, and requesting them to lay the same before their respective assemblies, in confidence that they will readily and cheerfully comply."

Indeed, Massachusetts, South Carolina, Rhode Island, Connecticut, and New Hampshire quickly followed suit, and eventually all the other colonies did so, though it would be the end of 1774 before the New York Assembly became the last to officially join the network. Meantime, however, the committees, also organized in hundreds of cities and towns about the colonies and estimated to have included as many as eight thousand individuals at any given time, would eventually come to supplant the colonial assemblies as the true voice of the people. The committees, many of them made up of the same leadership as the various Sons of Liberty chapters, could also operate in secret, sharing information, opinions, and strategies for dealing with the British without fear of reprisal. What Thomas Hutchinson had once dismissed as irrelevant and foolish would become a most effective intelligence-sharing and morale-boosting operation, uniting a far-flung and politically disparate group of colonies as never before.

And soon there would be much of import to share.

Shortly after the Massachusetts Assembly voted in June 1773 to form its own Committee of Correspondence, Samuel Adams learned that Thomas Cushing, the assembly's chairperson, had been sent a packet of potentially incendiary letters penned by Hutchinson and other British-appointed officials in the colony in the late 1760s. The letters, sent to a fellow government minister in London, presented the state of affairs in Massachusetts as precarious indeed. Hutchinson demonized

Adams and other Whig leaders, encouraged the maintenance of the onerous customs control, and suggested that the situation called for the curtailment of what Britons might think of as ordinary privileges of citizenship.

In a letter of October 4, 1768, Hutchinson told his confidant, "Many of the common people have been in a frenzy . . . too many of rank above the vulgar have countenanced and encouraged them, and the executive powers have completely lost their force." Indeed, troops were needed and quickly, he made clear: "For 4 or 5 weeks past, the distemper has been growing, and I concede that I have not been without some apprehension for myself."

Though Benjamin Franklin claimed he had given the letters to Cushing only to provide the assembly speaker and his associates with insight into Hutchinson's motives and intent, and only with the understanding that their contents would not be made public, the moment Adams learned of the letters, he calculated what would be the best use to make of them. With Cushing's approval, he announced to the assembly that he had obtained damning letters that proved the true intentions of their governor and Parliament as regarded Massachusetts. Furthermore, Adams would—upon condition that they not be copied or quoted—read them aloud to that body.

Of course, every delegate promised that not a word of what was to be quoted would pass beyond the chamber's closed doors, and Adams had his dreamed-of audience in the palm of his hand. Following the reading of the correspondence, the assembly proclaimed by a vote of 101 to 5 that Hutchinson (himself born in Massachusetts, it might be noted) clearly had no respect for the constitution of the colony and had willfully attempted to impose "arbitrary power" upon its citizens.

"Ignorant as they be," Hutchinson said of Samuel Adams and his fellow Sons, "the heads of a Boston town-meeting influence all public measures." As to the so-called trade restrictions and onerous enforcement by customs agents, he vowed, "I know of no burden brought upon the fair trader by the new establishment." In Hutchinson's estimation, only the "illicit trader finds the risk greater than it used to be."

The overall situation, he declared, "is most certainly a crisis," one for which the "licenciousness of such as call themselves sons of liberty" was responsible. Perhaps most damning was Hutchinson's declaration: "There must be an abridgement of what are called English liberties. . . . there must be a great restraint of natural liberty."

Though it would be a few months before the packet was printed in its entirety, excerpts sufficient to damn Hutchinson in the eyes of the public were printed in the June 28 issue of the *Boston Gazette* and were widely disseminated throughout the colonies. Following a vote of 80 to 11, a petition crafted by Adams and calling for the removal of Hutchinson as governor of the province was soon on its way from the Massachusetts Assembly to the king. If the Hutchinson Letter Affair suggested that the "quiet period" was over, other events suggested that cacophony would soon be the order of the day.

When news of the disclosure of the Hutchinson letters became public in England, a furor ensued. Those missives, along with a few from Andrew Oliver, who had ascended to the post of lieutenant governor under Hutchinson, had been penned to Thomas Whately, an influential member of Parliament who had died in 1772. Though Benjamin Franklin declined to say who had delivered the letters to him, Whately's brother William accused John Temple, a former lieutenant governor of New Hampshire and liberal sympathizer with the colonies. Whately and Temple fought a duel over the matter, and though Whately was wounded, the results satisfied neither man, and a second duel was arranged.

At that point Franklin intervened, publishing a letter in the *London Gazette* on December 27, 1773, that was eventually reprinted in the *Boston Gazette* of March 7, 1774. Franklin began by saying that unfortunately, Whately and Temple had engaged in a duel over a "transaction and its circumstances of which both of them are totally ignorant and innocent." Neither man had been involved in the procurement of the letters, the statesman declared. He alone had obtained and transmitted the Hutchinson letters to Boston. Furthermore, there had been no inappropriate sharing of private correspondence, as was alleged. The letters, said Franklin, "were written by public officers to persons in public station, on public affairs, and intended to procure public measures."

The correspondents quite frankly wished to stir up sentiment against the colonies in London, Franklin said, and certainly the letters had been effective in serving their intended purpose. Furthermore, the writers were concerned only that the letters not fall into the hands of any of the London-based colonial agents, "who the writers apprehended might return them, or copies of them to America."

In this regard, their fears had been well founded, Franklin continued, for he, being the first such agent who had laid his hands on them, had "thought it his duty to transmit them to his constituents." With that he ended the matter, sidestepping the question of just how he had obtained the letters, not making any apology for having sent them along, and signing himself as B. Franklin, "Agent for the House of Representatives of the Massachusett's-Bay."

Eventually, Franklin would be called before the Privy Council to explain his role in the matter further, but by the time he arrived in those chambers in late January 1774, news of an even more disturbing nature had reached the mother country. By the end of that interview, Franklin would have to reassess the whole of his diplomatic career.

The beginning of the end might be traced to the continuing economic woes of the British East India Company and the ensuing efforts of Parliament to prop up the unsustainable enterprise at the expense of the American colonies. When most of the provisions of the Townshend Acts had been repealed in 1770, leaving only the duty on tea, colonists had responded by either going without tea or consuming what was smuggled in from Holland. What was supposed to have been a boon to the struggling company simply had not materialized, so proponents in Parliament devised what seemed to be a foolproof plan.

Under the terms of the Tea Act of 1773, the present duty of 3 pence per pound, lingering since 1770, would remain. However, the tea company would no longer have to deliver its tea from India directly to Britain.

Instead paying the required import duties in London and selling the tea to wholesalers, who would in turn package it for resale to the colonies, the company would now be permitted to transport tea directly from India to the colonies. Even with the 3 pence import duty factored in, this cutting out of the middleman would enable colonists to buy good-quality India tea—far superior to the smuggled product—at about 2 shillings per pound, a penny less than Dutch tea. How could the miserly tea-drinking colonists resist? Lord North, the prime minister who introduced the bill, and the others responsible for its design must have congratulated themselves on their ingenuity and cunning. Soon enough, though, the joviality in London would cease.

Some commentators point out that the ensuing furor in the colonies was proof that the ultimate rupture from the mother country was idealistic in nature, for if greed had been the only factor motivating the colonies, the prospect of cheaper tea would surely have been met with widespread approval. In fact, though, there was dissatisfaction of a practical nature associated with the Tea Act.

Wholesalers in London were not happy with being cut out of the loop, to be sure, for export of tea to the colonies had once been a profitable enterprise. A second opposed group consisted of American shipping interests, which would no longer collect freight charges for transporting the tea to colonial ports. In addition, the British East India Company would be required to off-load its cargo only to agents licensed by the Crown in the major port cities of Boston, New York, Charleston, Philadelphia, and elsewhere. Those agents—who effectively were granted a monopoly—would necessarily be selected from the ranks of merchants deemed to have remained loyal through the trials and travails of the past decade, a matter that further infuriated those who had gone along with the nonimportation agreements. In Massachusetts, passions were further inflamed by the fact that Governor Hutchinson himself was financially involved in the firm chosen to receive British East India tea in Boston.

Added to all this was the dissatisfaction of the many colonial merchants who dealt extensively in illicit Dutch teas; if North's plan worked, they would find themselves out of business, along with the intrepid ships' captains and their crews employed in the smuggling. All in all, there were quite a variety of interests opposed to the Tea Act on pragmatic grounds.

No public referendum was ever held that might have provided insight as to just how many Americans would have gone along with the prospect of cheaper, better tea, though Franklin later scoffed at the notion that the saving of a few pennies per year would have been enough to sway a colonist: "They have no idea," Franklin said of the Tea Act's champions in Parliament, "that any people can act from any other principle but that of interest; and they believe that threepence on a pound of tea, of which one does not perhaps drink ten pound in a year (!), is sufficient to overcome the patriotism of an American."

Whether Franklin was right about "the people" in general will be forever uncertain, but it is undeniable that at an October 16 town meeting in Philadelphia a series of declarations was passed denouncing the Tea Act (with its life span of five years) as nothing more than an extension of the Townshend duty on tea and calling for any merchant who had signed on as an agent for the British East India Company to end the arrangement.

Nor is there doubt about the reaction of Samuel Adams, for on October 21, Adams drafted a letter for the Massachusetts Committee of Correspondence warning that the Tea Act would not only have ruinous effects upon the local economies but also support the notion that Parliament could "bind the colonies" in all cases it saw fit. "It is easy to see how aptly this Scheme will serve both to destroy the Trade of the Colonies & increase the revenue," he said before repeating what was by then a mantralike appeal for united action: "How necessary then is it that Each Colony should take effectual methods to prevent this measure from having its designd Effects."

With Governor Hutchinson having suspended the Massachusetts Assembly, Adams was cut off from his most effective channel of activism. Still, he gathered a number of associates for a meeting of the North End Caucus, a Whig organization, at the Green Dragon Tavern, where those present voted to prevent the sale of British East India Company tea in Boston, even if it cost them their fortunes and their lives. A handbill was drawn up and circulated advising that a committee would meet beneath the liberty tree at noon on November 3 and that all those who had agreed to serve as consignees for the British East India Company were requested to attend and hand in their resignations.

The five hundred or so Liberty Boys who gathered beneath the great elm at the corner of Essex and Washington Streets to witness this ceremony were disappointed, for the consignees did not attend. As the gathering was breaking up, however, word spread that a number of the consignees had been spotted at a nearby warehouse. William Molineux, one of the leaders of the North End Caucus and a colleague of Adams's on the city's Committee of Correspondence, placed himself at the head of a group that marched on the warehouse to reiterate the demands that the consignees relinquish their positions. When the consignees declined, Molineux warned of the "heavy resentment" that would come their way as a result. The consignees took this as a signal to withdraw behind the doors of the warehouse, and the encounter ended without further incident.

On November 5, the Boston Town Meeting reported a series of resolutions similar to those adopted in Philadelphia, asserting that the duty on tea was an unjust tax levied by Parliament and that the Tea Act was nothing more than an attempt to impose what Adams called an unconstitutional "Ministerial Plan" of government upon the colonies and "a violent attack upon the Liberties of America." It was the duty of every American to oppose the Tea Act, the resolutions continued, and anyone who participated in the enterprise in any way was to be seen as "an Enemy to America." A committee had been selected "to wait on those Gentlemen, who it is reported are appointed by the British East India Company to receive and sell said Tea," requesting "from a regard to their own characters and the peace and good order of this Town" that they immediately resign their appointment.

The response from the consignees—two of them sons of Governor Hutchinson—was not exactly what Adams and his fellow council members had wanted. "As they were not yet acquainted with the terms upon which the teas were consigned to them, they were not able to give a definitive answer to the request of the town," Governor Hutchinson would later write. "The answers were all voted to be daringly affrontive to the town, and the meeting was immediately after dissolved."

Meanwhile, it was discovered that seven ships carrying British East India Company tea were already en route to the colonies, three bound for New York, Charleston, and Philadelphia and the other four headed for Boston. The latter were expected to arrive any day, and tensions were mounting. To Hutchinson it seemed the most difficult situation that he had encountered in all his years in office. He was well aware that previous controversies had "had a tendency to deprive him of the esteem and favour of the people," but, he claimed, he had never been "apprehensive of injury to his person." Now however, he saw himself up against true villains, "a great proportion of them the lowest part of the people," from whom "acts of violence are to be expected."

Though one member of his council suggested that Hutchinson should simply order the tea returned to England, the governor was not inclined to do so, for it would have meant caving in to Adams and his colleagues and placing any consequent liabilities fully on his own shoulders. While he debated the best course of action, he struck an agreement with the consignees that upon the approach of the ships, their captains would be advised to drop anchor outside the entrance to the harbor. If they never actually arrived in Boston, Hutchinson reasoned, he could not be put into the position of ordering their ignominious return.

Though the protesters claimed that they would not resort to violent measures to keep the tea from being landed, Hutchinson very much doubted the sincerity of these assertions. On the evening of November 17, a mob demonstrated before the home of Richard Clarke, one of the consignees, and broke one of the windows in an attempt to gain entry. Only the fact that Clarke fired a warning shot over the crowd prevented his house from being pulled down.

On the following day, with the arrival of the tea ships considered imminent, the town meeting reconvened and once more voted to demand the resignation of the consignees. A committee, which included Samuel Adams, was deputed to serve copies of the resolution to the younger Hutchinsons, to Richard Clarke, and to Benjamin Faneuil and Joshua Winslow, partners in the third firm set to accept the tea. The consignees, encouraged by the governor, responded that their appointments had been arranged in London by other parties and that they were powerless to negate actions that they themselves had not undertaken.

It was the sort of sophistry that might have impressed Mad Hatters and spectacle-wearing rabbits, but when Adams reported the answer back to the town meeting, that assembly dissolved itself on the spot. "This sudden dissolution," Governor Hutchinson wrote, "struck more terror into the consignees than the most minatory resolves." The frightened consignees then petitioned Hutchinson to take the "property of the East India company" under the protection of the government.

On the following day, Hutchinson took all this to his council, but if he thought that helpful advice would be forthcoming from that quarter, he was sadly mistaken. Fingers were dragged about shirt collars, hemming was followed by hawing, and finally the one member who suggested that the consignees resign stood to proclaim forcibly against the council's now accepting responsibility for the tea, "lest they should make themselves liable to answer for any damage which might happen to it." In the end, the council determined that the best course of action was to adjourn until Monday so that the members might have more time to think things over. The exasperated Hutchinson agreed to give them the weekend, but he surely could not have expected much to develop in that time.

As it turned out, the equivocation of the Governor's Council was of little consequence. On Sunday, November 28, there sailed into Boston harbor the good ship *Dartmouth*, laden with more than three hundred chests of tea from India. Adams quickly dispatched an announcement to the Sons' committees in nearby towns, and soon a similar notice was posted on the boards about Boston: "Friends! brethren! countrymen! That worst of plagues, the detested tea, shipped for this port by the East India company, is now arrived in this harbour—the hour of destruction, or manly opposition to the machinations of tyranny stare you in the face. Every friend to his country, to himself, and posterity, is now called upon to meet."

They would gather at 9 a.m. on Monday at Faneuil Hall, Adams said, "at which time the bells will ring, to make an united and successful resistance to this last, worst, and most destructive measure of administration."

While Hutchinson and his council met on Monday, Adams stood before a body of several thousand at the Old South Meeting House, there being far too many to fit within Faneuil's walls. As Adams introduced a resolution demanding that the tea be returned to England in the same ship that had brought it, Hutchinson demanded one last time that the council give him authorization to land the tea under government protection. But that plea went nowhere, largely because of the understanding that once the tea reached American shores, the duty would be payable. The council members' best advice was that Hutchinson convene the local magistrates and ask them to take all necessary measures to keep the peace, and with that Hutchinson dismissed the group. "The people," Hutchinson lamented, had prevailed and were now "in possession of all the power of government, for any purpose they thought fit."

20

MAD HATTER'S BALL

Meanwhile, what ensued over the series of meetings that took place at the Old South Meeting House over the next two and a half weeks constituted a true revolutionary process. As the scholar L. F. S. Upton put it, Samuel Adams and his fellow leaders were engaged in nothing less than an attempt to convince the populace to accept "the alarming idea that the destruction of private property was necessary for the maintenance of public liberty."

The meetings that took place over this period were also of a distinctly different nature, according to Hutchinson. They were no longer "town" meetings, in which participation and voting rights were circumscribed by various conditions. Instead, they were convened as "body" meetings, in which anyone might speak, regardless of age, permanent place of residence, or voting status. To Hutchinson, it was the end of all reason. "Seeing the powers of government thus taken out of the hands of the legally established authority," he sent the sheriff to Old South with an order that the meeting disperse.

Though it was some time before the jeers abated, the sheriff was finally allowed to read the governor's orders, though boos and catcalls resounded all the while. Following the reading, the assembled multitude cast their vote, which to no one's surprise was a unanimous rejection of the governor's order, and the meeting went back to its principal business, to determine the proper disposition of the tea on board the *Dartmouth*.

The previous day, once the resolution demanding that the tea be returned to England had been passed, the owner of the *Dartmouth*,

Francis Rotch, had stood to protest. For one thing, he pointed out, his captain could not legally pass out of the harbor without a clearance from customs and a permit from the governor, neither of which was likely to be forthcoming. If he tried to sail without a permit, he might be apprehended by navy ships outside the harbor or anywhere along the voyage, his cargo confiscated and taken who knew where. And even if the ship did make it back to London, the unauthorized cargo might well be seized by agents there. Moreover, it did not seem fair to Rotch that he would not in any case be paid for the cost of carrying the cargo all the way to Massachusetts.

Samuel Adams listened patiently to all this, then asked Rotch if he was familiar with the precedent exempting a shipowner from responsibility for goods lost during a storm or other unexpected accident. Of course he was familiar with it, Rotch shot back, but what did that have to do with his present untenable position?

Adams may or may not have smiled at the question. But what he told the owner has become the stuff of legend: it was necessary only, he explained to Rotch, that he explain to anyone concerned that a mob of several thousand people had directed him to take the tea back without the duty being paid and that it was for the good of the safety of his person and his property that he comply; that should take care of the matter. The discussion was at an end.

Rotch was still protesting when the moderator ordered him out, along with the *Dartmouth*'s captain, James Hall. The *Dartmouth* was ordered to tie up at Griffin's Wharf, where the remainder of the ship's cargo could be taken out. But it would be "at their peril" if they tried to unload the tea, the pair were reminded, and the assembly immediately appointed a twenty-five-man guard to keep watch at the docks and prevent any such attempts.

Once all that was dealt with, John Hancock stood to inform the assembly that one of the town's justices had shared the news of Hutchinson's order to "use their endeavors to suppress any riot that might ensue on account of the tea." It was further evidence of Hutchinson's cynical manipulation of the government, "solely calculated to serve the views of Administration," he said, a sentiment that was quickly put into the form of a resolution and passed without debate.

Though they were eager to return to the primary business at hand, that being the proper disposition of the tea aboard the *Dartmouth*, a son-in-law of Richard Clarke, one of the consignees, rose to inform the body that indeed word had just arrived for the agents from the British East India Company. The consignees thus petitioned the body for time to consider this news before appearing with a proposal in hand. The request was granted, and with that the body adjourned until the following morning.

It was Tuesday morning when the sheriff arrived bearing Hutchinson's proclamation, however, and by the time that was done and Samuel Adams was finished with his vituperative response, an hour or more had passed. Adams raged for nearly twenty minutes on the specious nature of the governor's reasoning, going so far as to heap invective on Hutchinson's salutation, "In Faithfulness to my Trust and as his Majesty's Representative in this Province."

Even that commonplace sent Adams into near apoplexy: "He? He? is that Shadow of a Man, scarce able to support his withered carcase or his hoary Head! Is he a Representative of Majesty?"

Finally, it was time to return to more pressing matters. As one of the loyalists in attendance described the transition, "When he [Adams] had done remarking on every Expression he thought proper to remark on, the Audience testified their Approbation of what he had said, by Shouts of Applause, Clapping, etc." and the owners of two more tea-bearing ships on the way, the *Eleanor* and the *Beaver*, were invited to speak.

John Rowe, a part owner of the *Eleanor*, stood to proclaim that he was truly sorry if in fact his ship were indeed "concerned with bringing any of that detestable and obnoxious commodity" to Massachusetts. When that sentiment provoked cheers and applause, Rowe seems to have found himself carried away. According to one observer writing in a diary unearthed in 1965 by Upton, Rowe wondered, in fact, "whether a little Salt Water would not do it good, or whether Salt Water would

not make as good Tea as fresh." Some historians have argued that such
a long-standing Tory as Rowe would never have uttered such words,
but the unnamed diarist's account of the meetings suggests that indeed
Rowe *was* the first to predict the storied drama to come.

Shortly after Rowe's appearance, John Copley, a representative of the
consignees, was brought before the group to deliver the long-awaited response from the men who'd hoped to already be selling tea and turning
a handsome profit. They'd decided not to risk unnecessary incitement
by appearing before that body, their emissary said. And although they
still deemed it utterly impossible to send the tea back to London, they
were nonetheless "very desirous of seeing peace restored to the town."
To that end, the consignees said, they would consent "to storing the
Tea in any Store the People should think proper and submit it to the
Inspection of any Committee chosen by them, but that they could go no
further without ruining themselves."

At the end of this, Adams stood to observe that it was indeed a good
thing to find that the consignees were willing to negotiate, but he suggested that nothing in their response indicated a material change. The
tea should not be permitted to land under any circumstances, he said,
and in a subsequent resolution those in attendance agreed. Shortly
thereafter, John Hancock rose to close the meeting with fateful words:
"My Fellow Countrymen, we have now put our Hands to the Plough
and Wo be to him that shrinks or looks back."

When news of the body's actions reached him, Hutchinson found
reason to pause. The men had voted to oppose the landing of the tea
"at the risk of their lives and properties," he understood, which to him
signified "a more determined spirit . . . than in any of the former assemblies of the people." Despite the fact that the meeting had included all
social ranks, "no eccentrick or irregular motions" had been put forward,
and though it was not in his estimation a legal gathering, there was no
doubting the unanimity of will he was facing. Even though he was certain that the whole enterprise was the work of Samuel Adams and his
cohorts, the governor could scarcely dismiss the threat.

Immediately following the adjournment of the November 30 meeting,

reports from the Boston Committee of Correspondence went out across
the colonies. Committees from Roxbury, Dorchester, Brookline, and
Cambridge joined the Boston group to hold daily meetings in Faneuil
Hall and issued their own communiqués as well. There was a clock
ticking on the matter, as all concerned understood. The captain of the
Dartmouth was permitted twenty days after docking to declare his
cargo and pay the necessary duties. If he had not complied within that
time, the ship and its contents could be seized by customs agents and
disposed of. If the necessary business was not attended to by December
16, calamity was assured.

As the standoff between Hutchinson and the town continued, the *Eleanor* and the *Beaver*, laden with tea as well, sailed into the harbor and
were ordered to tie up near the *Dartmouth*. As the days to the deadline
dwindled, it became apparent that neither Hutchinson nor the Liberty
Boys of Boston would budge.

On December 14, another meeting of the body was convened at Old
South Meeting House and Rotch was summoned to give an explanation as to why he had not dispatched the tea back to London. Rotch
responded that he found it patently unfair that he, a simple trader operating in good faith, should be put into the middle of a dispute between
the colonists and the Crown. It seemed to Rotch that the townsmen
were intent upon destroying his ship or at least the tea inside it, and
if that were so, he hoped that all those engaged would bear their just
portion of his losses. He was willing to relinquish the ship and its contents to some board of appraisers who could determine its value and let
others decide its fate, but as for attempting to return the tea if it meant
risking his life not to go further in such attempts, Rotch said, so be it.

Some statements of sympathy for Rotch were forthcoming from the
crowd, but in the end he was directed to seek permission from the governor to move his ship. As such an appeal would scarcely endanger his
life, he agreed to try.

On December 16, the body, several thousand strong, convened again
at Old South and listened as Rotch recounted his efforts to comply
with their requests. He had petitioned the governor for the necessary

permit, and Hutchinson's reply had been this: "He was always disposed to oblige any person that appealed to him for a pass when there was just reason for one, but he could not think it his duty in this case and therefore could not."

It was nearing six o'clock by then, and dusk was falling in the streets outside. Anyone who noticed might have found it an all-too-appropriate reflection of the state at which relations with the mother country had arrived. Samuel Adams then rose to say that he could think of nothing more that could be done. He told those assembled that "they had now done all that they could for the salvation of their country." As for himself, he said, he intended to "go home, set down, and make himself as easy as he could." At that someone made a motion that they consider Mr. Rotch's conduct satisfactory, and upon approval of that sentiment, the meeting's close seemed imminent.

As one observer recalls, however, no sooner had merchant Rotch finished his recounting of the governor's dismissal than a number of men who were standing at the far end of the hall began to drift outside. A few minutes later, there came "an hideous Yelling in the Street . . . and in the Porch, as of an Hundred People, some imitating the Powaws of Indians and others the Whistle of a Boatswain . . . on which Numbers hastened out as fast as possible while Mr. Adams, Mr. Hancock, Dr. Young with several others called out to the People to stay, for they had not quite done."

The "powaws" and "whistles" were of course the preliminary calls to an action that has filled so many of pages history since. George Robert Hewes was one of those involved in the "hideous yelling," and he recounted the events that followed with the clarity of a born storyteller.

As Adams and the others tried to reestablish order inside the hall, Hewes and somewhere between sixty and a hundred others set out upon other business. "I immediately dressed myself in the costume of an Indian," Hewes said, "equipped with a small hatchet, which I and my associates denominated the tomahawk, with which, and a club, after having painted my face and hands with coal dust in the shop of a blacksmith, I repaired to Griffin's wharf."

As he hurried through the darkening streets toward the *Dartmouth*, the *Eleanor*, and the *Beaver*, Hewes recalled, he "fell in with many who were dressed, equipped and painted as I was, and who fell in with me and marched in order to the place of our destination."

At the wharf the men were divided into three parties. "We were immediately ordered by the respective commanders to board all the ships at the same time, which we promptly obeyed," Hewes said. "The commander of the division to which I belonged, as soon as we were on board the ship appointed me boatswain, and ordered me to go to the captain and demand of him the keys to the hatches and a dozen candles. I made the demand accordingly, and the captain promptly replied, and delivered the articles; but requested me at the same time to do no damage to the ship or rigging."

The propriety and calm with which events unfolded from there on were echoed by both sides. The boarders were ordered to open the hatches of the ships, remove the chests of tea, and toss them into the harbor, and Hewes reported that the men were happy to comply, "first cutting and splitting the chests with our tomahawks, so as thoroughly to expose them to the effects of the water.

"In about three hours from the time we went on board, we had thus broken and thrown overboard every tea chest to be found in the ship, while those in the other ships were disposing of the tea in the same way, at the same time." Hewes added, "We were surrounded by British armed ships, but no attempt was made to resist us."

According to Hewes's account, the assault concluded with the same surreal quality with which it had begun: "We then quietly retired to our several places of residence, without having any conversation with each other, or taking any measures to discover who were our associates; nor do I recollect of our having had the knowledge of the name of a single individual concerned in that affair. . . . There appeared to be an understanding that each individual should volunteer his services, keep his own secret, and risk the consequence for himself. No disorder took place during that transaction, and it was observed at that time that the stillest night ensued that Boston had enjoyed for many months."

Hewes was a Boston shoemaker who kept the details of the event to himself for almost fifty years, but his account squares with what has become legend, not only for the magnitude of the actions but for the deliberate manner in which they were carried out. Governor Hutchinson marveled at the efficiency of the operation: scarcely was the meeting at Old South dissolved, he said, when "the body of people repaired to the wharf, and surrounded the immediate actors, as a guard and security, until they had finished their work. In two or three hours, they hoisted out of the holds of the ships, three hundred and forty-two chests of tea, and emptied them into the sea."

Even John Adams, no advocate of mob action, wrote in his diary the next day, "There is a dignity, a majesty, a sublimity, in this last action of the patriots, that I greatly admire. . . . It must have so important consequences that I consider it an epoch in history."

Despite the mighty implications of the event, the atmosphere in Boston immediately afterward was preternaturally calm. There seemed to be no need for further action. There was only uncertainty as to how Great Britain would respond. As John Adams put it, "What measures will the Ministry take in consequence of this? Will they resent it? Will they dare to resent it? Will they punish us? How? By quartering troops upon us? By annulling our charter? By laying on more duties? By restraining our trade? By sacrifice of individuals? Or how?"

Certainly many Britons resented the actions of the colony's governor in the matter. In the opinion of a number of his critics, had Hutchinson simply issued the permit for the *Dartmouth* to leave port, the entire incident could have been averted. But the governor was resolute to the end. He was bound, as all the king's governors were, he insisted, "to observe the acts of trade," and he acted as he should have in refusing to issue an unlawful permit. As to the destruction of the tea itself, he had no means of preventing it. There were no longer sufficient troops stationed at the castle to allow a deployment at the docks, and even if he had sent armed soldiers to the scene, the catastrophe sure to have ensued would have been far worse than what had transpired.

What had in fact occurred was the destruction of about £9,000 or more of excellent tea, believed now to have come from the bohea-producing region of China and to be worth $1 million or so in modern tender. But the damages went far beyond the monetary. As Hutchinson himself admitted, a powerful precedent was established and the previous rule of law subverted evermore. Protesters had destroyed private property in the service of their subversive aims, and little was to be done about it. Offering a reward for the identification of the perpetrators would be a joke. And no grand jury of the people would charge a participant anyway, for the actions taken would never be considered a crime.

John Adams was not alone in ascribing great importance to the matter. Hutchinson called the events of December 16, which would not be referred to as a "tea party" for half a century or more, "the boldest stroke which had yet been struck in America. . . . The thing was done: there was no way of nullifying it. Their leaders feared no consequences." In the end analysis, the governor declared that the people had "gone too far to recede, and that an open and general revolt must be the consequences." The best he could come up with as a response was to dissolve the colony's assembly for a month or more. As he put it, "No advantage could be expected from its sitting."

Certainly the ripple effects of the riot were evident at once. Samuel Adams compiled an account of the events for immediate circulation and dispatched the Boston silversmith Paul Revere, a dependable messenger for the Committee of Correspondence, to ride at once to New York and Philadelphia with the news. It was Adams's position that he and "the people" had exercised every means at their disposal to see the tea returned safely but had been foiled by the designs of the governor, the consignees, and the customs council. At that final meeting, attended by as many as seven thousand men, including citizens of towns twenty miles away, frustrations had unavoidably boiled over, and in less than four hours, Boston harbor had become one giant teapot.

Furthermore, the leader of the Sons of Liberty in Boston could not have been happier. "You cannot imagine the height of joy that sparkles in the eyes and animates the countenances as well as the hearts of all we meet on this occasion," Adams wrote to his compatriot Richard Henry Lee in Virginia, "excepting the disappointed, disconcerted Hutchinson and his tools."

Adams was convinced that what happened in Boston was the event needed to unify the colonies once and for all, and it seemed that he was right. On December 25, the British ship *Polly* entered the Delaware River bound for Philadelphia, carrying nearly seven hundred chests of tea, twice the amount that had been dumped in Boston harbor. As the *Philadelphia Gazette* reported on January 3, 1774, townsmen had intercepted the ship at Chester, a few miles south of Philadelphia, forcing the captain to tie it off and accompany them to a meeting of thousands of citizens that spilled onto the common outside the state house on December 27. There, resolutions had been passed declaring that the tea aboard the *Polly* would not be permitted to land and the captain had been handed this message:

> *What think you, Captain, of a Halter around your Neck—*
> *ten Gallons of liquid Tar decanted on your Pate—with the*
> *Feathers of a dozen wild Geese laid over that to enliven your*
> *Appearance? Only think seriously of this—and fly to the Place*
> *from whence you came—fly without Hesitation—without the*
> *Formality of a Protest—and above all, Captain Ayres, let us*
> *advise you to fly without the wild Geese Feathers.*

If the captain thought at all, he did not think long. Shortly he was back on the *Polly* and bound for London, all thought of landing his cargo gone.

In New York, meantime, word that a tea ship was on its way led to a formal reorganization of the Sons of Liberty there. On December 16, committee members issued a broadside that was distributed about the city, calling for a meeting at City Hall on the following day to undertake "business of the utmost importance." Not only fellow Sons but "every other friend to the liberties and trade of America" was encouraged to attend.

At that meeting, which was well attended in spite of bitter weather, as John Holt reported in his *Journal*, John Lamb read aloud several letters from fellow committees in Boston and Philadelphia. Though they had not yet heard what their fellow activists had achieved in Boston harbor on the previous evening, those in attendance in New York voted to appoint a permanent fifteen-person Committee of Correspondence to communicate with the other colonies "on the subject of the dutied Tea."

Lamb then introduced a series of resolutions under the banner of "The Association of the Sons of Liberty of New York," dated November 29, 1773. The preamble of the document sketched out the history of the duties levied on tea in the colonies and the efforts of the British government to bail out the distressed East India Company. It had all devolved in a melancholy way: the company had chartered a number of ships to bring tea to the colonies, "which may be hourly expected, to make an important trial of our virtue," the document continued. "If they succeed in the sale of that tea, we shall have no property that we can call our own, and then we may bid adieu to American liberty."

To help prevent such a calamity, it was resolved that anyone importing tea into New York, so long as the duties were imposed, would be deemed "an enemy to the liberties of America." Anyone assisting in the landing or storage of that tea would be similarly regarded, as would anyone who sold or bought it. Furthermore, the Sons' declaration stated, any attempts to disguise the process by arranging for pre- or postpayment of the duties in England would not be tolerated. Finally, the document stated "that whoever shall transgress any of these resolutions, we will not deal with, or employ, or have any connection with him."

Hardly had those resolves been agreed to by those in attendance when an emissary of the governor arrived with a proposal. Since he had been informed that indeed the tea was on its way, the governor wondered if it might be agreeable to unload and store the tea in the fort while it awaited final distribution to its various consignees? After reading this message to the meeting, Lamb glanced about the crowded hall to ask, "Gentlemen, is this satisfactory to you?" The answer was of course a resounding no, and, following an equally vigorous statement of resolve that no tea should ever be landed under the terms of the Tea Act, the group voted to adjourn "till the arrival of the Tea Ship" and that meantime news of their resolves be broadcast to the other colonies.

In effect, then, the Sons of Liberty became the official voice of the people of New York. And when Paul Revere rode in shortly thereafter with news of the events in Boston harbor, Lamb and Sears were further heartened. A particularly enthusiastic subset of their associates formed a group they called "the Mohawks," promising to do the same as had been done in Boston with any tea ship that found its way to the New York docks.

Whereas Boston, Philadelphia, and New York kept tea away from their ports, the situation played out somewhat differently in Charleston. As the *South-Carolina Gazette* reported in its issue of December 6, the British ship *London* had arrived earlier in the week carrying 274 chests of tea. Christopher Gadsden and his followers immediately circulated handbills calling for a meeting to consider a response at the Exchange building on December 4. So many people packed the hall that the main support timbers of the floor were said to have cracked and threatened to give way.

No one was hurt, however; the greater injury accrued to merchants of the town, who argued that since there was tea aboard the *London* that had been ordered by merchants who had chosen not to join the nonimportation boycott prior to the passage of the Tea Act, they retained every right to accept it, and that, furthermore, there was no valid reason to prevent the off-loading of the tea that had been shipped by the East India Company.

Following two further meetings, the coalition between the planters and the mechanics engineered by Gadsden prevailed, resolving that the East India tea could not be landed and that its consignees should immediately resign their positions. The so-called private teas were permitted to be off-loaded, but Captain Alexander Curling of the *London* was instructed to take the British East India Company's tea back from whence it came. All the wrangling took time, however, and by midnight on December 21, Curling's ship was still tied off at the Charleston docks.

With the deadline for payment of duty on the East India Company tea now passed, the loyalist governor, William Bull, ordered the cargo seized and placed in the government's warehouse. Though the depth of passion expressed during the debates on the matter suggested that the citizens of Charleston might hold their own tea party, the dualistic nature of the opposition there dictated otherwise. The planters were not about to take to the streets over the matter, and the mechanics were not sufficiently galvanized to engineer such an operation on their own.

In the end, the customs master reported that the seizure and storage operations had taken place without incident. As the *Gazette* described it, there had never been "an Instance here, of so great a Number of Packages, being taken out of any Vessel, and thus disposed of, in so short a Time." The Earl of Dartmouth wrote Governor Bull to commend him on his actions, noting that although what had taken place in Charleston was "not equal in criminality" to what had happened in Boston and Philadelphia, the affair could be considered by the Crown "in no other light than that of a most unwarrantable Insult to the authority of this Kingdom." Though his lordship closed by assuring Bull that it was the king's intention "to pursue such measures as shall be effectual for securing the Dependence of the Colonies upon this Kingdom," the East India Company tea never would be distributed to the consignees. It would languish in the government's warehouse for more than three years, after which it was finally auctioned off in support of the revolutionary government.

21

INTOLERABLE

Though Samuel Adams might have seen the destruction of the tea in Boston as the event that would once and for all unite the colonies in opposition to the Crown, the immediate repercussions were not entirely favorable for the radical movement. Though most of the provinces—as well as forty other towns in Massachusetts colony—joined in declaring a boycott on dutied tea, the incident alarmed a number of the merchant class, especially outside the bounds of the Massachusetts seat of government.

Though the events of December 16 established a precedent for the destruction of private property in the service of a goal deemed worthy by proponents of political change, it was not the sort of thing that could easily be embraced by men whose livelihoods depended upon the orderly exchange of goods. The town of Marshfield, Massachusetts, actually condemned the violent acts in Boston and called for the conviction of those responsible. For similar reasons, the town of Littleton disbanded its Committee of Correspondence. Neither could Adams convince the nearby province of Connecticut to adopt resolutions favorable to the cause.

If only Parliament had been content to make a more reasoned response to the violence in Boston, a natural antipathy toward violence and mob rule in the colonies might have corrected the course toward independence, for a time at least. But when the news reached London on January 20, 1774, the results were predictable, with some calling for immediate military action against the colony.

On February 4, King George, after conferring with General Gage, recently returned from the colonies, wrote Lord North to suggest that it was time to end their tolerant stance. Gage was ready to return to the colonies "at a day's notice" and impose some much-needed order, the king assured North. "He says they will be lyons, whilst we are lambs; but if we take the resolute part, they will undoubtedly be very meek. He thinks . . . four regiments . . . if sent to Boston are sufficient to prevent any disturbance."

The king urged North to meet with Gage and hear for himself the general's sentiments on how Massachusetts might best be dealt with. The king went on to lament that the repeal of the Stamp Act had probably been an unfortunate mistake. "All men seem now to feel that the fatal compliance of 1766 has encouraged the Americans annually to encrease in their pretensions to that thorough independency . . . which is quite subversive of the obedience which a colony owes to its mother country." It was a statement attesting to the condescending attitude toward the colonies that many of the king's subjects continued to hold.

Still, overt military action seemed impractical to many Britons. To begin with, there were only 25,000 soldiers in the king's army in 1774, and it was thought that the Americans might muster as many as 100,000 troops of their own. In addition, the massive expense and logistic challenges of supply and maintenance of a fighting force thousands of miles across an ocean were the reasons why England had gotten itself into this position to begin with.

In the end, North determined to craft a set of punitive legislative measures, known as the Coercive Acts in England and termed the Intolerable Acts in the colonies, that would punish Bostonians and show the rest of the colonies that England meant business. "The Americans have tarred and feathered your subjects, plundered your merchants, burnt your ships, and denied all obedience to your laws and authority," he said, introducing the measures in Parliament, "yet so clement and so long forbearing has our conduct been that it is incumbent on us now to take a different course. Whatever may be the consequences, we must risk something; if we do not, all is over. . . . It is political necessity."

Though some members of Parliament opposed various of the measures as unnecessarily oppressive, North was adamant. He was not out to "enslave America. I deny it. I have no such intention." These were, he said, but necessary steps "to bring them to a sense of their duty."

As for any contention that the Americans now saw the error of their ways and were willing to indemnify the East India Company, North recounted the fate of the good ship *Fortune*, which had arrived in Boston harbor on March 6, bearing 28½ chests of tea. Though it had not been East India Company tea, it had been tea nonetheless, and on the following day, fifty or sixty men dressed as Mohawks had boarded the ship, locked a customs man in a cabin, pulled chests of tea from the hold, and dumped the tea overboard. "Is this, Sir, feeling their error?" North asked indignantly. "Is this, Sir, reforming?"

Though there were some who were willing to take on what North intended as rhetorical questions, most in Parliament were of the opinion that the reprehensible behavior of the Massachusetts colonists indeed needed punishing. The first of North's measures, the Boston Port Act, was passed on March 31, 1774, stipulating "WHEREAS dangerous commotions and insurrections have been fomented and raised in the town of Boston, in the province of Massachusetts Bay, in New England, by divers ill-affected persons, to the subversion of his Majesty's government, and to the utter destruction of the publick peace. . . . That from and after the first day of June, one thousand seven hundred and seventy-four, it shall not be lawful for any person or persons whatsoever to lade put, or cause or procure to be laden or put, off or from any quay, wharf, or other place, within the said town of Boston, or in or upon any part of the shore of the bay, commonly called The Harbour of Boston . . . any goods, wares, or merchandise, whatsoever."

In fact, the Port of Boston was to be closed to all commercial traffic until such time as the king was satisfied "that peace and obedience to the laws shall be so far restored in the said town of Boston, that the trade of Great Britain may safely be carried on there, and his Majesty's customs duly collected." A further provision made it clear that one condition of such satisfaction would be the reimbursement of the East India Company for its losses "by or on behalf of the inhabitants of the said town of Boston to the united company of merchants of England trading to the East Indies, for the damage sustained by the said company by the destruction of their goods sent to the said town of Boston."

Furthermore, the act stipulated, similar "reasonable" satisfaction would have to be made to the customs officers who had suffered in the melee. And to ensure that the provisions of the Port Act were vigorously enforced, the king appointed none other than General Gage as the new governor of Massachusetts colony.

When Gage sailed into Boston harbor in early May carrying word of his appointment as well as the passage of the Port Act, the results were predictable. At a hastily called meeting, the town's Correspondence Committee authorized Samuel Adams to draft a series of letters to all the colonies informing them of the news and calling for the support of their beleaguered colony.

"General Gage is just arrivd here, with a Commission to supercede Govr Hutchinson," the alarmed Adams wrote, adding that one of the first orders of business announced by the new governor had been the relocation of the government's center of operations. "It is said that the Town of Salem about twenty Miles East of this Metropolis is to be the Seat of Government—that the Commissioners of the Customs and their numerous Retinue are to remove to the Town of Marblehead a Town contiguous to Salem and that this if the General shall think proper is to be a Garrisond Town. Reports are various and contradictory."

It was a case of gross overreaction on the part of the British, Adams said. "It appears that the Inhabitants of this Town have been Tryed condemn'd and are to be punished . . . without their having been accused of any crime committed by them," he proclaimed, adding that Boston would not be able to survive the closing of its port without the aid of its neighbors, nor should any other colony suppose it would be spared such treatment should the Crown so decide. The only course of action was to unite. In a letter of May 13 to the Philadelphia Committee of Correspondence, Adams spelled out the situation with typical bluntness: "This Attack, though made immediately upon us, is doubtless designd for every other Colony, who will not surrender their sacred Rights & Liberties into the Hands of an infamous Ministry. Now therefore is the

Time, when ALL should be united in opposition to this Violation of the Liberties of ALL. Their grand object is to divide the Colonies."

In his various missives, Adams counseled fellow Sons in Massachusetts and elsewhere that it was surely the British ministry's hope that Bostonians would be left to languish by their fellow colonists. Therefore, he contended, the most effective way of proving otherwise and forcing the British to reconsider would be to form a pan-colonial boycott of all trade with the mother country. The town of Newburyport had already announced that it would no longer trade "southward of South Carolina nor to any part of Great Britain" until the port of Boston was reopened, and Adams drafted a call for similar resolutions, not only by all other towns in Massachusetts but by all other colonies as well.

Adams also supported the convening of a colonial congress to solidify plans for such a boycott but meantime pressed his colleagues to call for an immediate cessation of consumption of British goods, with the fine points to be dealt with later. At the same time, he was growing increasingly doubtful of the merchants' willingness to comply with any boycott. Since their very livelihoods were at stake, it seemed unlikely that he could count on unanimous support from that quarter. Increasingly, then, he directed his calls to "the body of the people" for support of his plan. Though "violence and submission" would prove equally fatal responses to the edicts of the "barbarians" in England, he counseled, economic warfare would bring them to their knees.

If some merchants did indeed waver in their support of the boycott, the punitive nature of the Boston Port Act stirred the moral outrage of other leaders throughout the colonies, many of them previously unmoved by calls for joint opposition to British rule. For one thing, the Port Act was clearly designed to punish. It was directed at one port and one colony and made no pretense of being cloaked among other "regulations of trade." The Port Act was retribution for the destruction of tea in Boston harbor, pure and simple, and furthermore it would bring great hardship on the citizens of an entire colony, the vast majority of whom had had nothing to do with the event and simply wished for an unbroken supply of food, clothing, and other necessities.

Christopher Gadsden wrote Adams that all supporters of liberty in South Carolina sympathized with Boston's suffering and pledged that shipments of rice were on the way from his colony to Massachusetts. The Virginia House of Burgesses met to declare a day of mourning for their northern brethren, committees in Maryland issued proclamations of support, and churches in Maryland and Philadelphia tolled their bells from morning to night on June 1, the day the Port Act took effect. Yet take effect the act did, and, soon thereafter, other news arrived in Boston that even more punishment was on the way.

The Massachusetts Government Act was passed by Parliament on May 20, removing the power of the colony to elect the members of the governor's executive council and granting the governor sole authority to appoint judges, sheriffs, justices of the peace, and jury members. Henceforth town meetings would be limited to one each year. There would no longer be a shadow government to meet as it pleased and issue proclamations willy-nilly. The government of Massachusetts was being taken from the hands of an irresponsible citizenry and put back where it belonged.

A companion piece of legislation, the Administration of Justice Act, was passed by Parliament on the same day, provoking equal outrage from colonial leaders, who quickly dubbed it "the Murder Act." In recognition of the attempts of the citizens of Massachusetts Bay to "throw off the authority of Parliament," the act stipulated that beginning August 1, it would be within the governor's discretion to move the trial of any government official accused of murder—or any other capital offense upon a person—while acting "in support of the public peace of the province."

If it was the governor's opinion that "an indifferent trial cannot be had within the said province, in that case, it shall and may be lawful for the governor . . . to direct, with the advice and consent of the council, that the inquisition, indictment, or appeal, shall be tried in some other of his Majesty's colonies, or in Great Britain." The very thought that a trial such as that of the troops involved in the Boston Massacre might be moved to Great Britain seemed beyond the pale of reason to any colonist. Indeed, the veiled message within the Justice Act seemed to be: "We will deal with you colonists as we wish and we will do so with impunity." Even to those who considered the destruction of the tea a reprehensible action, the Justice Act seemed little better.

George Washington, previously hardly known as a radical, took on something of an Adams-like flair in his letters of the time, decrying the Justice Act as a thinly veiled justification for the most tyrannical actions. Though he supported the notion that the East India Company should be indemnified for its losses, he informed his Tory friend George William Fairfax in a July 4 letter that he found the Coercive Acts "subversive of everything that I hold dear and valuable." Washington told Fairfax that the actions of General Gage since returning to Massachusetts (and calling the trade boycott "treason") had been nothing short of despotic and likened the new governor to a pompous Turkish pasha. Washington became a champion in the Virginia assembly for the Fairfax Resolves, a set of resolutions passed on July 18, which called for an end to the importation of slaves and a ban on trade with Great Britain.

A fourth piece of legislation often lumped with those acts specific to Massachusetts was passed on June 2. The Quartering Act of 1774 provided for the governor of *any* of the colonies to order the use of other buildings if barracks were not provided for the housing of British troops. Because it did not require that colonies supply provisions for the troops as previous such acts had, however, it did not occasion the same general outcry as did the provisions directed at Massachusetts.

"Will the People of America consider these measures, as Attacks on the Constitution of an Individual Province in which the rest are not interested," Samuel Adams asked Richard Henry Lee of Virginia in a letter of July 15, "or will they view the model of Government prepar'd for us as a Sistem for the whole Continent? Will they, as unconcern'd Spectators, look upon it to be design'd only to top off the exuberant Branches of Democracy in the Constitution of this Province? Or, as part of a plan to reduce them all to Slavery? These are Questions, in my Opinion of Importance, which I trust will be thoroughly weighed in a general Congress."

Adams was not the only one to call for such a gathering, of course, for the general feeling of the day was that the colonies would soon be faced with a momentous decision, and even moderate interests preferred that any pan-colonial actions be decided upon after discussion and judicious deliberation, not via letters between Committees of Correspondence. In his *History of the Province of Massachusetts Bay*, Thomas Hutchinson refers to a letter sent earlier in 1774 from Benjamin Franklin to the Massachusetts Assembly suggesting such a congress, and he was also aware that John Hancock was promoting the concept in letters and speeches. On May 15, 1774, Isaac Sears and Alexander McDougall wrote to Boston on behalf of the New York Committee of Correspondence in support of the boycott of British goods, so long as it might be "agreed upon by Committees from the Principal Towns on the Continent, to meet in a general Congress to be held here for that Purpose." And on May 17, the Rhode Island Assembly voted to propose a Continental Congress for the purpose of designing an effective plan of response to the British legislation; less than a month later it met again to select delegates to such a meeting.

In New York, the Sons of Liberty met in May with a delegation from the merchants, who feared being left out of any future meeting where serious measures might be adopted across the colonies. The result was the formation of a "Committee of Fifty-one," balanced between radical and conservative interests. When that committee finally met to choose delegates to the convention during the summer, a decidedly moderate slate was chosen, leaving radical Sons such as Sears and McDougall out.

By mid-June the *Massachusetts Spy* reported that "A Politico-Mercantile Congress seems now to be the voice of all the Colonies," with numerous sites having been suggested. The paper suggested that New York, where Sears and McDougall had originally proposed that the meeting be held, was now graciously granting the aggrieved colony of Massachusetts the right to choose the time and place.

In any case, on June 17, Adams convened a meeting of the Massachusetts Assembly and cleared the gallery for some serious work. When a loyalist observer gleaned Adams's intentions, he hurried out of the chambers to inform the governor. Gage, infuriated, sent an emissary with an edict declaring the meeting illegal. Those assembled were to quit the chambers at once. When Gage's minion arrived, however, he found the doors bolted, and no one answered his summons.

While the emissary read Gage's orders to the closed doors, Adams carried on his work inside, steadfastly guiding a momentous resolution through the chamber. There would indeed be a Continental Congress, to which all colonies would be urged to send a delegation, and it would take place in Philadelphia on September 1, 1774.

22

CONGRESS OF SONS

W hen the First Continental Congress convened in Philadelphia on September 5, there were fifty-six delegates present, representing every colony but that of Georgia. That colony's assembly had formed a Committee of Correspondence early in January 1774 and for a time had engaged Benjamin Franklin as its agent in London. In June, radicals had gone so far as to erect a liberty pole outside Tondee's Tavern in Savannah-Towne, "where gathered the Sons of Liberty" on July 24 and August 10. Still, outside its port city, the sparsely populated and conservative province (there were barely 50,000 residents, half of them slaves) traditionally provided little support for such a radical notion as independence. Though a few parishes voted to send delegates to Philadelphia, the lack of interest of most and the staunch opposition of the London-born governor, James Wright, determined that Georgia would not be represented in the Congress.

For Samuel Adams, the journey to Philadelphia would be the first time in his life that the fifty-two-year-old activist had ventured outside the colony of Massachusetts. Though the Harvard-educated Adams had contemplated a career first as a clergyman and then as an attorney, he had inherited an interest in liberal politics from his father that had led him into work with the Boston Town Assembly from the mid-1740s, shortly after his graduation.

Though it remains an open question as to whether Samuel Adams ever worked actively as a brewer (his father owned a malting house that produced one of the ingredients necessary for making beer, and Samuel was for a time a partner in that enterprise), he did work for a short period as an accountant and later as a not-so-assiduous tax collector for the town. With the help of a small inheritance from his father, his work for the assembly, and the willingness of his wife, Elizabeth, to work at menial jobs from time to time, Adams made do. But, as his biographers are agreed, money and appearances always took second place to his struggles against the British and on behalf of liberty. From time to time, friends, grateful for Adams's ever-whispering pen, stepped in to help with more practical affairs. As one associate, the Boston businessman John Andrews, put it:

> The ultimate wish and desire of the high Government party is to get Samuel Adams out of the way, when they think they may accomplish every of their plans: but however some may despise him, he has certainly very many friends. For not long since some persons (their names unknown) sent and ask'd his permission to build him a new barn, the old one being decay'd, which was executed in a few days. A second sent to ask leave to repair his house, which was thoroughly effected soon.

On the eve of Adams's departure for Philadelphia, others who were fearful that the activist's indifferent appearance might belie his eloquence took certain steps:

> A third [friend] sent to beg the favor of him to call at a taylor's shop and be measur'd for a suit of cloaths . . . which were finish'd and sent home for his acceptance. A fourth presented him with a new wig, a fifth with a new hat, a sixth with six pair of the best silk hose, a seventh with six pair of fine thread [stockings], a eighth with six pair shoes, and a ninth modestly enquir'd of him whether his finances want rather low than otherways. He reply'd it was true that was the case, but he was very indifferent about these matters . . . upon which the Gentlemen oblig'd him to accept of a purse containing about 15 or 20 Johannes. I mention this to show you how much he is esteem'd here. They value him for his good sense, great abilities, amazing fortitude, noble resolution,

and undaunted courage: being firm and unmov'd at all the various reports that were propagated in regard to his being taken up
and sent home, notwithstanding he had repeated letters from his
friends, both in England as well as here, to keep out of the way.

Adams was constitutionally unable to "keep out of the way," however, and, according to a story told by his daughter Hannah, shortly
before his travels turned down the offer of a sinecure from the newly
appointed Governor Gage in return for simply "making peace with the
King." Though the offer was never put into writing, some observers
say that had Adams agreed to put his pen down and keep his mouth
shut, he might have looked forward to a payment of as much as £1,000
per year.

Adams's reply might have been expected. The Puritan told Gage's
emissary that he had long ago made his peace with the "King of Kings"
and begged His Excellency to make no further insulting entreaties.
With that, he returned to preparing for his journey.

Adams and his fellow radical delegates did not envision an easy time
at the convention, for they well understood the dueling interests that
had brought the gathering into being. Whereas the Sons of Liberty and
other ardent Whigs were hopeful that the meeting would produce a
united call for the boycott on trade and a firm resolve for union, more
conservative interests, including many merchants, went to Philadelphia
in the hope that orderly relations with England—and certainly trade—
could somehow be restored.

The Massachusetts and Virginia delegations were viewed as the most
liberal of the group, their resolve hardened by Parliament's passage
that summer of the Quebec Act, another measure sometimes included
among the Intolerables. Among other contentious points, including the
recognition of the Roman Catholic religion, the act ceded large tracts
of frontier land coveted by Virginia developers back to Canada and
increased the fears of western Massachusetts farmers that the British
might also reclaim their own holdings on a whim.

The chief opponents of the liberal faction were the delegations from

Philadelphia and New York, where maneuvering by the merchants had produced agreement on the necessity of maintaining harmony with Great Britain and addressing any differences by petition to the king. Joseph Galloway, the speaker of the Pennsylvania Assembly, rose to prominence among the moderates on a platform that stressed such principles, including the insistence that ceding authority to various illegal conventions, committees, town assemblies, and mobs would in effect put an end to government itself. To Galloway and his proponents the so-called Intolerable Acts were simply the stuff of reason and order, and he counted on Adams and the Virginians to comport themselves so fearsomely that most delegates would turn to moderation.

Adams proved to be more than a match for Galloway, however. As part of a backroom agreement engineered by Adams, the Massachusetts and Virginia delegations threw their support for the position of secretary of the congress to Charles Thomson, the most liberal member of the Pennsylvania delegation and a man who, John Adams wrote in his diary, seemed "the Sam. Adams of Phyladelphia." Not wishing to portray his own delegation as fractured, Galloway joined the rest of the convention in approving Thomson unanimously.

In a move surely calculated to show his temperate self, Adams stood up as delegates began wrangling on the opening of the second day as to whether it was appropriate to begin with a prayer of benediction. Given the great divide between Episcopalians, Quakers, and Puritans, to say nothing of the Papists and Jews, all of whom had scrabbled from the beginning for a place on the new continent, several members opposed the motion on the grounds that it would be a divisive way to begin. After a bit of back-and-forth, Adams rose to observe that although he himself was a devout Puritan, he was no bigot "and could hear a Prayer from a Gentleman of Piety and Virtue, who was at the same Time a Friend to his Country."

With that introduction, Adams told the body that he was informed that the Reverend Jacob Duché, a noted Episcopalian minister, was such a friend, and then suggested that Duché might deliver a benediction. The group, struck by such moderate advice, readily concurred and

Duché, nominally a representative of the Church of England, rose to invoke Psalm 35, which beseeches the Lord to join in a fight against one's enemies and to scatter them "as dust before the wind."

If that was not sufficient portent of Adams's capabilities, what happened next put an end to any further speculation over the Congress's direction. When he had left Boston for Philadelphia, Adams had been well aware of an upcoming conference of Committees of Correspondence from Suffolk (which included Boston), Middlesex, Worcester, and Essex counties, called in opposition to the Massachusetts Government Act. Though Adams could not be at the meeting, which commenced on August 26, he entrusted his colleague Joseph Warren to oversee the meeting at Faneuil Hall. As a result of their deliberations, the committees produced a document known as the Suffolk Resolves, which stated that the signees, while acknowledging the sovereignty of and their allegiance to George III, were nonetheless agreed, among other things, to: (1) reject the provisions of the Port Act, the Government Act, and the Justice Act; (2) ignore the dictates of any court or official of justice claiming authority under the Government Act; (3) refuse the payment of any taxes until the Government Act was repealed; (4) require the resignation of the newly appointed members of the governor's council; (5) reject the provisions of the Quebec Act establishing Roman Catholicism as the state religion; (6) establish an armed militia in every town and require that the inhabitants of those towns "use their utmost diligence to acquaint themselves with *the art of war* as soon as possible" [italics added]; (7) withhold "all commercial intercourse with Great-Britain" and abstain from the use of British merchandise and manufactures; and (8) refrain from engagement in any "routs, riots or licentious attacks" or "outrage upon private property."

As Adams had arranged, a copy of the Resolves, signed in Massachusetts on September 9, was carried to Philadelphia by Paul Revere and read before the congress. In the eyes of the moderates, such declarations amounted to nothing less than an outright declaration of war, but the vote of the delegates, who included George Washington and Patrick Henry from Virginia, John Adams, John Dickinson of Pennsylvania, and Christopher Gadsden from South Carolina, was nonetheless to endorse the Suffolk Resolves. Furthermore, it was the decision of the congress to publish the text of the Resolves along with the news of their endorsement in colonial newspapers at once.

In the wake of such actions, the subsequent course of the congress was predictable. Galloway did his best, introducing a "Plan of Union of Great Britain and the Colonies" that called for the formation of a legislative association of colonies that would vote upon any act of Parliament before it could take effect, but as it seemed to yield to Parliament dominion over the colonies, only five delegations voted to approve it and the measure died.

Instead, the congress drafted a "Declaration of Rights and Grievances," which was addressed to King George, to whom the delegates professed their loyalty, yet it denied the right of Parliament to impose *any* legislation upon the colonies. The signees explained to the king that they could not submit to the acts pertaining to Massachusetts colony, nor to the Quartering Act, nor to the Quebec Act with its unfortunate establishment of the Roman Catholic religion and the dismantling of English law in favor of French law in that province. Until such time as those acts were revised or rescinded, the colonies said, they had no choice but to enter into an agreement suspending trade between the colonies and Great Britain as well as an agreement to suspend consumption of British goods and manufactures. In essence, the document cobbled together every complaint and stipulation that had accrued from the time of the Stamp Act to that moment. Despite the full force of the British government and the efforts of every loyalist in the provinces, the agenda of the Sons of Liberty now transcended local politics and became the guiding policy of the colonies as a whole.

Shortly after the declaration was drafted, the congress set about the formulation of a "Continental Association," designed to implement the provisions of the suspension of trade pact. Colonists would have to do without tea, sugar, lace and linen clothing, china, and manufactured goods such as muskets, silverware, and tools. In addition, the importation of slaves would cease. Nor would manufacturers in England any longer have access to American timber or by-products such as masts, staves, planks, turpentine, and tar. There would be no more iron, furs, wheat, corn for whiskey, rice, or tobacco, far and away the colonies' most valuable crop. Nor would there be any more of the finely wrought American ships built in Charleston and sent to Britain to become men-of-war.

Committees were to be appointed in every community in the colonies, their members charged with oversight of their neighbors. The names of any persons found in violation of the agreement would be published so that such enemies of liberty could be excommunicated from the main. In addition, local committees were authorized to form "enforcement" groups and adopt such measures as were deemed proper for enforcement of the association's aims. Though such might seem abhorrent to the modern reader familiar with the "block captains" and "building captains" common to Communist regimes, the promulgation of such extreme tactics also offers an insight into the degree of the colonists' desperation: in order to achieve liberty, it seemed understood, liberty would necessarily be curtailed.

And to ensure that all of those resolves did not go unnoticed in England, the congress capped its business by resolving to meet at a Second Continental Congress in Philadelphia on May 10, 1775. If there was not a satisfactory response to the petition by then, the colonists would meet to debate what further steps should be taken.

Of course, given the logistics of the times, all were aware that there would be no instantaneous response to those many brave actions. The resolutions of the congress would not reach London for six weeks or so. There would be a necessary period of deliberation there and another six weeks gone by before the British reply could return. Delegates knew that the new year would surely pass before they received any indication as to how their petition to His Majesty had been received.

In the meantime, the delegates traveled back to their respective communities and turned their attention to carrying out the wishes of the Congress—to the degree possible, that is. In Charleston, the "General Committee," as the Committee of Correspondence there called itself, took over most of the functions previously carried out by the colonial assembly. In due course, a Provincial Congress was formed, which then decamped from its original meeting rooms at Pike's Tavern and took over the former Assembly Room in the state house. As Henry Laurens, a planter who was slowly drifting toward the liberal side, wrote his son, the group sat and conducted its affairs in those chambers "with all the Solemnity and formality of a Constitutional parliament." As one of its first orders of business, the body quickly terminated any further suits for debt, an issue that had festered in the colony from the time that Parliament had invalidated the use of paper currency to settle such.

There was also another attempt to land tea in Charleston, when the *Britannia*, captained by Samuel Ball, Jr., arrived from London and attempted to land three chests sent to local merchants. Though it was not East India tea, it was tea nonetheless and the General Committee approached the merchants to whom the freight was consigned and advised them what would have to be done. On November 3, the merchants grudgingly boarded the *Britannia* and, as the *South-Carolina Gazette* reported in its November 21 issue, dumped the tea into the harbor "as an obligation to Neptune."

In New York, where the Committee of Fifty-one gave way to a more radical Committee of Sixty upon the return of its delegation to Philadelphia, a Committee of Inspection was formed to police ship traffic in the harbor. On February 1, 1775, the *James*, loaded with coal and various items of merchandise from London, attempted to dock at the wharf of the Quaker merchant Robert Murray. When a crowd quickly gathered to protest, the ship's captain sailed out into the bay. Eight days later, however, the *James* was back, this time accompanied by the British warship *Kingfisher*. The navy men were not about to set foot on the docks, however, and when the captain stepped ashore, he was snatched up by the protesting mob and paraded through the streets of the town until he swore to leave and never return.

Anyone else might have seen the folly of trying to run the gauntlet set up by the New York committee, but Murray, who owned an opulent home in what was then a distant suburb and is now known as Murray

Hill, was overextended. Thus he sought to land the cargo aboard a second ship, the *Beulah*, by sending a smaller boat out from New Jersey to meet the former near Staten Island. The goods were taken from the *Beulah* to Murray's warehouse in Elizabeth, but Isaac Sears, who was in charge of the Committee of Inspection, soon heard of the matter and intimidated Murray's employees into confessing their deeds.

When confronted, Murray promised to send the fabric and pepper bales he'd unloaded back to England, issue a public apology, and make a donation to a local hospital in Elizabeth. That was enough for the members of the Elizabeth committee, but Alexander McDougall wanted to make an example of the greedy Murray and his reckless disregard for the cause. At McDougall's urging, the New York Committee of Inspection announced that Murray and his business would be summarily banished from the city. At that juncture, according to a family biographer, Murray's wife wrote a letter to Sears and McDougall, appealing a decision that would unfairly place "innocent Wives and helpless children in Unspeakable Distress." Ultimately, Sears and McDougall gave in, and a neighborhood and a phone exchange in Manhattan would one day bear the family name, but more important, the dominance of the Sons in New York had been demonstrated in no uncertain terms.

In Massachusetts, owing to the presence of Governor Gage and the aforementioned four regiments of troops he had brought to garrison on the common, Samuel Adams was having a more difficult time of it. While still in Philadelphia, Adams wrote to Gage on October 10, expressing concern that the new governor was busy turning Boston into a military encampment. "It is with the deepest Concern that we observe that . . . your Excellency is erecting fortifications round the town of Boston," he wrote. "These Enormities committed by a standing Army, in our opinion, unlawfully posted there in a time of Peace, are irritating in the greatest Degree," he continued, warning that they would, if not removed, "endanger the involving [of] all America in the Horrors of a civil War!"

Such protests were to no avail, of course. In Gage's mind, war was exactly what Adams and his cohorts wanted, and he would do exactly what he felt was needed to keep the unruly population under control. Though meetings of the town assembly, the chief thorn in the governor's side, had been banned, Adams kept them going under the ruse that the gatherings were the continuation of a meeting originally convened and merely adjourned before the publication of the Governing Act. In December the town assembly appointed a sixty-two-person-strong Committee of Inspection of its own to enforce the directives of the Continental Congress, and Adams kept up a vigorous letter-writing campaign apprising the other colonies of the struggles in Massachusetts and thanking them for the continuing stream of relief supplies arriving in Boston.

But there was no sign of a softening by Gage regarding Boston. On January 29, 1775, Adams wrote to Richard Henry Lee in Virginia, saying, "We appear to be in a state of Hostility. . . . Regiments with a very few Adherents on one side & all the rest of the Inhabitants of the Province backd by all the Colonies on the other!" Still there was hope that the petition of the Continental Congress would have some effect and that "the new Parliament will reverse the Laws & measures of the old."

However, if such hopes were disappointed, he told Lee, "I am well informd that in every Part of the Province there are selected Numbers of Men, called Minute Men—that they are well disciplined & well provided—and that upon a very short Notice they will be able to assemble a formidable Army." Those Minutemen would not be the aggressors, he vowed, "but animated with an unquenchable Love of Liberty they will support their righteous Claim to it, to the utmost Extremity."

Much of the trouble in the colonies was because of the combative temperament of Gage and the meddling of former governor Hutchinson, Adams noted. The latter "has the Tongue & the Heart of a Courtier," he said, and now spent time in London spreading inflammatory lies about the colonists and their aims. "I earnestly wish that Lord North would no longer listen to the Voice of Faction," he told Lee, closing his letter not with a call to arms but with a call for reason to prevail: "If our Claims are just & reasonable they ought to concede to them."

Despite such hopes, there was not much sign of concession in

England. When the petition of the congress finally arrived in London in mid-December and the king was apprised of its contents, his reaction was swift. If such behavior kept up, he said, there would be "slaughter" in the colonies.

The petition was first delivered to Benjamin Franklin, in London, who was by now regarded as the de facto agent for all the colonies. Franklin was directed not only to lay the petition before the king but also to arrange for its publication throughout the United Kingdom. The king, however, refused to accept the document from Franklin, who was forced to deliver it to Lord Dartmouth, who in turn laid it before the king, who declared that he would turn it over to Parliament for disposition.

While this game of hot potato went on, Franklin toured the hustings of England as well as the caucus chambers of London, passing word of the colonists' proposals and attempting to lay the groundwork for a compromise that would necessarily involve repeal of the Coercive Acts. As Franklin told William Pitt during one such meeting, "The army cannot possibly answer any good purpose in Boston, but may do infinite mischief; and no accommodation can properly be proposed and entered into by the Americans, while the bayonet is at their breasts." The sentiment struck home with Pitt, who begged his fellow members in the House of Lords to join him in petitioning the king to remove the troops from Boston. Otherwise, Pitt warned his colleagues, "You will be forced to a disgraceful abandonment of present measures and principles which you avow but cannot defend."

All that was of little avail, however, for by now King George, that personage to whom even Samuel Adams and the most fervent of the Sons of Liberty pledged allegiance, had had his fill of outrageous behavior from the colonists. They would have to acknowledge the supremacy of Parliament, or else.

Although Prime Minister North and Secretary of State for the Colonies Dartmouth were engaged in secret talks with Franklin in an attempt to find some workable compromise, the two sides remained apart. Dartmouth proposed the sending of a "Peace Commission" to the colonies to consider the grievances of the citizens, but Franklin countered that such an endeavor would be of no avail unless the British first agreed that the colonies had the right to govern and tax themselves.

Meanwhile, word reached North that the king was impatient with his prime minister's shilly-shallying and that certain forces were at play within the cabinet—all champions of the authority of Parliament—to remove him from his position. Thus, at a cabinet meeting of January 12, just prior to the reconvening of Parliament, North threw off all attempts at conciliation and agreed to pursue policies that would cut off all trade with the colonies and declare all persons within the colonies not actively loyal to the crown to be rebels.

North's capitulation was a fateful step, of course, though any opposition on his part would have accomplished little. In any case, the colonial secretary was quick to follow the prime minister's lead. On January 27, Dartmouth wrote orders to Gage to arrest Samuel Adams and the rest of the leaders of the resistance in Massachusetts. Given the fact of "an actual and open Rebellion in that Province," he wrote, "the first & essential step to be taken towards re-establishing Government, would be to arrest and imprison the principal actors & abettors in the Provincial Congress (whose proceedings appear in every light to be acts of treason & rebellion)."

Gage was to move secretly and without warning, Dartmouth said, adding that the plan "can hardly fail of Success, and will perhaps be accomplished without bloodshed." It was the secretary's opinion that the inhabitants were surely unprepared to combat regular troops and in short "cannot be very formidable."

Even if such an action set off other "hostilities, it will surely be better that the Conflict should be brought on, upon such ground, than in a riper state of Rebellion." Such an operation was, in Dartmouth's opinion, "the best & most effectual means of vindicating the authority of this Kingdom."

As for the disposition of Adams and any other prisoners taken, Dartmouth left that up to Gage. Since the courts were not at present functioning, there was little hope of prosecution, but, as Dartmouth observed, "Their imprisonment however will prevent their doing any further mischief . . . and the continuance of that imprisonment will be no slight punishment."

Gage should be prepared for almost any eventuality as a result of the operation, Dartmouth warned, and he should use whatever means he thought necessary to prevail. Naval forces would be at his disposal if needed, and his conduct was to be governed "very much by your own Judgement and Discretion." Given that the charter of Massachusetts Bay colony provided that the governor declare a state of martial law "in time of actual War, Invasion or Rebellion," Dartmouth suggested that Gage was free to exercise such power, though "the Expedience and Propriety of adopting such a Measure must depend upon your own Discretion under many Circumstances that can only be judged of upon the Spot." With that, Dartmouth essentially approved the first strike of what would become a war.

23

SHOT AROUND THE WORLD

Dartmouth's letter would not reach Gage until April 16, but meantime other actions on both sides of the Atlantic gave portents as to how those orders would play out. On February 2, Prime Minister North appeared before the House of Commons to move for a declaration that Massachusetts was in fact in a state of rebellion and a reaffirmation of the sovereignty of Great Britain over all the colonies. Included was a stipulation that the king take all necessary measures to enforce the laws there. North also recommended authorization for an increase in military forces in America and an immediate cessation of trade between the colonies and Great Britain, Ireland, and the West Indies. Though there was some objection and debate, North's proposals won out by a 2-to-1 margin in the House of Commons and by 3 to 1 in the House of Lords.

About three weeks later, on February 27, North submitted two more proposals, the New England Trade and Fisheries Act—often referred to as the New England Restraining Act—and the Conciliatory Resolution. The former was a punitive measure that forbade the colonies from trading with any nation other than Great Britain and also declared the lucrative North Atlantic fishing grounds, claimed by England, off-limits to fishermen of all the northeastern colonies, a genuinely crippling move.

The Conciliatory Resolution, on the other hand, actually sounded like the stuff of the Continental Congress's dreams, for it provided for the removal of all taxes and duties from any colony that agreed to submit its rightful portion of the monies necessary for the maintenance of the common defense and the functioning of the civil government and court system. The colonies would be left to devise their own scheme of raising the funds and would thus be "voluntarily" bearing their fair share of such expenses.

There was more to the proposal than met the eye, however, for the true intent of the resolution, addressed not to the Continental Congress but to individual colonies, was to entice the more moderate provinces into a contest against such radical enclaves as Virginia and Massachusetts and thus break the resolve of the Continental Congress. By the time the news of the resolution reached the colonies, however, such blandishments would fall far short of convincing even moderates of any good intentions on the part of the mother country.

Meanwhile, in the colonies, the degree of strength apparent in the common resolve varied by locale. In New York, the state assembly balked at reconstituting itself as a Provincial Congress and actually voted down the various resolves of the Continental Congress by a small margin. When that body also refused to select delegates for the second congress, scheduled for May, the Committee of Sixty took matters into its own hands and in early March convened a public meeting of concerned citizens for the purpose of selecting congressional representatives, a matter it quickly concluded.

As debate on the elections ensued, the *Rivington's Gazette* of March 9 printed an account submitted by two men, William Cunningham and John Hill, complaining that scarcely had they arrived upon the grounds of the liberty pole to watch a boxing match when they were approached by a group of men who took exception to remarks the pair had made in favor of the king at one of the committee's meetings earlier in the day. Before long the two were surrounded by as many as two hundred men, who then dragged Cunningham to the pole, forced him onto his knees, and demanded that he "damn his Popish king George."

Instead, Cunningham said, he blurted, "God bless King George," whereupon he was dragged about the green, his clothes were torn off, and he was relieved of his watch. The same indignities were about to be visited on Hill, the complainants said, when a justice of the peace arrived with a group of deputies to rescue them.

On March 1, Charles Pinckney wrote to Sears and Lamb on behalf of the South Carolina committee to commiserate on the unfortunate circumstances faced by the Sons in New York. It was a disappointment to hear that the state assembly would not join the association, Pinckney said, but he wanted Sears and Lamb to know that South Carolina did not see it as a repudiation. Though Pinckney observed that "we cannot but think it would have been much more happy for the whole," had the New York Assembly gone along, he and his colleagues in the South were well aware of "the poison that is daily distilling from some of your pensioned presses, and the hireling writers that have crept in among you."

New York had for so long been a haven for "placemen, of contractors, of officers, and needy dependants upon the Crown" that a certain difficulty in achieving unanimity of purpose was to be expected. Nonetheless, the South Carolinians assured their counterparts, "love to Constitutional Liberty, to justice, and your posterity, however depressed for a little while, will at last surmount all obstacles, and do honour to New York." Pinckney did, however, press his fellow New Yorkers for some proof of that province's commitment to the cause, in order that the face of unity might be maintained. Pinckney's concerns vanished when word arrived that a New York delegation to the second congress had in fact been selected.

At the same time, Gadsden, Pinckney, and their fellow Sons were facing their own troubles in South Carolina. Though a Provincial Congress and Committee of Correspondence had been established, during debate on the trade boycott the influential planter John Rutledge had introduced a provision that would allow for the continuing export of rice to Great Britain. It was all well and good for the northerners to declare an end to exports, Rutledge argued, for they shipped out little. An end to the export of the staple crop of South Carolina, however, would lead to the collapse of the province's economy. Though Gadsden and other radicals vigorously opposed the exemption, the state congress voted by its pocketbook, and rice was approved for export.

Another flare-up took place in Charleston in March, when a planter returned aboard ship from a visit to England, bringing with him a consignment of horses, silver plate, and furniture that he intended for use at his plantation. Though the initial decision of Gadsden and the committee was to allow the landing of the horses, given that no mention of livestock had been made in the provisions of the Continental Association, the mechanics of the town protested, fearful that artists and skilled workers and craftsmen would end up bearing the brunt of the boycott if matters continued to be interpreted so. After heated debate, it was determined by a vote of 35 to 34 that horses and all would have to be returned to England.

Meanwhile, in Virginia, difficulties escalated between the newly formed Provincial Congress and Lord Dunmore, who had held the post of governor since being ignominiously shuffled off from New York in 1771. Dunmore's relations with his constituents were very nearly as contentious as Hutchinson's were in New York, and he had dissolved the House of Burgesses on more than one occasion during his tenure.

On March 20, 1775, while suffering under a prolonged order of dissolution by Dunmore, the House of Burgesses convened in Richmond, where Patrick Henry introduced a measure calling for the establishment of a state militia. When more moderate interests opposed the measure, Henry rose to deliver what is generally referred to as the most influential of all prorevolutionary speeches, inspired in large part by the experiences of the biblical prophet Jeremiah, who was told by God, "Attack you they may, overcome you they cannot."

Colonel Edward Carrington, listening outside a window of the church where the burgesses were meeting, wrote that Henry's oration had been so transcendent that he thought no experience was ever likely to exceed it. "Right here I wish to be buried," he said. Another reported that he had been "*sick* with excitement."

The references are, of course, to the famed speech that closed with the valiant assertion "Almighty God! I know not what course others may take, but as for me, give me liberty or give me death!" Henry's words, since immortalized, are credited with swinging a close majority of the burgesses, including Thomas Jefferson and George Washington, into agreement on the proposal to call troops to arms.

Considerable controversy has risen regarding the speech, owing to the fact that Henry kept no copy and, once again, no transcription was made of his remarks at the meeting. Galvanizing as all those who were there agree it was, it was nearly forty years later before Henry's biographer William Wirt made an attempt to reconstruct the remarks from the recollections of bystanders. Adding to the difficulty that the intervening years had intensified, Wirt found himself up against an issue often cited by those who found themselves under the famed orator's spell. As Thomas Jefferson explained it, "It was difficult to tell when [Henry] had spoken, to tell what he had said. . . . When he had spoken in opposition to my opinion, had produced a great effect, and I myself had been highly delighted and moved, I have asked myself, when he ceased, 'What the devil has he said?' and could never answer the inquiry."

There were those who recalled the speech in far more unflattering terms. The Tory James Parker wrote a loyalist friend that the speech had been an insolent offense: "He called the K—— a Tyrant, a fool, a puppet and a tool to the ministry." Parker added that Henry had characterized Britons as a set of spoiled wretches who "had lost their native courage and [were] unable to look the brave Americans in the face." Still, there seems little doubt that Henry closed his speech—directed as much at the less stalwart of his own colleagues as at the British, it should be noted—with some version of the stirring phrase.

Such moments and contests large and small might have continued indefinitely had it not been for the eventual arrival of the secret orders from Lord Dartmouth to Gage. The *Essex Gazette* of April 18 noted that the British ship *Nautilus* had arrived in Boston on Friday, April 14, bearing "dispatches for His Excellency" and that same issue reported the arrival of the *Falcon* on April 16.

As it turned out, the *Nautilus* was actually carrying a duplicate of the orders Dartmouth dispatched to Gage. His lordship's original letter was aboard the second ship to arrive. In any event, Gage now possessed authorization for the highly provocative operation that he himself had first suggested to the colonial secretary. As early as January 18, the governor had told Dartmouth that it was his opinion that "if a respectable force is seen in the field, the most obnoxious leaders seized, and a pardon proclaimed for all others, Government will come off victorious." Though Dartmouth would not be able to promise Gage the power to issue the pardons for some time, for the first time in the history of the conflict, a British commander was given the go-ahead to use force against the colonists.

Meanwhile, Samuel Adams, John Hancock, and the other "obnoxious" leaders of the resistance had been meeting since April 11 with the Provincial Congress in Concord, about twenty miles northwest of Boston, where they would be free of interference by Gage. Though Adams and Hancock were arguing there for the establishment of a militia in perhaps the most contentious of the colonies, it became a tough sell.

There was little money available for the purpose, and for all that had taken place, many in Massachusetts, as in Virginia, were not convinced that armed resistance was necessary or advisable, even though correspondence from London had recently arrived announcing that there would be no conciliation; in fact, the dispatches warned, the British were sending troops to quash what was officially termed "an open state of rebellion." Yet the most that Hancock and Adams were able to coax out of their Congress was a small amount for the stockpiling of supplies and a resolution of April 15 that proclaimed the upcoming day of May 11 as one of "Public Humiliation, Fasting and Prayer," in order that the people of Great Britain—and especially their rulers—might "have their Eyes open'd to them."

Though a number of accounts insist that the moment Gage read the fateful orders from the colonial secretary he set upon the design of a mission to apprehend Adams and Hancock in Concord, there is little evidence for that. During the Concord meetings, Adams and Hancock were actually staying in Lexington, five miles to the southeast, at the home of the Reverend Jonas Clarke, a fact of which Gage, who had an informant planted within the Provincial Congress, was well aware. With the frustrating session at Concord now concluded, the pair saw no reason to return to heavily fortified Boston. They planned to stay with Clarke in Lexington for a few more days before traveling directly to Philadelphia for the Second Continental Congress in May.

Still, it was apparent that something was up in Boston. Paul Revere had formed his own surveillance team made up of fellow mechanics from the city, and each night small groups patrolled the streets of Boston to keep an eye on what the troops were up to. Revere and his men noted that a number of small transport boats attached to the warships in the harbor had been hauled out of the water for repair and returned to the mother ships just before midnight on Saturday, April 15. Furthermore, Revere said, all the light infantrymen and assault troops had been removed from their normal duty stations. When he reported the news to Dr. Joseph Warren, who had stayed on in Boston, Warren suggested that Revere ride to Lexington on Sunday to let Adams and Hancock know.

When Revere delivered his report to Adams, the longtime activist realized that the moment he had long foreseen was at hand. Though he could not be sure just what Gage intended, it was clear that a British assault of some sort was imminent. Neither he nor Hancock would have assumed that they would be the targets of any sizable force, as was suggested by the number of boats and size of the force reported by Revere. Any attempt to take the two of them would have been more likely a stealthy enterprise involving a few men. It was more likely, Adams and Hancock reasoned, that Gage intended to move on Concord for the purposes of confiscating what munitions and supplies the Committee of Safety had managed to gather. Accordingly, they sent word to have the shot, powder, muskets, tools, and foodstuffs dispersed and hidden about the community of Concord. Then, while Adams and Hancock deliberated their next moves, Revere was dispatched back to Boston to keep watch. Should he observe any movement of troops out of the city, it would be his duty to ride ahead to Lexington and Concord and spread the alarm.

Revere, dedicated Son that he was, eagerly accepted the charge. Still he was a cautious man, troubled by the fact that word of a number of his detail's covert activities was inexplicably finding its way back to General Gage. What if someone were to learn that he was the messenger meant to warn Adams of the troop movement and decide upon a way to prevent his riding out? Or what if he was somehow delayed on his way to Lexington and Concord—crossing the sandbar-laden Charles could be a tricky proposition, particularly in the dark. Thus, on his way back to the city, Revere stopped in Charlestown to confer with Sons there on a backup plan.

The moment he observed troops moving in Boston, Revere told his counterparts on the north bank of the Charles, he would give a signal: "If the British went out by Water [directly across the Charles], we would shew two Lanthorns in the North Church Steeple; and if by Land [marching across the Boston Neck to the southwest], one."

Though what ensued has become the stuff of every American schoolchild's catechism, Revere's part in history went largely unknown for the better part of the ensuing century. In the immediate aftermath of subsequent events, the silversmith was called to provide a deposition of his actions for the town assembly, and in the late 1790s Revere provided a lengthy account in a well-written letter to a friend. But it would fall to Henry Wadsworth Longfellow, with a poem published in 1861, to make a rather unassuming workingman into an icon: "Listen, my children, and you shall hear / Of the midnight ride of Paul Revere." Thus did a Boston silversmith become a hero of a revolution.

At about ten o'clock on Tuesday night, April 18, Revere was summoned from his home by Dr. Warren and informed that a significant number of troops had been observed marching from the common. They were on their way to boats deployed on the banks of the Charles, and Revere should ride at once to Lexington with the news. He would not be the only rider, moreover, for Warren had already dispatched another man, William Dawes, along the overland route. "Two lanthorns" would be hoisted in the North Episcopal steeple, Warren assured Revere, but meantime he was to be on his way.

Friends rowed the silversmith across the river, where he picked up "a very good horse" and was also told that ten well-armed British officers had been spotted just after sunset preceding him up the Lexington road. If that fact concerned him, Revere made no mention of it. He thanked the safety man who'd provided the information and set out quickly for Lexington.

By then it was eleven o'clock on a clear and pleasant night, with enough moonlight to show Revere his way. He was not far past Charlestown Common when he saw two men on horseback waiting beside the road under a tree. Revere was almost upon the pair when he realized that they were part of the British detail that the safety man had warned him about. One of the officers spurred his mount forward, cutting off Revere's path, and the other came straight for him.

Revere, who knew the terrain well, cut abruptly from the road and through the countryside, with the second officer in close pursuit. As Revere skirted a bog on his way toward the northbound Medford road ahead, he heard a shout and a curse from behind him. The second officer had guided his horse straight into the clay pond Revere knew about and was now hopelessly mired in it.

Revere rode on without further interference to Medford, about midway to Lexington, where he roused the captain of the local Minutemen and advised him that troops were marching out from Boston, then headed on to Lexington, shouting out warnings at every settlement along the way. At Lexington, Revere made his way to Reverend Clarke's house, where he found Adams and Hancock and shared word of the detachment on its way. It was all news to the officers—Dawes, the first rider who'd been sent out, had not yet arrived.

While Revere was readying himself to ride on to Concord to help secure the stores, Dawes finally arrived and the two set out together, along with a third rider, Dr. Samuel Prescott, whom Revere described as a "High Son of Liberty." Revere warned his companions of the likelihood that they might be intercepted by others of the detail of officers, and hardly had he spoken of it than they topped a rise to find four men on horses blocking the road. All were armed with pistols and swords, Revere saw, and he guided his two companions off the road into a nearby pasture at a gallop.

Dr. Prescott veered off, jumping his horse over a stone wall. As he disappeared into the night, headed in the direction of Concord, Revere urged his own mount toward a woods up ahead. If he made it to that cover, he might lose their pursuers, he was thinking, when suddenly six horsemen burst from the trees and surrounded him, ordering him to dismount.

One of the officers leveled his pistol at Revere's forehead, demanding to know his name and his business. He'd blow the silversmith's brains out, he said, unless he got straight answers. Revere made no secret of what he'd been doing. The troops out of Boston had run aground in the middle of the Charles River, though, he told the officer, and there were five hundred Minutemen on their way to Concord as they spoke.

The officer ordered Revere searched, then had him placed back on his horse. They were riding back to Lexington, Revere was told, and if he attempted to escape, he'd be shot. About a mile outside Lexington, the mount of one of the grenadiers began to tire, and the commanding officer ordered the procession to a halt. "Take that man's horse," the captain said, pointing at Revere, who had little choice but to dismount.

He waited until the soldiers were gone, then hurried off across the fields to Reverend Clarke's house to alert Adams and Hancock, who hastily talked things over. Perhaps the troops were set on apprehending them and perhaps they weren't, but it seemed that a retreat to the nearby town of Woburn, about four miles to the east, was the wisest course.

Revere accompanied the pair to the home of a fellow Liberty Boy in Woburn and made sure the two were settled, then set back out with a man named Lowell for the Lexington Meeting House, where Hancock had left a trunk full of the Provincial Congress's papers. By the time Revere and Lowell reached the Lexington Tavern, it was almost dawn. He and Lowell went up to Hancock's chambers to retrieve the papers, when they heard a great commotion outside and glanced out the windows to see six companies of British troops, more than seven hundred men, marching toward the common.

Revere and Lowell hurried out of the tavern with the trunk, weaving their way through the ranks of local Minutemen who were rushing to draw a line of defense at Lexington Common. Revere and Lowell were scarcely a hundred yards from the tavern, on their way to hide the congress's papers at the home of Reverend Clarke, when they paused to survey the scene behind them. "British Troops appeard on both Sides of the Meeting-House," Revere said. "In their Front was an Officer on Horse back. They made a Short Halt; when I saw, and heard, a Gun fired, which appeared to be a Pistol. Then I could distinguish two Guns, and then a Continual roar of Musquetry."

Thereupon, they made off with the trunk.

24

THE CONQUEROR SILENT SLEEPS

What Revere overheard that dawn so many years ago was in fact "the shot heard round the world" later immortalized by Ralph Waldo Emerson in his "Concord Hymn," a poem written in 1836 for the dedication of a monument to the Sons of Liberty who had died in Lexington and Concord on that day in 1775. And the ensuing "roar of musquetry" that Revere described would continue for six and a half years, until October 17, 1781, when General Charles Cornwallis surrendered his troops at Yorktown, signaling that a new nation, indivisible, would at last be formed.

The record of the more than two hundred battles that ensued and the significant political events that punctuated them, including the signing of the Declaration of Independence and the adoption of the Articles of Confederation, have filled hundreds, perhaps thousands, of books large and small, and the books continue to come despite the observations mentioned at the outset of this one. Even the briefest summary of all that would transpire in the half-dozen years following Lexington and Concord is not only far beyond the scope of this book but outside its intention as well.

The intent from the outset has been to record the efforts of a group of men who avowed in their 1766 Constitution "to persevere to the last in the vindication of our dear bought Rights and Privileges" and to follow the inextricable sequence of events propelled by these patriots from the chill January night when a Dutch placeman was "corrected," through the struggles as diverse as those in New York City, Boston, Providence, and Charleston, up until the night one of the most dedicated Sons of all risked his life to ride out and warn the men whose mission he treasured above all else.

As it turned out, and despite the authorization that Lord Dartmouth provided for the capture of those "obnoxious leaders," Gage held no designs upon John Hancock or Samuel Adams when he sent his troops out from Boston under cover of darkness. His orders to Lieutenant Colonel Francis Smith, commander of His Majesty's 10th Regiment of foot soldiers, were explicit in their focus:

Sir:

Having received intelligence, that a quantity of ammunition, provision, artillery, tents and small arms, have been collected at Concord, for the avowed purpose of raising and supporting a rebellion against his majesty, you will march with the corps of grenadiers and light infantry, put under your command, with the utmost expedition and secrecy to Concord, where you will seize arms, and all military stores whatever. But you will take care that the soldiers do not plunder the inhabitants, or hurt private property.

Your most obedient humble servant
Thomas Gage

Accordingly, the troops went out of Boston on the evening of April 18, preceded by an advance party of Royal Marines under the command of Major John Pitcairn. As that contingent neared Lexington, Pitcairn was met by the officers who had earlier arrested and interrogated Paul Revere. There were five hundred armed militiamen waiting in Lexington, he was advised, and more were on the way.

As Pitcairn considered his strategy, two of his scouts galloped back to the place where the column was halted. They had just encountered a colonist near Lexington, they said, and the man had raised his musket to fire at them. The weapon had misfired, and neither of the scouts had been injured, but the intent of the enemy was clear.

At that Pitcairn ordered his men to load their own weapons and fix their bayonets. The order did not signify an intent to attack, but it would have been more than imprudent of Pitcairn to do otherwise. By the time that his troops were readied, Colonel Smith and his men had caught up with them. Pitcairn advised his superior of the situation in Lexington and finally turned to order his own troops forward. On no account was any man to fire unless given the order to do so, he called out, and then his men were on the move.

As the British troops readied their final approach to Lexington, a colonial scout galloped into the town to spread the alarm. The redcoats were only minutes away, he advised John Parker, the captain of the local militia. Parker nodded, then turned to issue orders for his men to fall in on the common. After ten years of escalating tensions, it seemed, the time to fight had arrived.

When Pitcairn rode into Lexington at dawn, accompanied by a small group of cavalrymen, he would have been heartened at what he saw. Instead of five hundred Minutemen, there were perhaps a hundred arrayed upon the green and before the tavern, clearly no match for his party should it come to fighting. He brought the mounted group to a halt at the west side of the field, waiting while the foot soldiers approached the tavern and green from the east.

As the marching column quickly reassembled itself into the familiar line-of-battle formation favored by British tacticians, Pitcairn called out to the Minutemen, "Lay down your arms."

According to most accounts, a number of Minutemen took a look at the British troops, who vastly outnumbered them, and complied, some quickly, some after a moment of hesitation. Others, however, held their ground and their weapons. What happened from that point on varies, according to what side the reports come from.

Captain Parker, in his report, stated that he called the militia to Lexington common at about one in the morning of April 19 to discuss reports that British troops were on their way. Parker said that the agreement of all the men was to "not meddle or make with said Regular Troops unless they should insult us."

When the troops did arrive in Lexington, Parker said, "upon their sudden approach, I immediately ordered our Militia to disperse and not to fire." According to Parker, his advice was of no avail: "Immediately Said Troops made their appearance and rushed furiously, [and] fired . . . without receiving any provocation therefore from us." There were a number of other depositions offered by townsmen, all agreeing that it was not a militiaman who had fired the first shot and a number insisting that it had come from the pistol of a British officer.

It will come as no surprise that Major Pitcairn saw things somewhat differently. In his report to Gage, he says that once he was advised that several hundred men were gathered in Lexington to prevent his party's march to Concord and that his advance scouts had been fired on, he readied his troops but ordered them "on no account to fire, or even attempt it without orders."

When he approached within a hundred yards or so of the rebels, he said, he noticed a number of those who had ignored his order to lay down their arms running to take cover behind a set of stone walls on his formation's right flank. "I instantly called to the soldiers not to fire, but surround and disarm them," Pitcairn said, adding that he repeated his orders several times, to no avail. "Some of the rebels who had jumped over the wall, fired four or five shots at the soldiers, which wounded a man of the Tenth, and my horse was wounded in two places . . . and at the same time several shots were fired from a Meeting House on our left."

It was the beginning of the roar that would send Paul Revere and his man Lowell dashing for cover at the good reverend's. "Upon this without any order or regularity," Pitcairn said, "the Light Infantry began a scattered fire, and continued in that situation for some little time, contrary to the repeated orders of both me and other officers that were present." Most of the other accounts from British soldiers present agree with Pitcairn's rendition, differing primarily in terms of the degree of carnage that resulted.

Following Pitcairn's repeated orders to disperse, said Jeremy Lister, one of the foot soldiers, "they gave us a fire then ran off to get behind a wall. We had one man wounded of our Company in the leg. . . . Major

Pitcairn's horse was shot in the flank. We returned their salute, and before we proceed on our march from Lexington, I believe we kill'd and wounded either seven or eight men."

Another solder of the 10th Regiment, Henry de Berniere, said that he heard Pitcairn issue his order to the militiamen to lay down their weapons and disperse at least two times: "But to no purpose, upon which he ordered our light infantry to advance and disarm them, which they were doing when one of the rebels fired a shot, our soldiers returned the fire and killed about fourteen of them, there was only one man of the Tenth light infantry received a shot through the leg. Some of them got into a church and fired from it, but were soon drove out."

Though the fighting was brief it was intense, and it was deadly. Ten Minutemen lay dead on Lexington Common and nine more were injured. They were the first official casualties of the Revolutionary War.

As Private Lister's report suggests, with the Lexington militia routed, Pitcairn and his men were soon on their way to Concord, which had been the object of their march all along. They were joined there by reinforcements that had marched across Boston Neck under Lord Percy, and raiding parties were soon formed to scour homes and nearby farms for munitions and stores of foods, a task that proved largely futile. One party found a pair of small cannon, which they quickly disabled, but for the most part, the reputed stores seemed to have vanished.

The search took time, however, and word of the outrage in Lexington spread about the countryside as swiftly as any ever had. Before long, a force of Minutemen that the British estimated at more than 1,000 ringed the hills above Concord. Though about half of the British troops who were garrisoned in Boston—1,800 or so—had by now arrived in Concord, it was clear that serious resistance was at hand.

As a British force guarding the north bridge entrance to Concord began a withdrawal to the center of the town, American forces moved upon them, opening a withering fire. Four British officers and three infantrymen were killed, and five wounded. It was the beginning of a panicked retreat of the exhausted British forces along the unfamiliar, dusty roads back to Boston, a movement that was marked by intense fighting on both sides and led to the deaths of any number of unsuspecting civilians caught in the cross fire between snipers and regulars or suffering the frustrations of enraged British soldiers.

One account tells of William Marcy, the village idiot of Cambridge, sitting happily on a stone wall along the road to Boston and wishing the sullen retreating troops a good day. In the next instant there was a muzzle flash from within the ranks and Marcy toppled off his perch with a musket ball between his eyes.

As one soldier wrote of the experience, "I never broke my fast for forty-eight hours, for we carried no provisions. I had my hat shot off my head three times. Two balls went through my coat, and carried away my bayonet from my side."

All in all it was a deadly day, with some fifty Americans killed and forty-one wounded. As for the British, what had begun propitiously in Lexington turned disastrous by the time the troops dragged themselves back to the banks of the Charles, desperate to regain the safety of their fort. Seventy-three were dead and some two hundred more were wounded.

George Washington would later write that had the British not rushed back to Boston so fearfully that day, they would have been cut off by other Minutemen and the entire force would probably have surrendered. And, indeed, had the British lost a tenth of the entire fighting force stationed in the colonies on the first day of military engagement, perhaps the six and a half years of fighting that ensued and the thousands of lives lost might have been saved.

But as it was, and as bad as it was, April 19 was only the beginning. Soon Boston was surrounded, and the siege of the city would last for nearly a year, until March 17, 1776, when British Commander William Howe, after a long stalemate with the newly constituted Continental Army commanded by George Washington, finally withdrew his troops to Nova Scotia. The war that had so many times been foreshadowed was at last under way.

◆　◆　◆

In a letter from Philadelphia of June 28 to his wife, Betsy, in Boston, Samuel Adams wrote of an engagement that had been described to him between troops and the "Rebel Army" in the Boston suburb of Charlestown. "I cannot but be greatly rejoycd at the tried Valor of our Countrymen, who by all Accounts behavd with an Intrepiditry becoming those who fought for their Liberities against the mercenary Soldiers of a Tyrant," he told her.

Furthermore, it was painful for him to imagine her fear at hearing "the Noise of War" so near her. He added, "I pray to God to cover the heads of our Countrymen in every day of Battle, and ever to protect you from Injury in these distracted times," and confided that he felt great affliction at the death of their good friend Dr. Warren, who had been killed while defending against a British advance on Breed's Hill on June 17. Though he had been commissioned a general in the Massachusetts militia, Warren had taken a place in the bunkers alongside all the other common soldiers who kept the British contained in Boston.

From the outset, however, Adams had not seemed daunted by the ultimate cost of the conflict. One contemporary scribe reported that he turned to John Hancock at the moment following receipt of the news from Lexington to say, "O! what a glorious morning is this." And indeed he did rejoice that the citizens of Massachusetts had responded to the call to arms issued by the Continental Congress, even if they had, in his words, been "driven to Resistance through Necessity." In any case, it was his unequivocal pronouncement that his compatriots might at last "justly claim the Support of the confederated Colonies."

Of course, any reader who can appreciate the tragedy of a simpleminded boy being shot dead off a wall for the crime of a cheery hello to a group of passing soldiers—or one who laments the folly of war in general—might have reservations about the propriety of any man's "rejoicing" over such a conflict's beginning. But Adams would not be the first activist to point out that there comes a time when it is clear that polite and peaceful petition to an oppressive master will not serve to bring about meaningful change. In the final analysis, as Malcolm X declared in his 1963 *Message to the Grassroots*, "You haven't got a revolution that doesn't involve bloodshed." Certainly, Adams would over time be reviled as an ultimate propagandist and rabble-rouser, but at the same time he is identified by many as the one individual above all who guided the country to a revolution that is alternately regarded as glorious, bloody, and inevitable.

25

SHADE OF PARADISE

On June 12, 1775, during the early days of the Siege of Boston, General Gage issued a proclamation meant to put an end to the armed conflict. "I avail myself of the last effort within the bounds of my duty, to spare the effusion of blood," he said, "to offer, and I do hereby in his Majesty's name, offer and promise, his most gracious pardon in all who shall forthwith lay down their arms, and return to the duties of peaceable subjects, excepting only from the benefit of such pardon, Samuel Adams and John Hancock, whose offences are of too flagitious a natur."

Gage's supercilious offer only hardened the resolve of those who had taken up arms, but it also announced to the world at last, and in no uncertain terms, the identity of the most effective Sons of Liberty in the American colonies. Gage's backhanded designation was hardly the only recognition of Samuel Adams's contributions. Comparing him to the helmsman of the Trojan warship, Thomas Jefferson would declare some fifty years later, "If there was any Palinurus to the Revolution, Samuel Adams was the man. Indeed, in the Eastern States, for a year or two after it began, he was truly the *Man of the Revolution.*"

For all that, after the war began Adams would become very much a backroom politician. (As Pauline Maier has pointed out, many studies of Samuel Adams have fixated on the rather shortsighted observation that his career climaxed in 1776.) Though active as a behind-the-scenes facilitator at the Second Continental Congress, he assumed no office there. Though he was a supporter and signer of the Declaration of Independence, the voluminous scribe's part in its creation was chiefly advisory, though he did serve as the Massachusetts representative on the

committee that drafted the Articles of Confederation, the loosely circumscribed precursor to the strongly federalist U.S. Constitution composed ten years later.

In late 1781, Adams left the Continental Congress and returned to
Boston to reenter the world of Massachusetts politics, though that time
he was attempting to refine the procedures of a new form of government, not prod his peers to battle. By that time Samuel Adams had also
fallen out with his old ally and now Massachusetts governor John Hancock, owing in large part to what the self-effacing Adams considered
extravagant, self-aggrandizing behavior on the latter's part. And later,
during the debate on the new U.S. Constitution, Adams further marginalized himself as a staunch opponent of the move toward a strong
central government. The effort reinvigorated his interest in national
politics, however, and his tireless work to amend what he considered a
flawed document led to the formulation of the Bill of Rights in 1791 and,
along the way, a rapprochement with Hancock.

In 1789, Adams was elected to serve under Hancock as lieutenant
governor of the state, a development that would surely have chagrined
Thomas Gage had he been alive to witness it: the two men he blamed
above all for his woes were now the lawfully elected leaders of his former colony. Gage, recalled in disgrace to England shortly after the
disastrous Battle of Bunker Hill in the early days of the Siege of Boston, died in 1787. He was preceded in his journey to the shades by a
fellow former governor and another legendary foe of Adams, Thomas
Hutchinson, who died in 1780 in London, where he had continued to
serve as a largely marginalized adviser to the British government and
work on his epic *History of the Province of Massachusetts Bay*, the
third and final volume of which was published posthumously in 1828.

Adams would assume the most significant political office of his life
in 1793, at the age of seventy-one, when Hancock died and Adams ascended to the governorship. The following year, he was elected to the
post in his own right, the first of four annual terms he would serve. In
the first ever contested presidential election, that of 1796, he was selected by fifteen members of the Virginia delegation in a move to place

him as vice president to his fellow anti-Federalist Thomas Jefferson, but the staunch Federalist John Adams won the election handily, and Jefferson, under the system that was then used, became vice president as the second-place finisher.

At the end of his gubernatorial term in 1797, Samuel Adams finally retired from politics, so afflicted with the condition of essential tremor that he could no longer write. He died on October 2, 1803, at the age of eighty-one, the old Puritan eulogized in the Boston press as "The Father of the American Revolution."

Of the several "old radicals" so prominent in the early days of the formation of the Sons of Liberty—and excepting perhaps the two-time governors Patrick Henry of Virginia and the more moderate John Hancock in Massachusetts—Samuel Adams had, by most accounts, the most significant postrevolutionary political career. Yet even that later success came to him grudgingly and nearly by default. The fact is that Samuel Adams was not a politician or a bureaucrat but a zealot; in terms of his public life, he viewed himself not so much as an individual but as the embodiment of an idea, and as such he was far more suited for the work of toppling an oppressive government than for the comparatively dull business of building and maintaining a better one.

Of course the other prime movers of the American rebellion— among them James Otis, Christopher Gadsden, Isaac Sears, and John Lamb—command their fair share of pages in the more obscure annals, but despite the courage they displayed at a time long before a war was declared, before public opinion swung unequivocally their way, before it was deemed politically correct to don a uniform and take up arms against the oppressor, it is chiefly the aficionados of history who recognize their names today.

Washington, Jefferson, Madison, and Franklin deserve their accolades, just as Philadelphia can justly lay claim to the sobriquet "birthplace of liberty." But it is just as truthful to say that the American Revolution was birthed on a chill night in 1766 in Albany, New York, and that Samuel Adams is in fact the real "Father of his Country."

It is a commonplace that history is written by the victors, but it is a lesser recognized corollary that the most popular of those histories are those most vigorously promulgated by the new regime in charge. In comparison with the actions of the Sons of Liberty, for instance, Benjamin Franklin and his city, said to have cradled liberty, actually came a bit late to the party.

In fact, Franklin was on board a ship bound for the colonies the day fighting broke out in Lexington and Concord. He had endured a very difficult time in London since accusations had surfaced regarding his role in circulating the Hutchinson-Whately letters, his reputation among the British forever sullied by a vicious attack concerning the matter by Solicitor General Alexander Wedderburn before the Privy Council in late January 1774.

Franklin arrived in Philadelphia on May 5, 1775, only to learn that the long-threatened war had begun and he was to be Pennsylvania's delegate to the Second Continental Congress, where his most celebrated contributions as a statesman would begin. He was a member of the Committee of Five deputed to draft the Declaration of Independence and served as minister to France from 1776 to 1785, during which time he would negotiate the Treaty of Paris in 1783.

As for James Otis, the onetime confidant of Samuel Adams and sometimes credited with coining the phrase that formed the backbone of rebellion, "No taxation without representation," his public life essentially came to an end following the ill-fated coffeehouse tussle with tax man John Robinson in 1769. In the wake of his death in 1783, it was widely reported that he had previously written his sister, Mercy Otis Warren, "My dear sister, I hope, when God Almighty in his righteous providence shall take me out of time into eternity that it will be by a flash of lightning." Though no copy of that alleged letter remains, this much is certain: Otis, by then adjudged "harmlessly insane," was standing in the doorway of his caretaker friend's house in Andover on an otherwise bright May afternoon in 1783 when a bolt from a lone dark cloud passing overhead struck him dead.

Christopher Gadsden, often called the "Samuel Adams of the South," attended the Second Continental Congress as a member of the South

Carolina delegation but left in 1776 to assume command of the state's
military forces, repulsing a British attack on Charleston in 1778.
Shortly after, he was appointed vice president (lieutenant governor) of
South Carolina, a post he held for two years, until the British captured
Charleston and remanded Gadsden to prison at the old Spanish fort of
Castillo de San Marcos in Saint Augustine, Florida.

Refusing various blandishments offered by the British, Gadsden
spent forty-two weeks in solitary confinement there, until he was finally
paroled to Philadelphia. He eventually returned to South Carolina and
served in its House of Representatives, though his deteriorating health,
exacerbated by his prison confinement, prevented any significant role
in the new government. He died after a fall in Charleston in 1805, at
the age of eighty-one, and is perhaps best known today for his creation
of the "Don't Tread on Me" rattlesnake flag, which he presented to the
first commander in chief of the U.S. Navy, Commodore Esek Hopkins.

The firebrand privateer Isaac Sears remained in New York following the Battle of Lexington, serving as the commander of that city's
militia until Washington's army arrived in June 1775. In one of his
more celebrated actions, he led a raiding party that November on the
offices of the Tory-controlled *Rivington's Royal Gazette*, destroying
the press and melting its lead into bullets for the revolutionary troops.
When the British captured the city in 1777, Sears fled to Massachusetts, where he resumed a profitable career as a privateer. He returned
to New York in 1783 when the British withdrew, living in grand style
in a mansion off Bowling Green and reestablishing himself in local
politics. A series of questionable financial transactions put him deep
into debt and led to his fleeing the city in 1786, whereupon he became
involved in a trading venture to China. He contracted a fever and
died in Canton on October 28, 1786.

John Lamb, along with Sears one of the original founders of the
New York Sons of Liberty, was also active in the early revolutionary
resistance in New York. As the commander of the militia's artillery
company, on August 23, 1775, he led a midnight raiding party intent on

capturing the twenty-one British cannon installed on the Battery, at the city's southern tip. They had hauled off eleven of the cannon before a man-of-war anchored nearby spotted them and began a barrage on the city that would end with a third of the population of 25,000 fleeing the island in terror.

Though that mission ended in a standoff, Lamb continued to serve as an artillery officer in the Continental Army with distinction and was appointed a brigadier general by the war's end. As a reward for his service, he was named the first customs collector of the Port of New York, a post he held until 1797, when the newly elected president, John Adams, removed him after a deputy was accused of embezzling tax revenues. Lamb, along with Samuel Adams, Isaac Sears, and many others among the original Sons of Liberty, maintained a staunch states'-rights, anti-federalist stance to the very end. He died in poverty on May 31, 1800.

Though the intrepid rider and messenger Paul Revere never aspired to a position of leadership within the ranks of the revolutionaries, he would become, after Hancock, the most enduringly successful businessman of them all. He served a somewhat controversial career as an infantry major during the war, then, after weathering charges of insubordination, returned to Boston to open a hardware supply store. Eventually, he established an iron and brass foundry in the city, becoming renowned as a caster of church bells and eventually a major supplier of ships' hardware and fittings. As the nineteenth century dawned, Revere opened the first copper mill in the United States, the Revere Copper Company, which endures to this day. Revere, whose business interests led him to the federalist position after the war, died in 1818 in Boston at the age of eighty-three and is buried in the Granary Cemetery, along with his former compatriots Samuel Adams and Isaac Sears.

Whether these men and the countless others who identified themselves as Sons of Liberty and Liberty Boys were motivated to risk everything primarily for principle or for their pocketbooks is surely an imponderable in the end. Perhaps principle was everything to the resolute Puritan Samuel Adams; but to merchants and traders such as Hancock, Lamb, and Sears, or workingmen and their supporters such as Revere and Gadsden, principle was as much a justification as a cause. And in the end, what does it truly matter?

Whatever their motivations, without the Sons of Liberty, there would have been no Revolution as we know it. As Pauline Maier makes clear in her discussion of the group in the formative Stamp Act days, the Sons set everything into motion. They legitimized the very notion of resistance and, in organizing as they did, provided a means by which momentous change might be implemented. They allowed—in Maier's words—that ultimately, "resistance could become revolution."

In desperation they found common cause, and, as unlikely as it initially seemed—even to themselves—they went to war against the most powerful military force in the world, emerged victorious, and created a new nation, devoted to principle and supported by practice.

26

WHAT REMAINS

Though the signing of the Treaty of Paris on September 3, 1783, put an end to the Revolutionary War and established an irrevocably independent United States, the Sons of Liberty enjoyed a brief reincarnation in New York, when, following the evacuation of the British, Isaac Sears and John Lamb reorganized their political activities around an antiloyalist platform. There was a great deal of lingering hostility on the part of those who had suffered at the hands of the British and their sympathizers during the occupation of the city from late 1776 through the end of the war. For weeks following the withdrawal of British troops, newspaper accounts described a number of beatings, tarrings and featherings, and various forms of threats and intimidation against those thought to be Tories, and by December, the Sons would win sufficient seats in the state assembly to ensure passage of a number of hostile measures directed against loyalists.

Anyone accused of Tory leanings by so much as a single citizen could be deprived of the right to vote, and those accused of collaborating with the British during the occupation were subject to an onerous tax. At a massive rally held on the city's common in March 1784, there were calls that any remaining loyalists be expelled from the state by May 1, and—in direct contravention of the treaty ending the war—that their property be confiscated and sold at auction.

Though some saw the proposed expulsion of so many longtime citizens as counterproductive to the revitalization of the war-ravaged city and considered such actions a direct contradiction of the principles that had fueled the Revolution in the first place, the radicals' hold on the populace remained solid until a scandal broke shortly before elections for the state assembly in June 1784. Sears, Lamb, and other influential leaders within the Sons organization, it was discovered, had been buying up the pay certificates of beleaguered veterans at a discount, then using the proceeds to invest in forfeited Tory properties in and around the city. As a result of the charges, the Sons were lambasted at the polls, and Sears was forced out of the city, in disgrace and deeply in debt.

Though the debacle of 1784 may have marked the end of the Sons of Liberty as an effectual political entity, the spirit of the organization has endured in any number of manifestations through the ages. During the Civil War, a group of northern Democrats opposed to the war, supportive of states' rights, and committed to rapprochement with the South and a condoning of the practice of slavery became known as "Copperheads." The name was given them, after the venomous snake, by Republicans supporting Abraham Lincoln and the war effort. The "Peace Democrats," as they were also called, did not resist the epithet but in fact adopted a clever response: the copper "head" referred to in their view was the likeness of the Goddess of Liberty then stamped on the face of the copper penny, which they adopted as their proud symbol.

A sizable group associated with the Copperheads was that of the Knights of the Golden Circle, formed by a colorful Cincinnati physician named George Washington Lafayette Bickley. Bickley, a schemer with a pedigree equal to that of any snake-oil salesman from a Mark Twain novel, had a long history of involvement with secret fraternal societies and decided to form his own in 1859, with the express intention of creating a paramilitary force for the seizing of Mexico. There, a vast new slave state would be created, with himself (he had somehow acquired the title of "General" to supplant that of "Dr.") at its helm.

Though it might seem vaguely lunatic to the modern reader, Bickley's idea found great favor in the South and was the subject of any number of laudatory news articles in that region. When the Civil War broke out, Bickley adroitly shifted his group's focus from an assault on Mexico to the support of Confederate interests, and soon enough, the Knights, primarily a southern-based entity, organized chapters in a number of states, including Ohio, Indiana, Illinois, and Missouri, where Copperhead activists were prominent.

Various financial and other irregularities plagued the group, however, and in order to distance themselves from scandal, as well as from its charismatic founder, leaders reorganized in late 1863 as the Order of American Knights, and then again in 1864 as the Order of the Sons of Liberty, influenced both by the lofty imprimatur of the former resistance organizations and by the Copperheads' own affinity with the symbol of liberty. As the Union gradually gained control of the war and the war's end became inevitable, the group lost its influence, however, and eventually disbanded.

As might be expected, there were any number of vestigial groups of Sons who maintained connections during their service in the Revolutionary War and afterward, though the purpose of such associations was far more fraternal and honorary than actively political. One claiming a connection to the original Sons endures to this day: the Improved Order of Red Men, headquartered in Texas and maintaining chapters in seventeen states, including California, New York, New Jersey, and Virginia. Like the similarly democratically inclined "Tammany" groups that were popular in the years following the Revolution (one of which grew to substantial political influence in New York), the Red Men honor the contributions of workingmen to the Revolution and fashion their regalia and nomenclature after the Iroquois, Algonquian, and other Native tribes, prompted in part by the disguises worn during the Boston Tea Party, as well as by the essential "American" nature of the Native inhabitants. Richard Nixon and former chief justice of the United States Earl Warren are sometimes cited as having been members of the group.

The exploits of the Sons of Liberty have also entered modern American popular culture from time to time. In 1943, a Houghton Mifflin editor, Esther Forbes, published a novel for young readers, *Johnny Tremain*, which follows the adventures of a fictive young apprentice silversmith injured while working on a sizable commission from none other than John Hancock. Tremain later meets Paul Revere and eventually becomes a stalwart of the Sons of Liberty—"those carefully organized 'mobs' who often took justice into their own hands." The book, which remains the sixteenth best-selling children's title of all time, won the Newberry Medal in 1944 for Massachusetts resident Forbes, who had previously been awarded the Pulitzer Prize for History in 1942 for— what else—a biography of Paul Revere.

In 1957, Forbes's book was adapted into a Walt Disney film with speaking parts for characters that included Samuel Adams, James Otis, Paul Revere, and even General Gage. The film, while serviceable, never rose to the heights of its literary predecessor, and failed to find much favor with critics, including the often dyspeptic Leslie Halliwell, who dismissed it as a "schoolbook history with little vitality."

A somewhat more intriguing film is 1939's two-reel short *Sons of Liberty*, directed by Oscar winner Michael Curtiz, of *Casablanca* fame. The twenty-minute film tells the true story of a Jewish émigré, Haym Salomon, played in the film by Claude Rains. Salomon, a financier from Poland, arrived in New York City in 1775 and became involved with local merchants attempting to continue foreign trade. Soon he was a member of the New York Sons, and in 1776 he was arrested by the British on charges of espionage.

Though the British later pardoned the German-speaking Salomon on the condition that he serve as an interpreter for the Hessian mercenaries brought in to aid the fight against the colonists, the financier was in short order working to help free American prisoners and encouraging the German soldiers to desert the British. He was arrested again by the British but escaped and made his way to Philadelphia, where he worked for the remainder of the war to raise capital for military operations.

Curtiz's film, part of Hollywood's anti-Nazi, pro-liberty campaign of the late 1930s and early '40s, is hampered by the attempt to pack a feature's worth of material into a twenty-minute frame, but Rains, often consigned to villainy in his roles, is redoubtable as Salomon and enlivens what could have been torturous. Though *Sons of Liberty* is seldom seen, the determined can find it packaged as extra material on the DVD of an Errol Flynn vehicle, *Dodge City* (1939), also directed by Curtiz.

Perhaps the most popular reminder of the Sons comes in the form of the various Samuel Adams craft brews that constitute the cornerstone of the Boston Beer Company and account for about 1 percent of the American beer market. Adams would no doubt be pleased by the fact that, following the 2008 sale of Anheuser-Busch to European interests, the producer of "Sam Adams" became the largest American-owned brewery in the country. As to whether Adams ever brewed beer himself, Boston Beer Company cofounder Jim Koch reports being approached in the late 1990s by a rare-documents dealer offering a receipt signed by Adams for the purchase of hops, something only a brewer would have purchased. Koch balked at the price being asked by the dealer, however, and the document has since disappeared.

A somewhat different vestigial reminder of the Sons comes in the form of efforts of contemporary Tea Party members to ally themselves with the aims of the prerevolutionary patriots. Generally decrying the steadily burgeoning federal government committed to a continuing "slide into socialism," and complaining of oppressive taxation and excessive government spending, such groups appeal to contemporaries by insisting that the radicals who brought the nation into being would be appalled by what government has become—and one supposes that there is at least a sampling of Samuel Adams Boston Lager consumed along with other American brews at their rallies.

Nor is there much doubt that Samuel Adams and many of his steadfast states'-rights compatriots would be appalled at the size and nature of the current federal government, its annual expenditures, and its dizzying array of taxes. However, for contemporary patriots supposing that Samuel Adams would champion any talk of rebellion or violent action against that government, they might consider the "old revolutionary's" comments regarding the violent uprising known as Shays's Rebellion, which took place in two far-western counties of Massachusetts in 1787, when Adams was serving as a senator in the State Assembly.

When some 1,500 armed and tax-burdened farmers under the command of former Continental Army captain Daniel Shays threatened to march upon the Springfield Arsenal as part of a plan to disrupt court and governmental proceedings in the state, the governor ordered a contingent of 4,000 state militiamen to meet them. The resultant battle left four of Shays's men dead and twenty wounded. When friends of Shays went to Adams, expecting support for a pardon of the rebellion's leaders, he gave them a stinging lesson in democracy.

According to his first biographer, William Wells, Adams's reply was curt and to the point. "In monarchies, the crime of treason and rebellion may admit of being pardoned or lightly punished," he allowed, "but the man who dares to rebel against the laws of a republic ought to suffer death."

Adams would have further occasion to echo such sentiments in 1794, when a group of western Pennsylvania corn farmers protested a new excise tax passed on whiskey they were distilling. After they shot at federal revenuers and some five hundred men stormed the home of a federal tax inspector, General John Neville, President Washington sent a force of 15,000 militiamen to put down the so-called Whiskey Rebellion. By the time the troops arrived, the rebellion had evaporated, but as then-governor Samuel Adams was quick to tell his legislature, "What excuse then can there be for forcible opposition to the laws? If any law shall prove oppressive in its operation, the future deliberations of a freely elected Representative, will afford a constitutional remedy."

That old Son labored long and hard to create a government in which every man owned a voice and no man bowed before another. In his view, the very fact of the republic's existence was an eternal guarantee of liberty. For Adams and his fellow Sons, disobedience to a monarchy had proved unavoidable, but disobedience to the republic that replaced it was simply unthinkable. They had fought desperately to make it so.

NOTES

M ost of the materials pertaining to the exploits of the Sons of Liberty and the American Revolution are contained within the public archive, and the principal details have been often cited in various divergent contexts. However, where I have made use of any singular piece of scholarship, I have endeavored to acknowledge that in the text or within these notes. I have also included a notation of primary and secondary sources consulted (and not otherwise referenced in the text) chapter by chapter, in order to aid the reader interested in following a particular line of inquiry more deeply.

AUTHOR'S NOTE

As to the nature of the continuing historical enterprise, I recently presided over a seminar at a major institution in the Northeast with doctoral students of history, all of them laboring on dissertations that were biographical in nature. During the discussion period, one student enthusiastically described his project, having to do with a certain American female who had accomplished something notable early on in her life. "She never did another thing of any importance so long as she lived," he told me proudly, "but no one has ever written about it!"

The title of a 1980 volume by Pauline Maier, a protégée of the well-known Bernard Bailyn and a noted historian in her own right, is *The Old Revolutionaries: Political Lives in the Age of Samuel Adams.* Beyond Adams, Maier there discusses the work and influence of Dr. Thomas Young, Josiah and Mary Bartlett, Richard Henry Lee, and Charles Carroll of Carrollton.

Maier also devotes a chapter of 1972's *From Resistance to Revolution: Colonial Radicals and the Development of American Opposition to Britain, 1765–1776* to the impact of the Sons on activities pertaining to the Stamp Act crisis: "The Intercolonial Sons of Liberty and Organized Resistance, 1765–1766."

For a thorough and evenhanded survey of the significant literature pertaining to the American Revolution, see Rothbard, "Modern Historians Confront the American Revolution." Along the way, the well-known libertarian laments, "Disgracefully, there has been very little work done on two vital revolutionary organizations and institutions in the pre-Revolutionary period: the committees of correspondence, and the Sons of Liberty."

1. *O Albany!*

William Kennedy's personal history of the town is a highly selective, subjective, and entertaining one for fans of the Albany novels or those with some other interest—whatever that might be—in the subject.

Stanford White, who went on to design one manifestation of Madison Square Garden, the Washington Square arch, etc., penned his feelings about Albany to his mother while he was twenty-three and still in the employ of Henry Hobson Richardson, a noted architect of the day, to whom the quote is sometimes mistakenly attributed.

The particulars of Van Schaack's travails are contained in McAnear, "The Albany Stamp Act Riots"; in Van Schaack, *Memoirs*; and in issues of the New York press (*New York Mercury, Gazette,* and *Post-Boy,* late January 1766).

Becker's article "Growth of Revolutionary Parties and Methods in New York Province" provides an overarching context for radical activities for the decade 1765–1774.

The most thorough treatment of the Stamp Act Crisis comes from Edmund S. and Helen M. Morgan in their aptly named volume, *The Stamp Act Crisis.* Edmund Morgan's article "Colonial Ideas of Parliamentary

Power" is a persuasive summary of the colonists' perception of their rightful place in the hierarchy limned by the British Constitution.

The most authoritative (and entertaining) source on Franklin comes from the statesman himself—his autobiography is available in various editions.

A most readable and carefully researched "people's history" of the American Revolution, deftly summarizing a welter of materials from public documents of the time, is Page Smith's two-volume opus *A New Age Now Begins.*

For a thorough treatment of the difficulties of comparing currency values across history, see McCusker, *How Much Is That in Real Money?*

2. Measures Illegal, Unconstitutional, and Oppressive

References to various acts of Parliament and associated debates are drawn largely from *Parliamentary History of England*, as well as from *History, Debates and Proceedings of Both Houses of Parliament of Great Britain.*

For more on Franklin and his observations on the currents of the Atlantic, see Lacoute, "The Gulf Stream Charts of Benjamin Franklin and Timothy Folger."

For a diverting treatment of travel in the period, see Fontenoy, *The Sloops of the Hudson River.*

4. Storm Before the Calm

Fictional narratives of import trace the efforts of a protagonist (Ahab/ Sons of Liberty) to accomplish some momentous task (harpoon the damnable white whale/go to war against tax-hungry oppressors). But that is not enough to make for real satisfaction. Unless there is some underlying psychological and thematic concern (vengeance/rights of man) that richly complicates the events that occupy the surface of the tale, a reader is left with the equivalent of an action thriller (*Moby-Dick* reduced to *Jaws III/American Revolution: The Video Game*). The best stories intertwine the physical and the abstract to create a sense of substance as they progress toward an inevitable end, as tragic or triumphant as it may be.

The debate between pragmatists and ideologists is voluminous, but the works cited in the text should suffice for most. For a summary of the Michener-Wright position on economic forces shaping the Revolution, see Arango, "A Revolutionary Recession: Did a Sour Economy Set Off the American War for Independence?" Hofstadter's assessment of Beard is found in *The Progressive Historians*, page 344.

Population figures come from the U.S. Census, immigration and employment statistics from the U.S. Department of Labor. The Smith volumes provide a comprehensive overview of general living conditions in colonial America, as do countless other volumes and websites, including that of Colonial Williamsburg.

5. Nourished by Indulgence

For further details of the Townshend-Barré debates, see *History, Debates and Proceedings of Both Houses of Parliament of Great Britain*.

For the role of Samuel Adams in local government and other details of the proceedings of the Boston Assembly, see *Boston Town Records*.

Smith's letters are collected in *Historical Memoirs of William Smith*.

For a treatment of the evolving role of newspaper reporting during the period, see Schlesinger, "The Colonial Newspapers and the Stamp Act," as well as his *Prelude to Independence: The Newspaper War on Britain.*

As noted, Henry's resolutions were widely reprinted in various forms in the colonial press. While Jefferson's account (see Randall) is well intentioned and that of Henry's first biographer (Wirt) is stirring, the most intriguing recounting of Henry's oration may be "Journal of a French Traveller," reprinted anonymously in *American Historical Review* in

1922. A recent blog posting by Joshua Beatty of the Feinberg Library, SUNY Plattsburgh, suggests that the eighty-year-old mystery of the "traveller's" identity may have been solved. See Beatty's "The 'French Traveller,' Patrick Henry, and the Contagion of Liberty" (*Lemonade & Information*, March 26, 2011). For a modern reassessment of the import of Henry's actions before the burgesses, see the 2011 article published by Australian scholar Rhys Isaac (librarian Beatty's former mentor).

6. UNLEASHED

Unger's *John Hancock: Merchant King and American Patriot* is the definitive, and highly readable, biography of the man with the most famous signature in the world.

Bernard's letters to the home secretary were not made public until 1769, though all the while Adams and others of the Sons in Massachusetts suspected that he was communicating surreptitiously with his superiors. An account of the means by which the letters were finally procured is in Walett, "Governor Bernard's Undoing." Copies of the letters are found in *Collections of the Massachusetts Historical Society*.

Huchinson's account is found in the *Diary and Letters of Thomas Hutchinson*.

The full account of the business of the Stamp Act Congress is found in *Journal of the First Congress of the American Colonies*.

The account of the disturbances in Charleston is found in the *South-Carolina Gazette* for the dates and is also part of the full-length narrative of Sons activity in the state by Walsh, *Charleston's Sons of Liberty*.

10. HORNETS AND FIREBRANDS

Montresor's *Journals*, Colden's *Letters and Papers*, and contemporary press accounts form the basis of the narrative of the Stamp Act disturbances in New York.

Also of interest are Dawson, *The Sons of Liberty in New York* (1859), and a contemporary eyewitness account, "tolerably correct in the main," reproduced as "The Stamp Act Riot: A Letter Written on the Day Following," in *New York City During the American Revolution.*

Commentary by Morgan and Morgan and Becker constitutes the definitive evaluation of the significance of the Stamp Act events in the evolution of the Revolution.

Another well-drawn narrative of the events is found in Engleman, "Cadwallader Colden and the New York Stamp Act Riots."

"An Excellent New Song" is quoted in Dawson, *The Sons of Liberty in New York.*

11. FROM AIRY NOTHING

According to the website People of Colonial Albany Live Here, the "Sons of Liberty Constitution" was first reproduced in 1876 in a Schenectady periodical, the *American Historian and Quarterly Genealogical Record* (vol. 1). Only a photocopy of the original document remains in the holdings of the Colonial Albany Social History Project.

Along with Dawson, Walsh, and Maier, a series of articles by Champagne, "The Military Association of the Sons of Liberty," "Liberty Boys and Mechanics of New York City," and "New York's Radicals and the Coming of Independence," constitutes the principal critical examination of the influence of the Sons of Liberty per se on the development of the Revolution.

12. FIRST TO BLINK

Franklin's examination before the House of Commons has been widely reproduced; the reprintings include an appearance in *The World's Famous Orations*, a multivolume set compiled by William Jennings Bryan in 1906.

Contemporary newspaper accounts, along with commentary by Montresor, form the basis of the narrative of the Stamp Act's repeal and its reception in the colonies.

13. BETTER DAYS

Carter's edition of *Correspondence of General Thomas Gage* is the source for letters attributed to the general, along with the Gage Manuscripts held at the University of Michigan libraries and discussed later in the text.

Schlesinger's "Liberty Tree: A Genealogy" is a captivating and thoroughgoing treatise on the principal icon of the Sons movement in colonial America. Jenkins (*The Greatest Street in the World*) also provides a lively account of the liberty pole's various manifestations in New York. See also "The Liberty Pole on the Commons" in the *New-York Historical Society Quarterly Bulletin*.

Schecter's *Battle of New York* provides the definitive overview of New York's convoluted politics during the run-up to the Revolution.

14. TOWNSHEND FANS THE FLAMES

Mayhew's letter to Otis is found in Bradford's *Memoir of the Life and Writings* of the good reverend.

Adams's letters are collected in Cushing's four-volume set, *The Writings of Samuel Adams*.

The observer of unmatched joy is John Rowe, who provides a rhapsodic account of the festivities in *Letters and Diary of John Rowe, Boston Merchant*.

Chaffin's "Townshend Acts of 1767" appears in the pages of that principal repository of scholarship regarding the American Revolution, the *William and Mary Quarterly*.

Modern editions of Dickinson's collected essays are easily found.

The account of the contretemps between Otis and Adams is found in *Letters to the Right Honourable the Earl of Hillsborough*.

The most recent treatment of Adams's activities is the meticulous account of John K. Alexander, *Samuel Adams: The Life of an American Revolutionary* (2011).

Details of the *Romney* confrontation were assiduously reported in the local press and are the subject of Dickerson's thoughtful "John Hancock: Notorious Smuggler or Near Victim?"

15. THE ROAD TO MASSACRE

John Adams's letter to Rush of May 21, 1807, is found in vol. 9 of *The Works of John Adams.*

The complete list of Sons present at the dinner in Dorchester is found in Palfrey, "An Alphabetical List."

John Adams's *Diary and Autobiography* referred to is the four-volume set edited by Butterfield.

As Alexander points out, Samuel Adams's reputation has waxed and waned among biographers over the years. Earlier writers such as Wells painted him in hagiographic fashion, as a saintly savior of his country, whereas the mid-twentieth-century view tended toward a portrait of Adams as a Machiavellian manipulator and master of propaganda management; cf. John Miller, *Sam Adams: Pioneer in Propaganda.* Maier's summary "A New Englander as Revolutionary," in *The Old Revolutionaries,* is an engaging portrait of an individual as the living embodiment of an idea.

A discussion of Gadsden as "country factor" is found in Rogers, "The Charleston Tea Party."

The detailing of Gadsden's activities in Walsh's *Charleston's Sons of Liberty* lays out support for the oft-repeated description of Gadsden as "the Samuel Adams of South Carolina."

A comprehensive summary of the DeLancey-Livingston political maneuvering is found in Klein, "Democracy and Politics in Colonial New York."

Events surrounding the so-called Battle of Golden Hill were drawn nowhere more colorfully than in the contemporary New York press, renderings that enliven the scholarship that has descended since.

The anecdote regarding the skull-splitting efficacy of the halberd is variously reported in accounts of the demise of Charles the Bold.

16. Affray in King Street

The brawl provoked by Otis is detailed in Tudor's 1823 *Life of James Otis* and has become a staple of renderings of the Sons' activities in Boston since.

The Gailer incident was duly reported by the local press. For an in-depth discussion of the practice of tarring and feathering, see Irvin, "Tar, Feathers, and the Enemies of American Liberties."

Phillis Wheatley is also believed to have penned a poem titled "On the Affray in King-Street," treating the events of the Boston Massacre. That title appears in a list for a collection she proposed for publication in 1772. However, the collection never appeared, and Wheatley scholars debate the legitimacy of various fragments said to be taken from "Affray"; no copy of the finished poem survives. See Minardi, *Making Slavery History*, p. 4.

There are many accounts of the events leading up to and making up what is commonly referred to as the Boston Massacre, including the contemporary press coverage and other contemporary accounts taken up later in the text. Of the modern accounts of the event, none is more complete or colorful than Hiller Zobel's aptly titled *The Boston Massacre* (1970).

17. Trial of the Century

The role of John Adams in the defense of Captain Preston and his men is one of the more intriguing anecdotes to come out of the lead-up to the Revolution, owing to the delicious irony involved, a fact of which Adams himself was not unaware. His own comments on the matter have fed a number of subsequent well-drawn assessments, including Reid's "A Lawyer Acquitted" (1974) and McCullough's rendering of the material in *John Adams* (2001).

John Adams's trial notes and a record of his speeches are found in Kidder's *History of the Boston Massacre* (1870).

18. Charred to the Waterline

Randolph Adams's reassessment, "New Light on the Boston Massacre," is also a stoic, evenhanded reflection on the endless malleability of history.

The early exploits of Isaac Sears, Alexander McDougall, and the labyrinthine twists of prerevolutionary New York politics form a compelling thread through the first third of Schecter's authoritative *Battle of New York*, which continues its narrative through the British evacuation of the city in 1783.

The unfortunate behavior of John Murray, Earl of Dunmore, is detailed in the diary *Historical Memoirs of William Smith*.

Details of the adventures surrounding the *Gaspée* incident are drawn from contemporary press accounts as well as the wealth of letters, depositions, and other accounts originally compiled by William R. Staples (*Documentary History of the Destruction of the Gaspee*) in 1845 and republished by the Rhode Island Publications Society in 1990. To this writer, the narrative deriving from such materials virtually dictates itself, with the characters rivaling those drawn from any novelist's imagination.

19. Prelude to a Party

Hutchinson's involvement in the events transpiring in Massachusetts is nowhere better rendered than in his *History of the Province of Massachusetts Bay, from 1749 to 1774.*

Close watch on assemblies heeding Samuel Adams's call for the formation of Committees of Correspondence throughout the colonies was kept by the contemporary press.

Copies of the Hutchinson letters were eventually published in Boston by Edes and Gill in 1773.

20. Mad Hatter's Ball

North's various strategies are limned in the voluminous correspondence carried on with the king, collected and edited by W. B. Donne in *The*

Correspondence of King George III with Lord North from 1768 to 1783.

As Upton ("Proceedings of ye Body") notes, the story of the Boston Tea Party has been the subject of endless retellings. Yet, though the event has reached near-legendary status, accounts of it derive from very few sources. The minutes of the various "tea meetings" appear in the local press, including the *Massachusetts Gazette and Weekly News-Letter*, the *Boston Evening Post*, and the *Massachusetts Spy*. Principal public records are to be found in the *Boston Town Records, 1770–1777*. There are a half-dozen or so private diaries and letter collections by both Tories and Radicals who attended meetings and witnessed the events of the evening of December 16, and a number of accounts from purported participants transcribed at sometime following, most of which agree in the main with events as reported in the press and elsewhere. The British viewpoint is expressed in thoroughgoing fashion by Hutchinson in his *Letters* and *History*, though his account varies little from those of the radical press save in tone. Upton's 1965 work adds the perspective of an anonymous observer who kept a record of his observations at the various tea meetings, including the transcription of Rowe's mixing-tea-with-saltwater comments and a careful detailing of the events of December 16. The anonymous accounts were found among the papers of Canadian judge Jonathan Sewell, a resident of Cambridge at the time of the disturbances in Boston. Evidence suggests, however, that the accounts were penned by one of Sewell's cousins and somehow found their way into the judge's hands.

Though legend has it that Samuel Adams gave the preordained signal for the descent upon the British tea ships at the end of the tea meeting on December 16, the documents unearthed by Upton suggest otherwise. When the disturbances began in the streets, our anonymous narrator reports, "Mr. Adams, Mr. Hancock [and] Dr. Young with several others called out to the people to stay, for they had not quite done." If indeed Adams was aware of plans for any upcoming "Tea Party," it seems at the very least to have begun without him.

Hewes's account of his involvement in the "Tea Party" was transcribed by Hawkes as *A Retrospect of the Boston Tea-Party* in 1834, at a considerable remove from the events themselves, and historians often cast a suspicious eye on such long-postponed narratives. However, there is little in Hewes's rendering to suggest prevarication, or any motive for it.

The account of the Philadelphia Tea Party is drawn from the *Philadelphia Gazette* and other press accounts as well as from Eberlein and Lippincott, *The Colonial Houses of Philadelphia and Its Neighborhood* (1912).

The irony of the Charleston tea being auctioned off for the benefit of the revolutionary government in South Carolina is reported in Schlesinger, *The Colonial Merchants and the American Revolution*, p. 298.

21. INTOLERABLE

The king's letter to North is included in Donne's edition of the *Correspondence*.

North's addresses and submissions to Parliament are found in *History, Debates and Proceedings of Both Houses*.

Samuel Adams's letters regarding Gage and matters related to the Intolerable Acts are found in his *Writings*.

Gadsden's letter to Adams pledging South Carolina's support is referenced in Walsh, *Charleston's Sons of Liberty*.

Washington's letter to Fairfax is contained in the Sparks edition of his *Writings*.

22. CONGRESS OF SONS

The work of the Continental Congress has of course been widely documented and analyzed. An early and comprehensive treatment is that of Burnett, *The Continental Congress* (1941).

A compelling discussion of the British maneuvering in response to the Continental Congress is found in Macksy, *The War for America, 1775–1783*.

The account of fellow Bostonians eager to burnish the appearance of Samuel Adams comes from the Sargent edition of the *Letters of John Andrews*.

Hannah Adams's narrative of Governor Gage's overtures to her father is included in Wells, *The Father of the Revolution*, p. 193.

An account of the difficulties in Charleston is found in Rogers, "The Charleston Tea Party." Rogers describes the activities of Laurens as a man who would transform from a conservative plantation owner to one who, at the reading of the Declaration of Independence, resolved to free his slaves on the spot. As he wrote his son John shortly thereafter, "I am now by the Will of God brought into a new World & God only knows what sort of a World it will be."

An account of Robert Murray's attempt to land tea in New York in early 1775 is contained in Monaghan, *The Murrays of Murray Hill*.

Dartmouth's letter to Gage is found in the *Gage Manuscripts* at the Clements Library, University of Michigan.

23. SHOT AROUND THE WORLD

The Tory-leaning *Rivington's Gazette* account of Cunningham and Hill's travails at Liberty Square in New York is collected in Moore, *Diary of the American Revolution from Newspapers and Original Documents*.

Pinckney's letter to Sears and Lamb is collected in *American Archives: Documents of the American Revolution,* a substantial digitized collection compiled by the Northern Illinois Libraries.

The escalating conflict in South Carolina is detailed in the *South-Carolina Gazette* and in Walsh.

A rendering of Carrington's stirring account as well as a summary of the controversy surrounding the true nature of Henry's oration is found in Cohen, "The 'Liberty or Death' Speech," in the *William and Mary Quarterly* (1981).

The lead-up to the events at Lexington and Concord and the battles of that fateful day have of course been the subject of much scrutiny. A thorough and readable version is Tourtellot, *Lexington and Concord: The Beginning of the War of the American Revolution*.

Paul Revere's detailed retelling ("A Letter from Col. Paul Revere to the Corresponding Secretary," 1798) of his actions in this legendary

drama make for far more compelling reading than many of the over-
heated retellings cobbled together since.

Warren's role in the events, as well as his overarching relationship
with Samuel Adams, is detailed by Frothingham in his *Life and Times
of Joseph Warren* (1865).

Pertinent correspondence between Warren and Adams is collected in
Warren-Adams Letters, vol. 1, *1743–1777*.

24. THE CONQUEROR SILENT SLEEPS

Emerson, as much a philosopher as a poet, distills into six simple words
the profound significance of the actions at Concord on April 19, 1775—
i.e., the world's astonishment that American colonists would actually
go to war against Great Britain. The brief poem, which has become the
veritable anthem for the Revolution, while acknowledging the fact that
the combatants were long dead at the time of its writing, closes with the
prayer to the spirit that prompted the actions: "that made those heroes
dare / To die, and leave their children free"; the sentiment is one that
might live on forever.

In addition to the encyclopedic overview of Smith (*A New Age Now
Begins*), the various scholarly analyses, and the more narrowly focused
volumes mentioned previously, general readers might find the works of
two so-called economic interpreters of the Revolution to be compan-
ionable summaries of the whole of the era, even if more ideologically
oriented historians question the precision of their research and findings:
see, for example, Stanford University professor John C. Miller's *Origins
of the American Revolution* (1943) and Merrill Jensen's *The Founding
of a Nation: A History of the American Revolution* (1968).

An interpretation of the significance of the Sons of Liberty movement
from the Marxist point of view is provided by Herbert Morais, "The Sons
of Liberty in New York," in Morris, *The Era of the American Revolution*, where the thesis is that the Revolution was as much a practical class
struggle to determine who would rule the roost—in New York, at any
rate—as it was an ideological struggle between colonists and Britons.

Gage's letter to Smith is found in the Carter edition of his *Correspondence.*

Alden's "Why the March to Concord?" provides a concise summary of British intention and its thwarting at Concord and Lexington.

A stirring summary of the events at Concord and the tragic end of the hapless William Marcy is given by Smith, *A New Age Now Begins.*

25. SHADE OF PARADISE

Gage's published offer of a pardon to every Son but Adams and Hancock is collected in the Printed Ephemera Collection of the Library of Congress, Portfolio 38, Folder 17.

Maier's astute estimation of Samuel Adams's career is found in "A New Englander as Revolutionary," in *The Old Revolutionaries.*

A readable summary of Franklin's return to the colonies and his eventual immersion in the American Revolution is given by Walter Isaacson in "Benjamin Franklin Joins the Revolution" (2003).

The account of Otis's unfortunate end is found in Sarah Loring Bailey, *Historical Sketches of Andover.*

A thoughtful appraisal of Gadsden's bedrock political identity is found in Walsh, "Christopher Gadsden: Radical or Conservative Revolutionary?"

Maier's summary estimation of the Sons' influence is found in "The Intercolonial Sons of Liberty," in *From Resistance to Revolution.*

26. WHAT REMAINS

An interesting summary of various secret fraternal organizations in the Civil War era is found in Fesler, "Secret Societies in the North."

Bickley's unlikely, if diverting, escapades are detailed by Crenshaw in "Knights of the Golden Circle."

On the contemporary Tea Party movement and the nature of its relations with the original Sons, see Lepore, "Tea and Sympathy: Who Owns the American Revolution?"

BIBLIOGRAPHY

Primary Sources, Newspapers, with Year Beginning Publication

The Boston Chronicle (1767)
The Boston Gazette (1719)
The Boston News-Letter (1704)
The Boston Post-Boy (1735)
The Connecticut Courant (Hartford, 1764)
The Massachusetts Spy (1770)
The Newport Mercury (1758)
New-York Chronicle (1769)
The New-York Gazette (1759)
The New-York Gazette, and the Weekly Mercury (1768)
The New-York Gazette, Revived in the Weekly Post-Boy (1747)
The Pennsylvania Chronicle (1767)
The Pennsylvania Gazette (1728)
The Pennsylvania Packet (1771)
The Providence Gazette (1762)
Rivington's New-York Gazetteer (1773)
The South-Carolina Gazette (Charleston, 1732)

Other Primary Sources

Adams, John. *Diary and Autobiography of John Adams.* 4 vols. Ed. L. H. Butterfield. Cambridge, Mass.: Harvard University Press, 1961.

Adams, John, and Charles Francis Adams. *The Works of John Adams, Second President of the United States.* Boston: Little, Brown, 1854.

Adams, John, Samuel Adams, and James Warren. *Warren-Adams Letters*, vol. 1, *1743–1777*. Boston: Massachusetts Historical Society, 1917.

Adams, Samuel. *The Writings of Samuel Adams.* 4 vols. Ed. Harry A. Cushing. New York: G. P. Putnam's Sons, 1904–1908.

Andrews, John. *Letters of John Andrews, Esq., of Boston, 1772–1776.* Ed. Winthrop Sargent. Cambridge, Mass.: John Wilson & Sons, 1866.

Boston Town Records, 1758–1769. Boston: Rockwell and Churchill, 1886.

Boston Town Records, 1770–1777. Boston: Rockwell and Churchill, 1887.

Colden, Cadwallader. *Letters and Papers of Cadwallader Colden.* New York: New-York Historical Society, *Collections,* v. 56, 1923.

Dartmouth, Earl of. Letter to Thomas Gage, January 27, 1775. Thomas Gage Manuscripts, William L. Clements Library, University of Michigan.

Dickinson, John. *Letters from a Farmer in Pennsylvania, to the Inhabitants of the British Colonies.* New York: Outlook, 1903.

Emerson, Ralph Waldo. "Concord Hymn." In *The American Reader: Words That Moved a Nation.* Ed. Diane Ravitch. New York: HarperCollins, 2000.

Franklin, Benjamin. *The Autobiography of Benjamin Franklin: A Genetic Text.* Ed. J. A. Leo Lemay and P. M. Zail. Knoxville: University of Tennessee Press, 1981.

Gage, Thomas. *Correspondence of General Thomas Gage,* vol. 2. Ed. Clarence Edwin Carter. Hamden, Conn.: Archon, 1969.

George III, King. *The Correspondence of King George III with Lord North from 1768 to 1783.* 2 vols. Ed. W. Bodham Donne. London: John Murray, 1867.

History, Debates and Proceedings of Both Houses of Parliament of Great Britain, 1743–1774. 7 vols. London: J. Debrett, 1792.

Hutchinson, Thomas. *Copies of Letters Sent to Great Britain by His Excellency Thomas Hutchinson.* Boston: Edes and Gill, 1773.

———. *Diary and Letters of Thomas Hutchinson.* Ed. Peter Orlando Hutchinson. London: Samson Low, Marston, Searle, and Rivington, 1883.

"Journal of a French Traveller in the Colonies, 1765." *American Historical Review* 26 (July 1921): 726–747.

Journal of the First Congress of the American Colonies, in Opposition to the Tyrannical Acts of the British Parliament. New York, 1765. Reprinted in *Niles' Weekly Register,* vol. 2, 1812, pp. 337–342, 353–355.

Kidder, Frederic. *History of the Boston Massacre, Containing Unpublished Documents of John Adams and Explanatory Notes.* Albany, N.Y.: Joel Munsell, 1870.

"Letter from the General Committee of Charlestown, S.C. to the New-York Committee, March 1, 1775." *American Archives: Documents of the American Revolution,* ser. 4, vol. 2. DeKalb: Northern Illinois University Libraries, 2001.

Letters to the Right Honourable the Earl of Hillsborough, from Governor Bernard, General Gage, and the Council for the Province of Massachusetts-Bay. Boston: Edes and Gill, 1769.

Massachusetts Historical Society Collections, 6th ser., v. 9, nos. 123, 143, January 30, May 10, 1769.

Mayhew, Jonathan. *A Discourse Concerning Unlimited Submission and Non-Resistance to the Higher Powers.* Boston: D. Fowle, 1750.

———. Letter to James Otis, June 8, 1766. In Alden Bradford, *Memoir of the Life and Writings of Rev. Jonathan Mayhew, D.D.* Boston: C. C. Little, 1838.

Montresor, John. *Journals*. Ed. G. D. Scull. New York: New-York Historical Society, 1881.

Moore, Frank. *Diary of the American Revolution from Newspapers and Original Documents*, vol. 1. New York: Charles Scribner, 1860.

Otis, James. *The Rights of the British Colonies Asserted and Proved* (1764). In *The American Republic: Primary Sources*. Ed. Bruce Frohnen. Indianapolis: Liberty Fund, 2002.

Palfrey, William. "An Alphabetical List of the Sons of Liberty who din'd at Liberty Tree, Dorchester, 14 August 1769." Boston: Archives of the Massachusetts Historical Society.

Parliamentary History of England from the Earliest Period to the Year 1803, vol. 17, *1771–1774*. London: T. C. Hansard, 1803.

Revere, Paul. "A Letter from Col. Paul Revere to the Corresponding Secretary, Jan. 1, 1798." In *Collections of the Massachusetts Historical Society*. Boston: John Eastburn, 1835, 106–112.

Rowe, John. *Letters and Diary of John Rowe, Boston Merchant, 1759–1762, 1764–1779*. Ed. Anne Rowe Cunningham. Boston: W. B. Blake, 1903.

Smith, William. *Historical Memoirs of William Smith, from 16 March to 9 July 1776*. Ed. William H. W. Sabine. New York: Colburn & Tegg, 1956.

"The Sons of Liberty Constitution." www.nysm.nysed.gov/albany/solconst.html.

"The Stamp Act Riot: A Letter Written on the Day Following." In *New York City During the American Revolution*. New York: Mercantile Library Association, 1861, 41–49.

Staples, William R. *Documentary History of the Destruction of the Gaspee. Compiled for the Providence Journal*. Providence: Knowles, Vose, and Anthony, 1845.

Washington, George. *The Writings of George Washington*, vol. 2. Ed. Jared Sparks. New York: Harper & Brothers, 1847.

Wheatley, Phillis. "On the Death of Mr. Snider." In *The Poems of Phillis Wheatley*. Ed. with an introduction by Julian D. Mason, Jr. Chapel Hill: University of North Carolina Press, 1989, 131–132.

White, Stanford. *Stanford White: Letters to His Family*. Ed. Claire Nicolas White. New York: Rizzoli, 1997.

X, Malcolm. "Message to the Grass Roots." In *Malcolm X Speaks*. Ed. George Breitman. New York: Grove Press, 1990.

Other Sources

Adams, Randolph C. "New Light on the Boston Massacre." *Proceedings of the American Antiquarian Society* 47 (1936): 259–269.

Alden, John Richard. "Why the March to Concord?" *American Historical Review* 49, no. 3 (April 1944): 446–454.

Alexander, John K. *Samuel Adams: The Life of an American Revolutionary*. Lanham, Md.: Rowman & Littlefield, 2011.

Arango, Tim. "A Revolutionary Recession: Did a Sour Economy Set Off the American War for Independence?" *New York Times Upfront,* January 12, 2009.

Bailey, Sarah Loring. *Historical Sketches of Andover.* Boston: Houghton Mifflin, 1880.

Bailyn, Bernard. *The Ideological Origins of the American Revolution.* Cambridge, Mass.: Harvard University Press, 1967.

Baker, Jean. *Affairs of Party: The Political Culture of Northern Democrats in the Mid-Nineteenth Century.* Ithaca, N.Y.: Cornell University Press, 1983.

Beard, Charles A. *An Economic Interpretation of the Constitution of the United States.* New York: Macmillan, 1913.

Becker, Carl. "Growth of Revolutionary Parties and Methods in New York Province, 1765–1774." *American Historical Review* 7, no. 1 (1901): 56–76.

Bell, J. L. "Looking for 'Taxation Without Representation,'" April 25–27, 2009, http://boston1775.blogspot.com/2009/04/looking-for-taxation-without.html.

Burnett, Edmund Cody. *The Continental Congress.* New York: Macmillan, 1941.

Chaffin, Robert J. "The Townshend Acts of 1767." *William and Mary Quarterly* 27, no. 1 (January 1970): 90–121.

Champagne, Roger J. "Liberty Boys and Mechanics of New York City, 1764–1774." *Labor History* 8, no. 2 (1967): 115–135.

———. "The Military Association of the Sons of Liberty." *New-York Historical Society Quarterly* 41 (July 1967): 38–50.

———. "New York's Radicals and the Coming of Independence." *Journal of American History* 51, no. 1 (1964): 21–40.

Cohen, Charles L. "The 'Liberty or Death' Speech: A Note on Religion and Revolutionary Rhetoric." *William and Mary Quarterly* 38, no. 4 (October 1981): 702–717.

Crenshaw, Ollinger. "The Knights of the Golden Circle: The Career of George Bickley." *American Historical Review* 47, no. 1 (October 1941): 23–50.

Dawson, Henry B. *The Sons of Liberty in New York.* Poughkeepsie, N.Y.: Platt & Schram, 1859.

Dickerson, O. M. "John Hancock: Notorious Smuggler or Near Victim of British Revenue Racketeers?" *Mississippi Valley Historical Review* 32, no. 4 (March 1946): 517–540.

Eberlein, Harold Donaldson, and Horace Mather Lippincott. *The Colonial Houses of Philadelphia and Its Neighborhood.* Philadelphia and London: J. B. Lippincott, 1912.

Engelman, F. L. "Cadwallader Colden and the New York Stamp Act Riots." *William and Mary Quarterly* 10, no. 4 (October 1953): 560–578.

Fesler, Mayo. "Secret Societies in the North During the Civil War." *Indiana Magazine of History* 14, no. 3 (September 1918): 183–286.

Fontenoy, Paul E. *The Sloops of the Hudson River: A Historical and Design Survey.* Mystic, Conn.: Mystic Seaport Museum, 1994.

Frothingham, Richard. *Life and Times of Joseph Warren.* Boston: Little, Brown, 1865.

Gombrich, E. H. *A Little History of the World*. Trans. Caroline Mustill. New Haven, Conn., and London: Yale University Press, 2005.

Hawkes, James. *A Retrospect of the Boston Tea-Party, with a Memoir of George R. T. Hewes*. New York: S. S. Bliss, 1834.

Hofstadter, Richard. *The Progressive Historians: Turner, Beard, Parrington*. New York: Knopf, 1968.

Hutchinson, Thomas. *The History of the Province of Massachusetts Bay, from 1749 to 1774*. London: John Murray, 1828.

Irvin, Benjamin H. "Tar, Feathers, and the Enemies of American Liberties, 1768–1776." *New England Quarterly* 76, no. 2 (June 2003): 197–238.

Isaac, Rhys. "Lighting the Fuse of Revolution in Virginia, May 1765: Rereading the 'Journal of a French Traveller in the Colonies,'" *William and Mary Quarterly* 68, no. 4 (October 2011): 657–70.

Isaacson, Walter. "Benjamin Franklin Joins the Revolution." *Smithsonian*, August 1, 2003.

Jenkins, Stephen. *The Greatest Street in the World: The Story of Broadway, Old and New*. New York: G. P. Putnam's Sons, 1911.

Jensen, Merrill. *The Founding of a Nation: A History of the American Revolution, 1763–1776*. New York: Oxford University Press, 1968.

Kennedy, William. *O Albany!: Improbable City of Political Wizards, Fearless Ethnics, Spectacular Aristocrats, Splendid Nobodies, and Underrated Scoundrels*. New York: Viking Press, 1983.

Klein, Milton M. "Democracy and Politics in Colonial New York." *New York History* 60 (July 1959): 221–246.

Lacoute, John. "The Gulf Stream Charts of Benjamin Franklin and Timothy Folger." *Historic Nantucket* 2 (Fall 1995): 82–86.

Lepore, Jill. "Tea and Sympathy: Who Owns the American Revolution?" *New Yorker*, May 3, 2010, www.newyorker.com/reporting/2010/05/03/100503fa_fact_lepore.

"The Liberty Pole on the Commons." *New-York Historical Society Quarterly Bulletin* 3, no. 4 (January 1920): 108–130.

Macksy, Piers. *The War for America, 1775–1783*. Cambridge, Mass.: Harvard University Press, 1964.

Maier, Pauline. *From Resistance to Revolution: Colonial Radicals and the Development of American Opposition to Britain, 1765–1776*. New York: Alfred A. Knopf, 1972.

———. *The Old Revolutionaries: Political Lives in the Age of Samuel Adams*. New York: Alfred A. Knopf, 1980.

Maneres, Francis, ed. *A Fair Account of the Late Unhappy Disturbance at Boston in New England*. London: B. White, 1770.

McAnear, Beverly. "The Albany Stamp Act Riots." *William and Mary Quarterly* 4, no. 4 (October 1947): 486–498.

McCullough, David. *John Adams*. New York: Simon & Schuster, 2001.

McCusker, John J. *How Much Is That in Real Money?: A Historical Price Index for Use as a Deflator of Money Values in the Economy of the United States.* Worcester, Mass.: American Antiquarian Society, 2001.

Miller, John C. *Origins of the American Revolution.* Boston: Little, Brown, 1943.

———. *Sam Adams: Pioneer in Propaganda.* Boston: Little, Brown, 1936.

Minardi, Margot. *Making Slavery History: Abolitionism and the Politics of Memory in Massachusetts.* New York: Oxford University Press, 2010.

Monaghan, Charles. *The Murrays of Murray Hill.* Brooklyn: Urban History Press, 1998.

Morais, Herbert M. "The Sons of Liberty in New York." In *The Era of the American Revolution.* Ed. Richard B. Morris. New York: Columbia University Press, 1939, 269–289.

Morgan, Edmund S. "Colonial Ideas of Parliamentary Power 1764–66." *William and Mary Quarterly* 5, no. 4 (July 1948): 311–341.

Morgan, Edmund S., and Helen M. Morgan. *The Stamp Act Crisis: Prologue to Revolution.* Chapel Hill: University of North Carolina Press, 1995 (1953).

Randall, Henry S. *The Life of Thomas Jefferson,* vol. 1. New York: Derby and Jackson, 1858.

Reid, John Phillip. "A Lawyer Acquitted: John Adams and the Boston Massacre Trials." *American Journal of Legal History* 18, no. 3 (July 1974): 189–207.

Rogers, George C., Jr. "The Charleston Tea Party: The Significance of December 3, 1773." *South Carolina Historical Magazine* 75, no. 3 (July 1974): 153–168.

Rothbard, Murray N. "Modern Historians Confront the American Revolution." *Literature of Liberty* 1, no. 1 (January–March 1979): 16–41.

Schecter, Barnet. *The Battle of New York.* New York: Walker, 2002.

Schlesinger, Arthur M. *The Colonial Merchants and the American Revolution, 1763–1776.* New York: Columbia University, 1917.

———. "The Colonial Newspapers and the Stamp Act." *New England Quarterly* 8, no. 1 (March 1935): 63–83.

———. "Liberty Tree: A Genealogy." *New England Quarterly* 25, no. 4 (December 1952): 435–458.

———. *Prelude to Independence: The Newspaper War on Britain, 1764–1776.* New York: Alfred A. Knopf, 1958.

Smith, Adam. *Wealth of Nations.* New York: Prometheus, 1991.

Smith, Page. *A New Age Now Begins.* 2 vols. New York: McGraw-Hill, 1976.

Tourtellot, Arthur B. *Lexington and Concord: The Beginning of the War of the American Revolution.* New York: W. W. Norton, 1959.

Tudor, William. *The Life of James Otis of Massachusetts.* Boston: Wells and Lilly, 1823.

Unger, Harlow. *John Hancock: Merchant King and American Patriot.* New York: John Wiley & Sons, 2000.

Upton, L. F. S. "Proceedings of ye Body Respecting the Tea." *William and Mary Quarterly* 22, no. 2 (April 1965): 287–300.

Van Schaack, Henry Cruger. *Memoirs of the Life of Henry Van Schaack.* Chicago: A. C. McClurg, 1892.

Walett, Francis G. "Governor Bernard's Undoing: An Earlier Hutchinson Letters Affair." *New England Quarterly* 38, no. 2 (June 1965): 217–226.

Walsh, Richard. *Charleston's Sons of Liberty: A Study of the Artisans 1763–1789.* Columbia: University of South Carolina Press, 1959.

———. "Christopher Gadsden: Radical or Conservative Revolutionary?" *South Carolina Historical Magazine* 63, no. 4 (October 1962): 195–203.

Wells, William. *The Father of the Revolution: The Life and Public Services of Samuel Adams*, vol. 1. Boston: Little, Brown, 1888.

Wirt, William. *Sketches of the Life and Character of Patrick Henry*. Philadelphia: Webster, 1816.

Wood, Gordon S. *The Idea of America: Reflections on the Birth of the United States*. New York: Penguin, 2011.

Zobel, Hiller. *The Boston Massacre*. New York: W. W. Norton, 1970.

INDEX

ABOUT THE AUTHOR

LES STANDIFORD is the bestselling author of twenty books, including *Bringing Adam Home*, the John Deal mystery series, and the works of narrative history *The Man Who Invented Christmas* (a *New York Times* Editor's Choice) and *Last Train to Paradise*. He is the director of the creative writing program at Florida International University in Miami, where he lives with his wife, Kimberly, a psychotherapist and artist.

mL   12-12